Miriam Yahil-Wax & Roni A. Einav

Nordau to NASDAQ

The Evolution of an Israeli High-Tech Start-Up

KIP - Kotarim International Publishing, Ltd.

Nordau to NASDAQ:
The Evolution of an Israeli High-Tech Start-Up

First U.S. Edition: 2012

First Published in Hebrew: 2009
by Kinneret Zmora-Bitan

www.Nordau-to-NASDAQ.com

ISBN 978-965-91415-8-6

English Translation by Dan Gillon
Edited by Judy Gitenstein
Cover Photo: Getty Images
Cover Design: Imri Zertal

Publisher: Moshe Alon, Kotarim International Publishing, Ltd.
Graphic Design: Laura Gryncwajg

Copyright © 2012

Table of Contents

	Introduction	5
	Preface	7
1.	Inside Information	9
2.	Geniuses' Alert	21
3.	Three Memories	36
4.	A Snapshot of Childhood	46
5.	Never a Hired Hand	50
6.	Iran 101	65
7.	The Errors of Youth	78
8.	Seeds	83
9.	All My Prodigies	95
10.	The Birth of Software	108
11.	The Wizards	123
12.	Moving On	132
13.	Friends in Need	138
14.	Childhood Promises	143
15.	Discovering America	148
16.	The Year of the Paradox	157
17.	Throes of Independence	168
18.	A European Friend	176
19.	Uri, a Passion	187
20.	Obstacles	193
21.	Due Diligence	208
22.	Laurels	214
23.	Childhood Heroes	230
24.	Troubles in America	235
25.	A Place at the Top	244
26.	Hubris	256
27.	The End of the Beginning	263

Introduction

For many years I felt the desire to share the memories of my professional experience primarily with my family, then with the general public. I believed that my story could inspire younger members of my clan as well as young entrepreneurs everywhere. It is possible to start with nothing and scale the heights. All you need is brains, a decent education, determination, and a little bit of luck.

I wanted also to build a kind of heritage for software pioneers in general, and 4D personnel in particular.

My story is also that of Israel in my time. It is primarily based on facts and figures, and is mixed with my memories and those of other people. The passage of time may have modified those memories as did, of necessity, the rules of storytelling. And we decided to change some of the names, for obvious reasons.

On a professional level I have contributed to progress and increased the wealth of individuals and the state. I helped integrate many gifted new immigrants in Israel, and a few in America. On a personal level, my very dear wife, Matia, and I raised four capable boys, who continue the family legacy in academia, industry, and culture. With this book, our great-grandchildren will better understand the origin of their wealth while they enjoy it.

The story in this book ends in the year 2000, but not my business activity. Today it is centered on advising young entrepreneurs, new start-ups, and on my various hobbies: cycling, reading, and attending cultural performances. Today I eat the same food and drive the same car. From my high-rise apartment I see the Mediterranean, and the horizon looks even brighter.

I owe a debt of gratitude to my wife, Matia, who supported me along the long and demanding "journey" while handling the major duties of raising our four sons, Liran, Tsach, Ramon, and Yoav, on top of her career. And thank you to my brother Amnon Einav, my nephew Yiftach Einav, and Zippi Gon-Gross for their help to ensure the accuracy of this book.

I am eternally grateful to my friend Gabriel Wax, pilot and architect, for suggesting that his wife, Miriam Yahil-Wax, write my story. I cannot thank Miriam enough for undertaking the task.

Many thanks to my colleagues in Israel and abroad for their contributions: Ariel Gordon, Eli Mashiah, Shmuel Lahman, Amos Magor, Eyal Diskin, Alex Eldor, Han Bruggeling, Mickey Spigelman, Adam Gur, Nitza Meimon-Shashua, Rudolfo Vick, Dan Eitan, Lieutenant-Colonel (retired) Shaul Nagar.

My advisors on the history of Israeli high tech were the learned Amiram Shor, Prof Emanuel Greengrad, Yechezkel Zeira, Baruch Gindin.

The book was published first in Hebrew by Kinneret Zmora-Bitan, Dvir, in 2009, and was generally well received. As a kind of start-up by itself we move now to the global scene, starting in English, and eager to explore the outcome.

Roni Einav
February 2012

Preface

The world of action always appealed to me, but I had lived in the world of the imagination: literature and the theater. I found the ascent of Israel's high-tech industry fascinating yet knew nothing about it. What made tiny Israel into a leader in the global economy? Why in this particular field? Roni's appeal to me to help write his story was my own initiation into the realm of action.

For some two years he told his story and I listened and asked questions, till I became familiar with his world. I was pleasantly surprised to discover it did not lack in drama, and that imagination played as big a role in it as did professionalism and money. I was reassured there was enough to write about.

While the business story seemed to flow easily, Roni remained reticent about the personal aspects. Yet I felt the narrative would not be compelling if we did not reveal the unique background of the Israeli "battlefield entrepreneur" as he had been called elsewhere. Painstakingly I guided Roni to reconstruct his army and childhood memories, and together we brought to life little Tel Aviv of the '50s, the ambience of an urban pioneer's family, the view that education is the be-all and end-all, that all Israel has and will ever have to build on is human capital.

When we began this journey I told Roni that I was his first audience: if his story appealed to me, it may also appeal to the general public. I was certainly fascinated.

Many thanks to my spouse, Gabriel, who patiently read and commented on more than one draft. I am deeply grateful to my son, Jonathan Wax, a high-tech entrepreneur himself, who advised me on the inner workings of his field. And last but not least, I thank my friend Glenn Garelick for suggesting the English title.

Miriam Yahil-Wax

February 2012

Chapter 1

Inside Information

"Roni, Koichi is calling!" my receptionist bellowed clear across the workspace. The lines of programmers in the room between us looked up angrily from their computer screens.

Five minutes earlier I had left my desk to mingle with the development team and paused, as usual, beside the big windows overlooking Tel Aviv. From up high, the "white city," as it is poetically described, sparkled. The steel-and-glass skyscrapers reflected the autumn sun. The Tel Aviv of my childhood, with its modest low-rise houses, muddy streets, and open seashore, was now hidden under the rising metropolis. No doubt there are cities more beautiful, but none had Tel Aviv's special charm.

"Lonnie," the receptionist screeched again, mimicking Koichi's Japanese confusion of the letters "r" and "l." "Telephone, it's urgent!" The collective anger was now replaced by chuckles of appreciation. Even I was having difficulty suppressing a smile. I returned to my office to pick up the call.

Koichi was our representative in Japan. On the way past the rows of programmers back to my office I glanced at the clock, or rather clocks. After a series of mix-ups and hitches we had placed a row of clocks on the main wall. At any given moment we knew the time in any city in the world in which we were represented.

It was October 30, 1998, right before lunchtime. In Koichi's Tokyo it was 7:45 p.m. There was no reason at the time to think this was anything but a routine call, yet it was to be the start of an adventure that would change my life.

Koichi and I had known each other for eleven years. We'd been introduced by our European distributors, Boole & Babbage, when my company, New Dimension Software, was looking for a way to expand its customer base in East Asia. His English was good, and we were favorably impressed by his energy. We appointed him and his company to represent us in Japan.

We would meet from time to time—at our offices in Israel, in Europe, or in Japan. Koichi was hard-working and thorough, and did a good job of bridging the culture gap. His accent sometimes caused amusing mistakes—he would say, "walk" and mean "work," for example—but we never corrected him. I even got used to answering to the name "Lonnie San." He had helped us gain control of a significant share of the market for our operations software packages in Japan, and at the same time made a fair amount of money himself.

I wondered what could be so urgent that he was calling after his office hours. Money. It's never too late to talk about money. He probably wants us to raise his commission again. I settled into my chair and picked up the receiver.

To my pleasant surprise, something other than money was on Koichi's agenda. He wanted to check the details of a sales transaction that was in its final stages. A Japanese bank was buying two of our software products, which were designed to streamline operations and reduce costs dramatically. We stood to make a handsome profit from the deal, so I was glad to answer his questions and promised to phone Boole & Babbage Europe the next day to clear up the unresolved issues.

"Why don't you just ask BMC?" Koichi said. "After all, they're about to buy Boole & Babbage." I heard him but it didn't quite register.

"What did you say? Who's buying whom?" My other

telephone had started ringing and I was getting cranky.

"BMC is buying B&B." Wait a minute, I thought. That's impossible. Maybe I didn't understand him because of his accent. Maybe the connection was bad.

"Koichi San," I said, speaking slowly and clearly to make sure there was no misunderstanding. "Did you say that BMC is buying B&B?"

"Yes, yes, that's what I said. Tomorrow or the next day there will be a press release. BMC is buying B&B." So I'd heard him right. Koichi was telling me that the giant Texas-based company BMC Software was buying Boole & Babbage (USA), the parent of our European distributors. This was critical inside information on a huge transaction that affected us directly, and for a moment I felt completely lost.

"Lonnie San? Don't tell me you didn't know?"

I was still shocked and utterly speechless. I didn't want Koichi to know how surprised I was by his news so I avoided replying and ended our talk as calmly as I could.

Programmers began to get up from their computers to stretch their legs and get ready for lunch. Outside it was a glorious, bright autumn day, and everyone was looking forward to something hot and tasty. Poor fools! If they only knew what I'd just found out, they would quickly lose their appetite. How many of them would I soon have to fire? Where would they be eating lunch in a month's time? Only BMC knows! My loud receptionist also got ready to go up to our rooftop cafeteria. On her way to the elevator she smiled impishly at me, and my heart filled with sorrow. It was as if I'd already dismissed her.

What a blow! If the news was right—and I had no reason to doubt it—there was a real possibility that BMC would simply liquidate our business in Europe. The excellent network we had worked so hard to build would collapse, and our customers would take their business elsewhere. We had done very well with B&B Europe for more than a decade, and now everything was about to go down the drain. Bang—we'd be finished. And? Do I just sit here with my arms folded and wait for the final curtain? No way! I had to do something or I'd go out of my mind.

I needed to think about what to do and in what order. I had to update our CEO, Dan Barnea. Then I'd have to call my business partner, Galia Streiker, who was in California. It was nearly four in the morning there. I decided to wait till she'd had her morning coffee. Right now I needed to check the agreement. Maybe there was something in it that I could latch on to.

Our third distribution agreement had been signed nearly two years earlier. I found it and took it back to my office. Then I did something uncharacteristic: I closed the door. I believe in the open-door policy and love eye contact with my colleagues. But this time I couldn't rely on my poker face and didn't want anyone to see how worried I was.

The document was thick—twenty pages plus numerous addenda—and that made me even more nervous. A software distribution agreement should be small and simple: the price of the product, the distributor's commission, and the payment terms. But such contracts tend to become huge because during negotiations the lawyers try to outdo one another with implausible-sounding scenarios. They elaborate on imaginary calamities and expand the document with dozens of hypothetical clauses to cover every eventuality and misfortune: if Party A does this, Party B will do that. Lawyers say that in a complicated business, a dispute is only a matter of time. We'll soon see.

I start reading the huge document, looking for any reference to a scenario like the one we were now facing. The agreement time period was three years. Not good! Our company, New Dimension Software, would be tied to our European distributors, B&BE, for another whole year. Next. Clauses, sub-clauses, sub-sub-clauses. So much legal babble. Does the contract contain any protection for Party A, in the event that someone buys its distributor

(Party B), causing said party to cease operating as an independent entity? That's what I wanted to know. There was something about that in the contract somewhere. I'm sure there was. My search was now focused and I could reconstruct things.

Most of the negotiations leading up to the signing of the agreement had taken place between me and Han Bruggeling, the manager of B&BE. As we were about to close the deal, Han flew to the U.S to meet his boss, Paul Newton, CEO of the parent company, B&B, to get final approval. Newton, who attended to everything in minutest detail, blocked the signing of the agreement, and summoned us both to California. "Roni, my friend," he told me, "your products account for 35 percent of our sales in Europe; you're very important to us. If someone buys you, it'll cause us a lot of damage." Back then in 1996, Newton's concern was that a competitor would buy us, distribute our products with its own, and wouldn't have any need for B&BE's distribution services. Almost half of B&BE's sales volume would be wiped out. That was definitely cause for concern.

The tension in the air was palpable. They say that flattery gets you nowhere but I reckoned it could do no harm, perhaps even ease the strain. My tone became almost obsequious.

"That is right, Mr. Newton," I said. "If competitors buy us, you'll suffer a lot of damage. In your opinion, what will the extent of the damage be?" "That is a huge unknown," he replied. "I have to think and calculate." I agreed. "Instead of guessing, let's look at the worst-case scenario."

At that time, we knew of three companies that were likely to have an interest in acquiring New Dimension Software so as to reduce competition in the field. They were IBM, CA, and Platinum—all American companies that were developing similar products and had distribution systems capable of selling our software programs as well. Newton added BMC and Sterling to the list, and we continued to discuss the compensation calculations. "Mr. Newton, the duration of the agreement we are discussing is three years, 1997 to 2000. If someone buys us in 2000, what's the compensation that will be due to you for the loss in sales? And if it happens in 1999, how much?"

We drew a parabola that showed the various options. If they bought us one month after the signing of the new distribution agreement, B&B would have to be paid about six million dollars in compensation. If the purchase took place halfway through the agreement, that would be when maximum damage would occur and so the maximum compensation would be due. It could run to 12 million dollars. Beyond that point, the amounts due in compensation would steadily decrease. If we were bought two months before the end of the agreement, B&B's compensation would be a lot less, because by then their distribution rights would have almost expired. We worked together on these various calculations and reached agreement on the compensation we would pay. That set Newton's mind at ease.

And then I played what I thought was my trump card. "Mr. Newton," I said, "what will happen if someone buys you? What will then happen to us?"

Though somewhat taken aback, he gave me the answer I'd hoped to hear: "The same, Roni, my friend."

Nevertheless, I insisted on clarifying matters: "And what about the numbers?"

"The numbers are also more or less the same," he replied. "Let's not complicate things any more than they need to be." And that's what we settled on. In the new agreement there would be symmetry on the compensation issue—in other words, full reciprocity.

I said goodbye and took the draft to my board of directors for their approval. After my presentation they pounced. "How could you agree to such high compensation? After all, it would be total lunacy if we had to pay. You've lost it!" Calmly, I explained that the understanding stemmed entirely from Newton's legitimate demand. To put the two parties on equal footing, I had negotiated a balance to that demand. "Besides, there's a 70 percent chance that a competitor would buy B&B before they buy us, and don't ask me how I know—clairvoyance or maybe divine inspiration—but I urge you to approve this agreement because reopening the negotiations simply won't work." They were angry and scared, but they approved it.

It was that clause—the one that had so upset the board—that I was now feverishly searching for. Then, suddenly, there it was in black and white: "Agreed Compensation: If one of the parties is sold prior to the end of the Agreement Period ..." What the clause affirmed was that as of that day, B&B, or in this instance, BMC, who was buying B&BE, had to pay us about 10 million dollars in compensation. But I was still anxious. I called the company's lawyer, Mickey Spigelman, and then phoned Galia in California. Both assured me that the clause was valid and binding, and that we definitely had the right to demand the compensation that had been agreed to. Very well. What had seemed to me at the time a major risk was now turning into a substantial opportunity.

Two days later, there was an official announcement of the acquisition deal. Good. Now they'll pay, I reassured myself. Boy, are they going to pay! An acquisition process of this magnitude, with its many details and pitfalls, would take several months. The best thing for me to do was to wait a few days before calling Han Bruggeling at B&BE in Holland. I couldn't hold it against him that he hadn't even dropped a hint of the impending takeover—in his shoes I would have done the same. Nonetheless I was livid. Keeping my cool, I offered my congratulations and wished him and BMC good luck. Now would he be so kind as to arrange a meeting for me with the new management before they receive my demand for compensation.

"Does BMC know about us at all?" I asked casually. "Do they know that New Dimension accounts for 35 percent of

B&BE's sales, more than the sales of B&B's own products in Europe?" Han replied that they would soon find out when they look more closely. I detected tension in his courteous tone. "As to a meeting with them," he went on, "it's a great idea. It's always better to talk face-to-face." The marketing VP of BMC, Rick Gardner, Number 2 in the company, would soon arrive in Germany to organize the merger, which involved hundreds of B&B employees and thousands from BMC. Han suggested that we should come to Europe, where he would arrange a meeting for us with Rick Gardner. Till then could we please hold off saying anything about compensation, to avoid tainting the atmosphere?

The agreement allowed the injured party thirty days in which to make a claim, so I agreed not to rock the boat, and thanked him for the invitation. Behind the politeness and niceties, I was hopping mad. Who could tell what, if anything, would come out of the meeting in Germany? Even if the compensation were agreed to, it would be ages before we were paid. No one likes to part with money, not even a large, reputable company like BMC. I consulted my board, and we made a unanimous decision to strike a preemptive blow and set up a base for an independent branch in Europe, something we'd planned to do in the past, but had put off. We would act quickly because now that the acquisition of B&B had been announced, customers might start to make other arrangements. B&BE sales and support staff who worked with us might disperse, and they were people we would want to hire for our contemplated new branch.

I flew to London, Madrid, and other capitals in Europe, to meet some of the key people whom we had already talked to during our 1994 round of recruiting and to interview new people. A European company was engaged to headhunt personnel for management and sales positions. In short, we laid the foundation for establishing New Dimension Europe.

On my return to Israel, my wife, Matia, met me at the

airport with two pieces of news. Our daughter-in-law Shirit was pregnant with our first grandchild. The other news was worrying. Ramon, our third son, was on unexpected leave from the army. Matia knew I was going through a rough patch, so she had put off telling me about it.

One side of Ramon's face had become paralyzed, a condition known as Bell's palsy. In patients of Ramon's age, late teens, the paralysis usually goes away within a short time, but it was worrying. When I was in college I had the same condition, and it went away without treatment. I hoped his case was similarly mild. "Have you brought him what he asked for? He hasn't touched the piano since he got home," Matia said. Of course I'd brought what Ramon had asked for. No matter how much pressure my work puts on me, I always keep my promises to my children.

Ramon had played piano since childhood, but his army service in a Patriot missile unit meant he could play only when he was on leave. Before I went to Europe, I'd been given a list of sheet music to buy for him in London. I was there a short time and went by cab from the airport to get it, so that the cost of this present turned out to be higher than it would have been had I bought it in Israel. But obviously there's nothing like a gift that Dad brings from abroad.

We went into the house and I felt a pang in my heart when I saw the serious expression on Ramon's face, due to the paralysis, and the lopsided smile when he saw me. He gave me a hug, opened his present, and, to my joy, began to play. Matia breathed a sigh of relief and I immediately went to the phone in the bedroom and started looking for a specialist in neurology.

The BMC conference in Germany was drawing near, but I decided not to go. My heart and mind were occupied with Ramon. A paralyzed nerve was preventing the eyelid from closing and moistening the eye, and it had to be watched to ensure that it didn't dry up. He had to have frequent checkups, and needed transportation. Matia and I made every effort to be at his disposal. We came back early from work and welcomed his army buddies when they came to see him. The IDF gave him a temporary leave of absence, and the music I'd brought for him worked overtime.

Gradually the treatments began to have an effect, and time did its part too. The sleeping nerve woke up, Ramon was better, and once again I was able to focus on my work. As it turned out, I was even able to travel to Germany for the conference. Galia arrived there from the U.S., and the delegation from Tel Aviv consisted of New Dimension's CEO Dan Barnea and me as chairman of the board. Han Bruggeling went out of his way to be gracious. He even sent a car and driver to pick us up at the airport.

Just as BMC was an unknown to us, we were a mystery to them. B&B hadn't lied to them about us, but it takes several months for such an acquisition deal to be realized. The buyer makes an offer, the parties agree to it, and then the due diligence process begins. The buyer, for his part, begins looking for hidden snags; the seller tries to ensure that there aren't many. All that takes time. We attended the meeting that Han had arranged for us with Rick Gardner, without knowing whether BMC had already realized that B&BE without us was no great bargain or, as I'd surmised, they were still very much in the dark on this issue. We had come in order to pave the way for us to receive the agreed compensation in as positive an atmosphere as possible—only an idiot would pick a fight with a giant like BMC.

Because we didn't know the people involved, or what they wanted, we decided to go with open minds and hear what they had to say. There was no point in trying to make plans. We were going on a "blind date," without knowing whether we were heading for a stormy love affair or the war to end all wars.

The conference took place in a village near Frankfurt, at an austere German hotel that reminded me of the spa guesthouses

that my mother had loved in the Israel of the 1950s. Rick
Gardner turned out to be a genteel fellow, a man of the
world. Rather quickly it became clear to us that my hunch
was right. When they signed the acquisition deal, BMC had
been unaware of our importance to B&B, and had no clue that
there was a reciprocal compensation clause in our distribution
agreement. In fact, until this meeting they had not really been
aware of us at all.

My concerns about the true nature of our negotiating partner
vanished as the discussion became ever more positive. I was
frank in my explanation of where we all stood, and told him
without false modesty that New Dimension was the core of
B&BE's business. As for the compensation due to us, I pointed
out that the payment couldn't be put off. We needed the money
to hire salespeople now employed by B&BE, and to set up New
Dimension Europe.

"What's the compensation due to you?" asked Rick Gardner.

"Ten million dollars. And it's urgent," I said politely. "People
will disappear. There'll be employees who'll leave, and those
who won't want to work at BMC. That's why we have to move
right away."

Gardner shook his head, poured wine into Galia's glass, and
was silent. Han took up the conversation, and soon it flowed
smoothly, even though we were all aware of the gravity of the
matter that had just been put on the table. We waited for Rick
Gardner's reaction. In light of the sum I had just mentioned, I
was bracing myself for an unpleasant response. But when Rick
decided to end his silence, he smiled pleasantly and said, "Why
are you concerning yourself with ten million? We're talking
about hundreds of millions here." As if I hadn't heard I stuck
with my line. "We have to catch the people as soon as possible
… we have to move all kinds of mountains …"

"You're not on the right track, Mr. Einav. What's ten million
dollars? Small change. It's not at all the issue. I'm talking about

hundreds of millions, so let's not be hasty. What do you think of the wine?"

At that point we already had an annual turnover of one hundred million dollars in dozens of countries, had set up our own distribution network in the U.S., Australia, and Mexico, and were about to do the same in Brazil. We knew that on the NASDAQ our shares were flying high, and that provided us with a valuation of the company. Exactly how much did BMC think we were worth? That we didn't know. We also didn't think that the subject interested them. After all, they were engaged in acquiring B&B. Now, at the German restaurant, after Rick Gardner had for the second time said "hundreds of millions," I suddenly realized where we were heading, and that Dan and Galia had also figured out which way the wind was blowing. Han Bruggeling raised an eyebrow.

What did those high numbers that Mr. Gardner had thrown into the air actually mean? Was BMC interested in buying us? The twinkle in Galia's eye indicated that the same thought had just crossed her mind. Dan Barnea sat up straight in his chair. "So how much are we worth, in your opinion?" I asked. "Just in case someone, maybe you, wants to buy us tomorrow morning, how much are we worth?" Rick Gardner, obviously delighting in the wine's clarity as he held it up against the light, replied, "In my estimation, New Dimension is worth six hundred, maybe six hundred and twenty million dollars." Then he laughed, and emptied his glass.

Chapter 2

Geniuses' Alert

Instead of entering a three-year mandatory service in the IDF at age 18 like my peers, I had entered a special program, enabling me first to complete a BA at Technion-Israel Institute of Technology in industrial and management engineering. Having graduated, I was now enlisting to serve in the IDF's prestigious weaponry development unit, founded by professor (then colonel) Yuval Ne'eman, with the aim of coordinating security research and development. The unit's policy of recruiting only the best provided the IDF with a reservoir of exceptional brainpower, compensating for the limited purchasing power of the young state. Though it is best known for the innovative Arrow missile system, the unit's range of operations was numerically large and multifaceted. The most successful among them will remain shrouded in secrecy for as long as Israel survives.

The night before reporting for duty I was plagued by doubts: What am I truly worth? I wondered. Did I have what it takes to cope with the demands of this very special unit? Was I good enough to handle the competition? The unit only took the best of the crop. Was I one of them? Would I succeed or fail? At Technion, I had acquired a vocational skill, broadened my horizons, had a great time, and made lifelong friends. The demands of academia were no problem. Now I was about to face a test for which there was no preparation—the real world. Throughout that sleepless night, I longed for and feared the morning.

It was the summer of 1966. The Six-Day War loomed. The army was at its peak, ready and highly creative, awaiting the opportunity to demonstrate its real worth. The same was true of me. The expectations I had of myself were sky-high. Nothing could have sobered me up as much as my reception or, to be precise, the lack thereof, as I reported for duty.

The regular conscript arrives at the enlistment base accompanied by a large peer group, tearful parents, friends, and flowers. I reached IDF headquarters red-eyed, alone, and without a hint of ceremony. No one was waiting for me; no one came to greet me. For what seemed an eternity I hung about in the entrance hall of the picturesque stone building that housed the weaponry development unit. Conscripts and officers, cheerfully chatting, walked past me. The female soldiers giggled, amused, no doubt, by my rumbling stomach protesting my failure to eat the breakfast my mother had prepared. Knowing that the brand new shoes I had bought for this occasion squeaked, I stayed rooted to my place, feeling exposed and abandoned.

This was far from the way I had imagined my entry into the real world. All my painstaking preparations seemed foolish. Through that interminable night my mind had rehearsed what I would say to my commander, but no officer was there to receive me. Adding to my discomfort was the fact that everybody else was in uniform, whereas I came dressed as a civilian. True that in those days no one really believed that "clothes make the man." Rich and poor dressed in more or less the same blue shirt, combat jacket, mass-produced trousers and on Shabbat, the same white cotton shirt. Yet there I was in those familiar clothes that had served me well for years, feeling utterly out of place.

My wait came to an end as a clearly bored female clerk, addressing me by the lowly rank of acting officer, took my name, scribbled something, and escorted me into the unit's offices. Not bothering to introduce me to those present, she handed me a note and told me, "Go sit in the library and read up on this stuff." The note listed subjects such as simulation, war games, probabilities, permeability, and shrapnel.

What a disappointment! I shelved the clever little speech I had prepared, sat closeted within the library's four walls for three whole days, and did nothing but read. No one paid me the slightest attention. This is to be my task in the elite unit? Reading up on shrapnel? If so I don't have a cat in hell's chance to prove myself. So profound was my disappointment that I decided I wouldn't talk about it either to my girlfriend, Matia, or my parents.

On the third day of torment came salvation in the form of my direct commanding officer, Lieutenant Colonel Raffi Snir. He promised I would soon be on a course to complete my officer training, changing my status from acting officer to real officer. After that, I'd take a programming course. My hopes were reborn. I hadn't been abandoned after all. Soon I too would be able to contribute something to this important unit.

During my period of service, the weaponry development unit's commander was the legendary Yitzchak Ya'akov (Yazza), whom I met after completing my first research assignment, which began on my fourth day of service. Raffi Snir had instructed me to investigate "the optimal manner for a battleship to navigate its way out of the Port of Haifa, assuming that Syrian forces had mined the bay on the previous night."

The scenario Snir described was far from hypothetical. The Syrians had adopted a highly aggressive stance, and were they to translate their verbal threats into action, Israel could easily find itself facing precisely such a situation. I saw no imminent threat of war, but dealing with a mined port was clearly significant and, deterred neither by the gravity of the subject matter nor by my inexperience, I was more than happy to tackle the challenge. Determined to produce a perfect piece of research, I opted for Game Theory—at that time an innovative approach. I had knowingly taken a risk on my proposal, and worked round the clock to ensure a comprehensive outcome. Snir was impressed, calling my work "exceptional" and, as a reward, sent me off to deliver it in person to Yazza himself.

As he leafed through the report, I could see that the commander was taking it seriously and indeed, he instructed that it be kept for a future "D-Day."

Snir sent me off as promised to complete my officer's training and attend the programming course. I returned to the unit a full-fledged second lieutenant and qualified programmer, a systems analyst working on weapons systems, logistics, and various other military systems. My assignments included determining the type of minefield that would be most effective against vehicles, tanks, infantry; defining the desired characteristics of a sea missile; and devising the optimal way of building an armored personnel carrier (APC).

For me, this period of training was a dream come true. The experienced geniuses serving in the unit involved us beginners in everything they did, encouraging originality and creativity. They allowed us a great deal of freedom through their non-hierarchical approach. In marked contrast to the situation in the civilian marketplace where novice engineers begin as apprentices on the lowest rung, these old-timers encouraged us to participate in major projects and, on occasion, they even put us in charge. I thanked my lucky stars for giving me precisely the kind of start I had hoped for, a desk, pen and paper, plus an open invitation to use my brains alongside the most gifted people in the country. Could a young man of ambition ask for anything more?

And then the Six-Day War erupted. During the War of Independence in 1948, I had been a child. I remember the Sinai Campaign of 1956 mainly because the blackouts prevented us kids from playing outdoors in the evenings. By the Six-Day War I was an adult, an officer in the army, serving my country.

Though weaponry development was a non-combat unit, the 1967 war would prove to be as much of a test for us as it was for all other soldiers serving in the IDF. Had we dealt with the relevant subjects? Had we prepared effective solutions for real-life events about to unfold on the battlefield? And, from a more personal perspective, was I of value in the eyes of the IDF? The day of reckoning was at hand.

The outbreak of hostilities was preceded by a three-week high alert that historians were to call the "waiting period." Even before that nail-biting interlude had begun, serious cross-border incidents on the Syrian front, plus years of Palestinian terrorist incursions across Israel's borders with Jordan and Egypt, had brought increasing pressure on the government to retaliate. We shot down six Syrian warplanes that penetrated Israeli airspace, but the Syrians ignored the message. In our unit there was talk of their trying to mine the Port of Haifa, and my piece of theoretical research was pulled off the shelf and passed on to Operations as a working paper. Was D-Day approaching?

The so-called waiting period began in May 1967 when Egypt's president, Gamal Abdel Nasser, expelled UN observers and started to pour troops into the Sinai Peninsula. While our other Arab neighbors equivocated, Israel sat tight but prepared for war. When Nasser closed the Straits of Tiran to Israeli shipping, the blockade in effect forced Israel's hand, making war the only option.

But the war was slow in coming, and the IDF seemed to have forgotten all about its highly praised weaponry unit. Not a single assignment came our way. Nonetheless, we continued to get together every day in the basement of our headquarters in Tel Aviv to brainstorm. We visualized scenarios in every military area we had ever dealt with, and planned the most effective solutions. We compiled a list of about twenty-five urgent issues, such as the monitoring of convoys supplying fuel, munitions, and food, to analyze the logistical performance along their route. We knew that if our initial air strike proved to be indecisive, infantry and armored divisions would have to penetrate deep into Sinai. There, they would encounter severe problems traversing the sandy desert roads. We added issues linked to the operational performance of tanks and other armored vehicles. If remembered and called on, at least we would be prepared. Stony silence was all we got from HQ. They were up to their necks in getting the real warriors ready for battle.

During the high alert at the weaponry unit, which some joker had dubbed "geniuses' alert," we newcomers spent long hours in the company of the old-timers. Among those serving with me at that time were a number of luminaries-to-be. People like Eilon Kolberg, now a professor at Harvard; Yehuda Kahana and Arik Tamir, who would both become professors at Tel Aviv University; Miki Samuel, professor at the Weizmann Institute of Science; Moshe Ben Bassat, a professor in operations research and a highly successful entrepreneur. They formed an outstanding coterie of highly intelligent individuals with the finest possible education, courtesy of the small and impoverished state of Israel, that had the good sense to appreciate the potential of the "Hebrew brain" and gave education top priority. All of us, youngsters and veterans alike, were itching to play a significant role in the war that surely now was just around the corner.

Until then, we were able to go home in the evening. Matia and I used to go to the Angel Café on Arlozorov Street, where it was business as usual, except that the radio was left on, broadcasting a steady stream of bad tidings: Israel in the grip of a deep recession; Libya joining the campaign against us, followed by Iraq. Between sips of coffee, Matia wondered if Technion's postponing of the graduation ceremony on account of the massive reserves recruitment was troubling me: no ceremony, no diploma. I had to admit that I'd completely forgotten about it.

Every morning, we returned to HQ to rejoin the "geniuses' alert" in our two-story stone house with the red tile roof. Built by the Templars in the nineteenth century, it was one of the most eye-catching buildings in the compound, although it certainly did not meet IDF safety standards. A large proportion of the general staff was housed in randomly available buildings, which was a hodgepodge of graceful Templar stone houses, various IDF shacks and an assortment of asbestos-roofed huts from the days of British Mandate in Palestine. Within this ramshackle complex was the bunker intended for the IDF's top brass. This modern construction certainly did conform to safety regulations, but it was for the bigwigs, not for us ordinary mortals.

For three nerve-racking weeks, the best brains in the country sat in a basement unshielded against missiles. No one had the time to think that it might be a good idea for the sake of the country's future—if indeed it had any—to transfer us to a safer location. The entire population was sitting in unsafe buildings enveloped in darkness. Yet for them, the blackout was merely a petty nuisance. Far more distressing was the psychological gloom, the real sense of doom that had gripped us all. Civil defense wardens instructed the general population to tape their windows, but exploding glass was the least of anyone's worries. The real fear was the destruction of Israel. Here we were, a tiny country surrounded by hundreds of millions of hostile Arabs and an indifferent world that not so long ago turned away while Jews were being exterminated. What if this time around the miracle of Israel's victory in the 1948 War of Independence was not repeated? A joke circulated, reporting a notice to the public at Israel's international airport, asking the last person to leave the country: "Please turn off the lights."

War broke on the morning of June 5, 1967. We too were summoned to do our duty, though no specific mission was assigned. Apparently, the general staff really had forgotten us. The four reservists in the unit known as "the docs," for their Ph.Ds, were given a requisitioned civilian vehicle. We youngsters got jeeps. Having not been able to afford the fee to get a license, I joined my friend Mishka, who knew how to drive. The entire weaponry unit boarded a fifteen-vehicle convoy and headed off to implement the list of missions we had compiled in advance. We were instructed to go south, where we would be given further orders. Just before sunset we reached Beersheba. We camped out in a youth hostel and listened to the news. We had come directly from HQ but had no more idea of what was going on than the civilians did.

In the morning, the jubilant locals gave us the latest: "Hey guys, guess what? The air force destroyed the enemy's planes on the ground. The war is over!" We were happy, of course, except that it sounded so improbable. No doubt we have a great air force, but the war couldn't have ended in one day. And if the war had indeed ended, there would be nothing left for us to do. We showered, shaved, had some coffee, and made a decision. "Go south you sons of Zion," we had been told, and south is where we headed. We drove quickly toward the border. But the troops at the roadblock stopped us. Now what? Our commanding officer grumpily made his way to the command post. "We're sorry," they said. "In case you hadn't noticed, there's a war going on here. We're not about to let you eggheads run around in the Sinai. It's dangerous."

For what was known as the best army in the world, our experience was incredibly haphazard. We came, we saw, we said, "Hello, we're from the general staff-intelligence branch-weaponry unit. We're here to gather data from combat areas. Tell us where to go." After trying to brush us aside, the combat-hardened soldiers eventually agreed to cooperate. "OK, since you geniuses want to investigate—please yourselves, investigate!" No escort was suggested or any other help given. They seemed utterly unconcerned by what might happen to us. "You want to explore, go ahead. You're keen on getting killed, be our guests." Their disdain for us was undisguised, but we persevered until finally they gave us some sort of a map. By the time we had decided what we should focus on, and were at last allowed to enter the combat zone, the war was already in its third day.

There were reasons for our insistence that our mission was important. First, this in all probability would not be the last war and it was our job to learn its lessons for the next round. Second, it was essential to learn from what actually happened in the field, rather than from second-hand information. In real combat conditions things would certainly be different from what they were in experiments. Our first task was to look at tanks in the combat zones as soon after the battles as possible.

During our first journey into the vast desert, I was so excited that I simply forgot we were in the middle of a war zone. Sand, sand, and yet more sand lay before us, a golden ocean with soaring waves stretching as far as the eye could see. We had to make do with a brief glance at the fantastic landscape. Like insurance assessors, we hurried to the scene as quickly as possible, while the evidence was still uncontaminated. We knew that we would need to spend more than one day in the battle zones, so we decided to sleep over in an adjacent area occupied by a combat unit. At the end of each day, we would have to argue with combat soldiers for their permission just to lay our weary heads among them in their encampments; the fact of the matter was that the war was highly chaotic, and it wasn't clear who belonged where or who was in charge at any given moment. In the mornings we returned to the battlefields and continued our own war.

This became the daily routine. We would extract information from the reluctant command posts as to the sites of tank battles, then head to those locations where disabled or destroyed tanks had been abandoned. For most of us, the only prior sighting of a tank had been either in battle simulation exercises or in the Independence Day Parade. Now in the Sinai desert, the gaping holes in a tank's armor inflicted by Egyptian shells were within reach. Our hands touched the blackened frame of a tank that had been torched; our feet stumbled on a bloodied turret that had been shorn from the hull and had rolled into the sand.

This was indeed our baptism by fire. We were not engaged in the fighting, nor were we directly exposed to danger. Nevertheless, for the first time in my life I was seeing corpses, mostly those of the Egyptian dead, many just lying where they had fallen. Others had met their deaths in minefields from which it was impossible to remove them. The air all around us reeked of rotting bodies. It was, to say the least, a distasteful sight. My friends and I tried not to think that these corpses were once men like us; that somewhere in their country a mother, a wife, or a child was waiting for them to return. It was not easy to ignore the bodies and get on with what we were doing as if they were not there.

Nevertheless, that is precisely what we did. Meticulously we inspected one tank after another and wrote up to two pages of analysis for each. We strained to overcome the nauseating smells and horrific sights all around us to focus on our mission, which was to note fuel marks on the ground, shredded wrapping sacks, scattered metal fragments. Here we saw an unfinished ration, there an axe—a standard piece of equipment on a Russian tank. We were no longer watching a simulated battle in the calm of the base. This was the real thing: dirty, bloody, shocking.

We began as a bunch of novices who knew nothing, and gradually became tougher and better at our trade. In the field, we learned to identify different types of fuel, distinguish between the impact of a high-explosive squash head shell (HESH) and that of a hollow charge projectile. We became skilled at differentiating between the perforation of an armor piercing shell and the damage caused by armor piercing shells with discarding sabots. And so on.

We developed operational procedures that enabled us to function in the field as effectively as in the lab. Our secret weapons? Rulers, rolls of measuring tape, pencils, and cameras.

We marked the angle of each point of impact on the pre-prepared silhouette charts, numbered it, noted whether it had penetrated the armor, and what specific damage it had caused. The findings were also photographed from every angle. We saw a variety of armored vehicles, the remnants of anti-tank companies also known as "tank hunters," and Armored Personnel Carriers (APCs), and checked the efficacy of various tank munitions. The damage assessment analysis we produced was comprehensive. The same can't be said about the other objects of our investigation, because three days later the war really did end.

On our way home, our small convoy came across hundreds of Egyptian soldiers making their way to the Suez Canal. I heroically grabbed my rifle, not realizing that I had forgotten to put the gun in safety mode, and a bullet whizzed past my ear. Our entire convoy came to a screeching halt as the "docs" jumped from their vehicles and sought shelter, convinced that we were under Egyptian attack. The fleeing Egyptians, thinking they were under assault, also halted and raised their hands in surrender. I took pictures of the debacle, souvenirs of the scene of my shame.

The unit's real achievement was the speedy research we'd managed to do in the battle zones. In the space of a few weeks we'd been able to inspect some three hundred and fifty tanks— one hundred of them during the war, and the rest after the victory. We went north to the Golan Heights to visit a number of tank repair depots to view armor that had sustained relatively minor damage. We didn't want to miss anything relevant to the full picture we were after. In fact, we crisscrossed the country, which was now four and a half times bigger than it had been before the war. By the time we'd finished we had inspected over six hundred tanks and had amassed the data needed for comprehensive research.

Back at HQ I was nominated to compile the material. A new group of academic draftees was being enlisted and I picked two of them to help. We had to sort the material, analyze it, and draw conclusions. Without complaining and with great attention to detail, the new recruits did a magnificent job. After all the material had been collated and categorized, we wrote a detailed summary, complete with pictures, and printed fifty copies that were classified top secret. I thought we had accomplished something important, but the decision on that belonged to our superiors.

In September 1967, on the eve of the Jewish New Year, we delivered the final report to General Ezer Weizmann, the chief of the general staff's operations branch. Known for his mischievousness, he took the report, put it on his head, smiled impishly and said: "OK, so what am I supposed to do with this? Use it as a sun hat?" He wasn't the only one who belittled our efforts. Quite a few of the combat unit's top brass who regularly received our reports were skeptical. On the one hand they called us geniuses, on the other they failed to appreciate the importance of the systematic and scientific work we had done with actual combat. If our conclusions happened not to conform to their practices, they as often as not dismissed them out of hand.

Ezer Weizmann's reaction to our report was by no means an exception. The work of Adam Sheffi, for example, a gifted officer with a Ph.D. from Stanford University, suffered a similar fate. He had been fiddling with an almost obsolete word-processing program installed on our Linolex computer, to create something that resembled a logarithmic table. By programming the results, he obtained an extremely accurate computerized firing range chart. Such a chart would enable an artillery gunner to feed the relevant data into a computer, instantly get a fix on the target's range, and fire. But when Sheffi offered it to the chiefs of the artillery corps he was given the cold shoulder. Used to manual calculations, they pooh-poohed the concept, not realizing that had they gone for it they would have been trading base metal for gold. Again and again they turned it down, until finally one of them actually tried it out and saw the light. Adam Sheffi's brilliant improvisation led eventually to the development of the field artillery digital automatic computer (FADAC), now an integral part of the IDF's equipment.

Our report also eventually gained the respect it deserved. Recognition came after it reached someone in Operations, who realized its true value and offered to sell it to the German army for a substantial sum. Only after it had been praised abroad did the IDF finally wake up and take our work seriously. To this day it's used locally and internationally as a teaching manual. Moreover, as I was told recently by retired major general Amos Horev, it proved significant to the design of the Israeli Merkava tank. The importance of our report derives from the fact that we had realized that a tank's performance in action is different than in maneuvers. In the actual theater of war temperatures are higher, the machine is covered with dirt, it loses fuel, and the availability of ammunition fluctuates. We had the foresight to gather this data from the field of battle, analyze it scientifically, and reach definite conclusions. That effort was to influence R&D and the army's readiness.

What we had accomplished was one of many testimonies to the strength of Israel's human capital and a further justification for the existence of this very special unit. The National Geographic Channel reported recently that experiments conducted after the war by Americans led to the development of what is known as "Active Protection." Today, Active Protection is viewed as the-state-of-the art technology in armor design.

As a result of the work I did in the field of armor and my participation in the war, I was promoted from second to first lieutenant a few months ahead of schedule. The first thing I did after Israel's stunning victory was to learn to drive. Under the guidance of Mishka I already had a good deal of practice on the difficult roads of the Sinai desert. I borrowed money from my brother Uri, invested a few months of my army pay in lessons, and passed the driving test.

The second thing I did after the war was to take my family in the unit's pickup to my graduation ceremony at Technion. As I drove to our Tel Aviv apartment on Nordau Boulevard—cautiously, as befits a newly qualified driver—I saw my father and mother, with my younger brother, Amnon, between them, waiting on the balcony. They were all dressed up in their Shabbat best, beaming. I could see that my mother's lovingly tended cactus plants, and my little brother had grown taller. Only my parents seemed smaller than I remembered. In the short time I had been away, much had changed.

When everyone was settled in the car, we picked up Matia in Haifa. She was still studying at Technion and was waiting for us in her apartment. Well before we got to her house I had already spotted her, a picture postcard of a sabra (native Israeli) girl: long legs, no makeup, flowing black ponytail and a perfect smile. We had a joyful family meal at the Balfour Basement, paid for by my modest army salary, and then drove off to Technion for the ceremony. When my name was called I thought I could see my mother holding back tears. My father shook my hand and gave me a bear hug. Mine was the family's first academic degree. Making sure no one was looking, Matia gave me a warm kiss. Sadly, my brother Uri couldn't make it to the event. He was a kibbutz farmer whose first duty was to the land—a master that doesn't stand in wait for anything, not even a brother's graduation.

The war taught me a number of things about myself and about the world—some practical, some philosophical. I witnessed the transience of life but, being young, I camouflaged my fear with the thought, "It won't happen to me." I experienced the enemy at close quarters, close enough to smell its humanity, which made things just that much more difficult. I realized that being a man was neither a function of biology nor an adopted pose, but rather a mission in life. It demanded not only courage and resourcefulness but also hard work and tenacity. I became aware of my responsibilities to myself and to my country; of the strength that comes from the unity of a group and of my own strength as an individual.

The personal and professional wealth of experience I amassed during the war and before it was immense. I became aware of the significance of Israel's base of human capital and the powerful influence that a talented and cohesive team drawn from its own ranks could exert. The mix of the analytical and the practical fired my imagination. Brain-paper-pencil turned out to be an effective weapon system. I began to get some idea of my own worth. I also realized that my intellect had its market price.

Chapter 3
Three Memories

1

Uri was only fifteen when our father asked him to leave school and get a job. Dad worked in a printing cooperative, his meager salary barely enough to support the family. Mom had worked for the electric company until Amnon was born, and then quit to look after him. My brother willingly left high school, found work in a bank, and went to evening classes to complete his matriculation. My parents were deeply appreciative of his sacrifice.

Uri, who would later join Kibbutz Yiftach in the Galilee, had no hesitation about leaving school. He was inspired by the socialist youth movement's powerful ideology of tilling the land so that the Jewish people will "be planted in our natural soil from which we have been uprooted, and strike our roots deep into its life-giving substance" (A.D. Gordon, the Israeli Labor movement ideologist). During my childhood, I had similar thoughts, mostly because I admired my brother and what he stood for, but also because those were the ideals of our time. The bonus of being part of the youth movement track was that you could do your military service with your friends, and ultimately join a kibbutz with them. But I was essentially a city boy, a bookworm, and a lover of intellectual rather than physical challenges. I dreaded the time when I'd be asked to follow my brother's example, to leave school and help support the family.

My father believed that work comes before education. He was a highly disciplined, self-educated man. He emigrated from Poland to Palestine on his own in the 1930s, took evening classes in accounting, and didn't consider a formal education to be really necessary. He felt you could expand your horizons and learn everything you needed to know by reading books. I admired him for being self-made, well read, and broad-minded, but felt he lacked foresight. The world was changing and where matriculation was once enough, a college education would soon be a must. Early on, I had felt that without money, only intellect and education would make it possible for me to shape my future.

My parents, however, did not agree. As members of the "all-for-one and one-for-all" generation, they didn't attach much importance to personal fulfillment. The homeland, after all, was barely established, and the new nation had not yet fully formed. People had to make a living, not pick and choose. I was torn between my aspirations and my respect for my parents. The closer I got to my fifteenth birthday, the more troubled I became. How could I bridge the two worldviews? What could I do to persuade my parents to let me stay at school?

One evening, about two weeks before my birthday, I decided to consult the encyclopedia. If I could find an academic profession that my father would approve of, maybe he would let me finish high school. Because they were heavy, the thick volumes were on the top shelf, the widest in the bookcase, with the smaller books organized neatly below.

I took a chair and climbed up to the encyclopedia shelf. I made it safely to the top but on the way down, the heavy volume slipped from my hands, knocking Yosef Haim Brenner's book *Bereavement and Failure* off the middle shelf and into the fish tank on a small table below. I didn't know where to hide my embarrassment. Dad, who was immersed in reading on the balcony, had noticed the little drama. He rose, scooped the book out of the water and carefully laid it out to dry. Shaking his head at me, he murmured, "Oy, Roni, Roni," as if to say that I was a hopeless case. Then, he delivered a scientific lecture on water, the enemy of print. Dad was proud that the writings of important Hebrew authors had been produced at "his" printing press, and there I was, criminally negligent, feeding the fish with his creation. "Anyway, what were you looking for up there, my little Tarzan?"

Here it comes, I thought, the moment I had dreaded. Mom sensed a storm was looming and quickly grabbed Amnon's hand. "We're going to Aunt Sima's." Dad nodded a farewell, but his gaze remained fixed on me.

"Roni, soon you'll have to pitch in and help shoulder the family's responsibilities," he began, getting straight to the point. "You'll be able to continue your studies in evening classes, of course." Instead of refusing outright as I had planned, I began to stammer. "I'm … a good … student, Dad. I want to finish school with high grades and a good matriculation certificate, and I can." My feeble voice got firmer then faded out again. "Learn in the evening," my father said, "just like Uri did, and you'll get the same matriculation certificate." This time it was his voice that developed a nervous hoarseness.

"It's not the same at all! They're not the same pupils or the same teachers at night," I cried out from the bottom of my heart. "I'm not quitting school now. I'm not, and that's that." There. I had uttered the rebellious words. Tears choked me as I fought for the right to decide my own future, but I stood firm and presented my arguments until he was won over. "OK," he said at last. "I will respect your wishes. You can stay at school, but bear in mind that you'll have to work hard to earn your keep during vacations." I was overjoyed. I was doing that willingly anyway; the main thing was that my schooling wasn't going to be interrupted.

The encyclopedia hadn't been needed after all, and Dad put it back on the top shelf by himself. Better safe than sorry.

2

Three years later, we were sitting on another balcony in our new apartment at the corner of Nordau and Dizengoff, fourth floor, no elevator. I had matriculated with the high grades I had hoped for, and was awarded a full scholarship to join the Israeli army's prestigious academic program, called Atuda. This would enable me to complete my university studies before doing my army service, and then serve in my chosen field. I was filled with ambition but at that point I had no idea what profession I wanted to follow, or where I should study.

In those days, a decent young Israeli, one of Zionism's "new Jews," was supposed to help build the motherland by the sweat of his brow, in the fields or in the citrus groves. A nice city boy was expected to choose a productive occupation that made a contribution to society.

When my father saw my excellent matriculation results, he wrote to Technion-Israel Institute of Technology to request information and application forms. When the paperwork arrived in the mail, he and I sat on the balcony and began to pore over the catalog. We sat together, father and son, discussing and debating with ourselves, but nothing really appealed. Wise as we were, we hadn't the faintest idea of how to choose among the subjects listed in the catalog. On the balcony across the boulevard, our neighbor, the poet Nathan Alterman, sat reading a newspaper. Maybe we should consult with him, my father whispered. Government ministers did. But Dad was only thinking aloud and would never have dared approach the famous poet. So we continued leafing wisely through the catalog, unable to reach any decision.

A breeze began to blow in from the sea, and Alterman rose, nodded to us, and went inside. As darkness descended on the city, we tried to finish the catalog. Just as my brother Amnon returned home from the youth movement's center and my mother called us to come in for dinner, we got to the very last listing.

"Electrical engineering and electro mechanics," my father read out reverently. It sounded good. "Pick this, Roni, pick this. Electricity is the future." He'd probably heard that prophecy from Artek, his admired brother-in-law, who was a senior engineer at Israel's electric company.

I started reading about the terms of admission and retorted: "It's the hardest course to get into. Just one in five or one in seven is accepted." The challenge only made Dad's eyes sparkle even more.

"OK, Dad," I said, "write 'Electrical Engineering' on the form." Enormously satisfied, he recorded our choice in his meticulous handwriting. "Shifra!" he called out to Mom, who had just come out of the kitchen with a bowl of salad, "Roni is going to be an electrical engineer."

That's how I ended up enrolled in electrical engineering. I had no idea what to expect at Technion, but it was exciting just to think about living away from home. Soon I would start my adult, independent life, without the close supervision of my parents.

In our room, before we went to sleep, I saw that Amnon had made my bed. I knew he was depressed, as I'd been when Uri was about to go into the army. This was a small gesture of love at parting. I wanted to say something to him as his big brother and from my heart, but in our house we didn't talk about feelings. Instead I joked with him about the omelet Mom had burned slightly. We played a game of chess, and he beat me. For winning, I gave him a fancy pocketknife that I knew he'd coveted for a long time. Afterward we went to bed, he full of sorrow, and I filled with excitement.

3

In June 1968, exactly one year after the Six-Day War, I was in the army and coming home almost every day. I was preparing for an interview at the Tel Aviv campus of Hebrew University, where I was thinking of enrolling in a master's degree program. Not in electrical engineering, though. Electrical engineering had turned out not to be for me. Instead of continuing to be bored for another three years, I decided to change courses and switched to Industrial Engineering & Management. I didn't know any more about this subject than I'd known about electricity a year earlier, but the field sounded broader and more diverse. My second choice was just a little more informed than the first one had been but, though it too was a shot in the dark, I'd hit a bull's-eye.

On the day of my interview my mother was ill. Before leaving the house I made her some tea and sat with her for a while. She had been indisposed for quite some time. Sitting up in bed, she was barely able to sip her drink, and the little that was drunk was just to please me. She had no appetite, and didn't even taste the hot chicken soup that her sister, Aunt Sima, Artek's wife, had brought. It had taken all the strength she possessed for her to write a letter to Uri. She managed to put it into an envelope, but not to close it. "Fix mistakes and send it, Ronile. Don't forget." I nodded and put the envelope into my shirt pocket. I was pressed for time, afraid I'd be late for the interview. As for her mistakes, I thought it better to leave them alone. They would surely make Uri smile. Unlike my father, who like her was of Polish birth, she never fully mastered Hebrew.

I went into the kitchen to make myself a quick cup of coffee, gulped it down, and returned to my mother's bedside to remove the teacup and say goodbye. "I'm going, Mom," I said. "Go, Ronile, and succeed. Thank you for tea. And tell Dad he doesn't have to come home early. I'm fine. And don't forget letter in pocket."

I went to the front door, opened it, and noticed there was a fresh breeze. I don't know what made me pause and go back into my parents' room. "Mom–" She didn't answer. I touched her. She didn't respond. Her eyes were shut. I tried again. "Mom ... Shifra!" Silence. I remember exactly what she was wearing, how she looked, the pen that had slipped from her open hand. I could see that she had died. I don't remember what I felt—I don't want to remember. I don't think I've ever talked about it since. It's hard for me to talk about it now. I was twenty-four years old.

My first thought was of Amnon, the one most attached to our mother. He was serving as a signalman in an armored brigade in the Suez Canal Zone. How was I going to tell him?

My second thought was regret that Matia and I had not married before this. I knew my mother was waiting and hoping, quietly, patiently, without saying a word to us. We had met two years earlier, on June 6, 1966, just one month before I had finished my degree at Technion and had begun my army service, a year almost to the day before the Six-Day War. Since then, her parents had become friendly with mine, and just a week earlier they'd gone together to the theater. Matia and I were already living together, and both sets of parents failed to understand what we were waiting for.

My third thought was that I should cry out, call for help, do something, even though nothing could be done. I didn't need a doctor to tell me she was dead. I called for an ambulance and gave the address. Then I rang my father and told him to go immediately to Ichilov Hospital. Uri was at his kibbutz. He too had to be told—but first I had to tell Amnon. It was impossible to call a serviceman from a civilian phone, so to speak to my brother I had to go to my military office. Even there I couldn't dial Amnon's unit directly. Every call had to go through a military switchboard.

The ambulance came and took my mother and me to the hospital. When we arrived, my father was already there waiting. A doctor, looking as if he were just out of school, pronounced her dead on arrival. Gently, he covered her face, and advised my father to go home. Dad nodded sadly and I set off as quickly as I could for my office, which was in the IDF Headquarters close by, to tell Amnon.

I sat by the phone and called the military operator. "Connect me with unit 210. This is an urgent family matter." From the tone of my voice it must have been obvious to her that I wasn't joking. She did everything she could to reach Amnon's unit in the Canal Zone. Finally she got through and asked for my brother. We waited—she, at her end, facing the flickering switchboard, and I at mine, staring at the blank wall.

"He's coming," she said suddenly, half talking, half shouting. "Here he is. Speak."

"Amnon!" No reply. All I could hear was static and the sound of ringing. "He's not hearing you," the operator explained. "What shall we do?"

"Can he hear you?" I asked. "Yes, he can hear me. Do you want me to give him a message?" She sounded eager to help. "Yes, I do. I know it's hard, but you have to tell him this: 'Roni says that Mom is dead. Come home immediately.'" A heavy silence, broken only by static. "I'll tell him," she said. "How are you two connected?" "I'm his brother." "Wait on the line, Roni." The static waited with me. Then I heard her voice, as if from a great distance, reverberating like an especially bad recording: "Am-non-non, your mom-om-om—died-ied-ied. Roni says come home-ome-ome."

After the funeral, I gave Uri the letter Mom had written him. My brother read it quickly while leaning on a dusty cypress tree. Our mother's mistakes produced no smiles this time. Instead his lower lip trembled. Then he gave it to his wife, Bruria, who read it and cried. Finally she handed it to me and I put it back in my pocket.

Amnon, who had come to the funeral straight from the Canal, suggested that we sleep at the house with Dad so he wouldn't be alone on his first night as a widower. Dinner was a somber affair. When it was over, my father went to his bedroom and we brothers to our old room. There we once again read our mother's last letter. She had addressed it to "Urik and Brurik and my dearest, dearest grandchildren." She wrote about Matia's father, who'd returned from a trip abroad bearing gifts for everyone, and how glad she was that she and my father were going to the theater with Matia's parents. She'd been alone on Saturday because, she wrote in her inimitable style, "Roni is all his time staying at Matia and Dad was working. He is always doing things outside house ..." She ended the letter with an appeal to her grandchildren on the kibbutz: "Who knows how to write, please write ... I have lot of time to read. Who knows to draw, please draw ... waiting for very, very long letter." She didn't mention the illness that was sucking the life out of her or that she had been feeling lonely ever since her youngest son had been drafted. Many years later when my youngest son went into the army and the house was empty of children I understood how much had been left out of that letter.

Needless to say, I didn't make it to the interview at Hebrew University. All I could do was to send a note of apology. My endless vacillation about what I should study ended with a decision to go for a master's degree in operations research at Technion. This involved one day a week in Haifa and one evening a week in Tel Aviv. I also submitted a proposal for my doctoral dissertation, but somewhere along the way I changed direction. Matia realized that given the reality of the times in which we lived, it would be difficult for her to work as an architect and raise a family. She decided to switch to a course in traffic engineering.

In 1969, a year after my mother died, Matia and I were married in a modest ceremony. A year later, a pregnant Matia began working in transport engineering. Without even noticing, we were drawn into the struggle to advance our careers and start a family. Her path was clearly defined. Mine was still unknown. I had a college education and extensive job experience in the IDF. I already had quite a clear idea of where my strengths lay, but I still hadn't decided what path my life would take.

Chapter 4
A Snapshot of Childhood

Under the cover of darkness, the pirate ship creeps up the Yarkon River estuary straight into the sleeping city. Wearing a plumed hat, my sword already drawn, I lie in wait by a thicket of tall reeds, my band of courageous footballing musketeers just behind me. As the vessel reaches the Hapoel Tel Aviv gym I give the order. "Fooooollow me! Stooooorm the ship!" And, brave commander that I am, I lead the attack. My loyal friends, like devoted Tarzans, scale the ropes that had dropped on cue from the eucalyptus trees all around us. Swiftly as monkeys, we land on the deck. Barely recovering from the jolt of the fall, I hear a menacing voice: "Get up Roni; get up, get dressed." But I am up! And dressed. And in the midst of a raging battle. My eyes seek out the pirates hiding under mounds of rope and sails.

"Get up Roni, get up." Can this be my father calling? "The train won't wait for us." Train? Hold on a minute, I'm on a ship. Hey, what is happening to my ship? Slowly the vessel slips away beneath me. In a minute I will surely drown.

"Get dressed!" My eyes are open now, but there is nothing except the blackness of night. "Dad, hold on tight or you'll drown." A small light is switched on in the hallway. I see my father all dressed up and holding my coat, ready to leave the house. We are at home. There is no ship. It's the middle of the night. Something bad is happening—that is why my father wants me. Afraid to ask what it is I get dressed quickly and quietly so as not to wake up my little brother. The pirate ship lingers in my mind's eye, now clearly just a dream.

My father and I leave the house in silence. Amnon and my mother are still asleep. My brother Uri's bed is empty, he's away on a school trip. It's a cold November day. We hurry to the waiting bus, already full of silent passengers. I recognize one or two, friends of Dad's from the Ahdut Press Collaborative. Yazek, the typesetter, offers me a tangerine. "Thank you," I whisper, and he smiles amiably. We set off, arriving soon at a railway station. A special train is waiting, most of the carriages already full. Ours is the last bus to arrive, holding up the departure. We too board the train.

At long last my father explains what this is all about. "We're going to pay our respects to Weizmann." Now I remember that my parents had been talking about this. It had been announced on the radio that Israel's first president, Dr. Chaim Weizmann, was dead. Every Israeli child learned that Weizmann was a distinguished scientist and a remarkable person, a role model whom we should try to emulate. I had once gone with my father to hear the great man give a speech at the Municipality on Bialik Street. Against the backdrop of Tel Aviv's muddy, bleak landscape, his neatly trimmed beard, black top hat, and elegant walking cane made a big impression on me. So we're going to pay homage to His Honor the president.

On the train, I did my best to revive the images of the pirate ship dream but they had evaporated like mist. I peeled and ate the tangerine Yazek had given me and tucked the peels into my pocket, far too drowsy to look for a waste bin. When the train slowed down I woke up. "We've arrived," said Dad. The train continued its journey for a few meters past the station, and then came to a halt, its wheels spewing luminous sparks into the night. "We'll be heading back in an hour," somebody announced. All the passengers got up, made their way down to the gravel a few meters past the platform, and began walking silently toward the Weizmann Institute. My teacher Ricky told us that President Weizmann had lived there with his family, and that the presidential quarters were surrounded by beautiful gardens.

"Why is the path round?" I asked quietly. We seemed to be going in circles and not getting anywhere. "All the paths here are circular," Dad explained, "so that the visitor can lose himself in the beauty of the place." We walked a little farther on the circular path and then Dad said, "This is where we have to turn right. This is the path to the house."

We found ourselves at the beginning of a straight path with a point of light at the end—a single glimmer in the otherwise darkened garden, drawing us toward it like a beacon. With us in the lead, everyone began walking along the straight path that led to the front courtyard of the president's house. I could feel my heart pounding faster and faster. My father, sensing my excitement, took my hand. As we approached, all eyes, including mine, were transfixed by four shafts of light that beamed from the ground, illuminating a canopy above draped in blue and black ribbons. The canopy was suspended by metal chains attached to high poles, not unlike the masts on the pirate ship of my dream—except that instead of a skull, each one supported a golden Star of David.

The coffin lay under the canopy. Next to it stood an armed guard of honor. Our small Tel Avivian procession walked past the coffin. Dad told me to walk ahead of him. I paused for a moment, though I didn't really know why, probably just imitating the grown-ups. I was a bit frightened—more by the proximity to death than by the enormity of the occasion.

On a table nearby lay Weizmann's top hat, walking cane, and crocodile briefcase. "Now that he's gone," Dad told me, "these will become national symbols." Then he fastened the top button of my coat and said something that didn't seem at all relevant to the death of a president. "You should know, Roni, that people, children too, are duty-bound not only to their families but also to their nation." I was much too young to understand what these words really meant, yet wise enough to store them in my memory. I have a duty to my nation, I thought to myself with concealed pride. That's what my father said.

The president's funeral was attended only by the very most important people: representatives of the Histadrut (unions), senior civil servants, foreign diplomats. The nocturnal visit, the special train, and the opportunity to pay last respects—these were small tokens granted to men of my father's standing. They were close enough to the ruling elite to be singled out in some way, but not important enough to take part in the funeral itself. From this I learned that all men are equal, but some are more equal than others.

Chapter 5
Never a Hired Hand

"I'll never be a hired hand!" This was Dad's constant response to Mom's demand that he look for a second job. Her complaints about our increasingly difficult circumstances shook him to the core, but he refused to compromise. He was proud to be a member of the urban working class, and steadfastly objected to the degradation of working for a boss. "Anything but a hired hand" was his battle cry.

Dad loathed capitalism because it divided the world into capitalists and wage slaves. He abhorred totalitarian Communism for subverting the ideal of equality. His search led him to the cooperative movement, specifically to a printing cooperative known as Dfus Achdut. This was the second of two cooperatives founded in 1910 by David Ben Gurion (who was to become the first prime minister of Israel), Yizchak Ben-Zvi (who became the second president of Israel), and Ben-Zvi's wife, Rachel Yanait. It was run exclusively by and for the benefit of its working members without the involvement of outside salaried staff. The mission was to print and publish a newspaper, Ha–Achdut, as well as a selection of Zionist literature. My father, who identified with the founders' ideals, discovered his spiritual home.

In time, the press had moved to a beautiful Art Deco building on Levontin Street in Tel Aviv, where it operated until the end of the millennium. It printed books by Bialik and Ravnitzky, stories by Chekhov, Arlozorov's quarterly *Achdut Ha'avoda*, and refused point- blank to print books counter to its ideology. At the height of the war of independence, the press printed free of charge Alterman's poem *Al Zot (For That)*, which denounced Israeli soldiers' killing of Arab civilians during the conquest of Lod. The poem was censored and the Labor-associated newspaper *Davar* refused to publish it. This infuriated Prime Minister Ben-Gurion, and he ordered that the free copies printed by Achdut Press be made compulsory reading for all soldiers.

These and many similar stories were Dad's way of passing on to us his spiritual and political legacy. He had joined the cooperative during the 1930s, initially as its director of finance. He waited his turn for the better part of thirty years until finally, on February 17, 1967, he became the press's manager. Throughout his adult life, Yizchak Einav was a shareholder and active member of the cooperative printing press, an equal among equals, in an establishment he passionately identified with. He was never a hired hand, never subordinate to anyone, and even the financial distress at home didn't persuade him to give up his dignified independence. Mom's demands pained him, but her refusal to understand how he felt wounded him even more.

His solution was to cut back, save, and get his children to pitch in as soon as they were old enough. Indeed, since our early youth, all three of us had worked during our vacations. I had always earned my own pocket money. Dad appreciated that, and sometimes arranged temporary work for me at the printing press. "You must be a hired hand now, you're still young, but when you grow up …" It wasn't easy for him to ask one of his sons to do something he himself wouldn't do, but it didn't bother me in the slightest. From the moment I began to earn money and taste independence, I worked willingly, even joyfully, and was glad to do what I could to help support the family.

My bonus was being with him at the printing house, being treated like an adult, eating lunch with him in the canteen, listening to his views on cooperation and equality and the importance of work. I loved watching the typesetters, skillfully placing row upon row of mirrored lead letters upside down into printing blocks. I marveled at their ability to transform handwritten texts full of deletions and corrections into neat, clean blocks.

Later, as a student at the Technion, I also worked, not only to ease my parents' burden, but also to pay my own tuition, because for each year I received an Atuda scholarship, I would have to serve an additional year in the army. Reducing that commitment to the minimum was my main goal. Although I'd been raised on the values of the Labor movement and the importance of manual work, I chose not to earn money in the industry for which my academic training was preparing me. Hebrew Labor is a beautiful ideal, but the smell of print at the press was like Chanel No. 5 compared to the stench emitted by Hebrew factories at the height of summer. My course at Technion included periods of fieldwork at the Ata Clothing and Assis Juice factories in Haifa. The noise, pollution, overcrowding, and sweat instantly sent me looking for a cleaner line of work, where I could use my intellect and education and be independent—not exactly like Dad, but in the same spirit.

Teaching was the obvious choice. I had a go at it but the salary was an insult and the workload insane. Twice a week I ran around like a headless chicken, back and forth by train between Tel Aviv, which is in central Israel, on the Mediterranean, and Haifa, farther north, also on the coast. At the beginning of the week I would leave Tel Aviv for Technion, stop on the way in Hadera to teach physics at the high school, and then arrive late for class in Haifa. In the middle of the week I would go back to Tel Aviv in order to stop off again in Hadera, and again be late for my course at Technion. I was in perpetual motion between work and school. Inevitably, my grades were affected. As a result, the army stopped my grant payments, which forced me to step up the pace even more in order to finance myself.

Necessity is the mother of invention. With my friend Shmuel Lachman, I created my first marketable product—a booklet of solutions in thermodynamics. We began by meticulously working out the answers to all the exercises in the standard textbook for that difficult branch of physics. Then we hired a typist, proofread the material she produced, printed it at the Achdut Press, and bound hundreds of copies manually. The booklet sold successfully in student union shops, and the two of us felt as if we had struck gold.

On the day I realized that I was no longer a burden to my parents and could shorten my period of bondage to the IDF, I was walking on air. When I paid the tuition for my last two years at Technion, I was in seventh heaven. How good it was to earn money! How nice it was to have a steady income. And what fun it was to allow myself some small luxuries, like eating Wiener schnitzel with the gang at Stefan's little eatery near Technion in Neve Sha'anan.

Once I'd finished my military service, completed the required course work in Operations Research at Technion, and submitted my thesis, I received my master's degree. Much more important, I became father to Liran. Fatherhood spurred me on to find a proper job. At least for now, my dream and Dad's directive never to be a hired hand was on the back burner. I began to look into teaching, no longer as a sideline but as a career. If I could support my family as an employee in the academic world, that's what I would do. Adapt or perish is, after all, nature's directive.

The transition from student to teacher in my department at Technion was a challenge I embraced with great enthusiasm. I taught a few core classes in the master's degree program, and was also able to develop an innovative course on game and decision theory, which was becoming a special interest for me. Before long, I was offered a half-time job at the fledgling Ben-Gurion University in Beersheba, where I pioneered a course in a new area, Computer Applications in Planning and Engineering. Job offers streamed in, and I said yes to them all, regardless of the distance I'd have to travel and the amount of work that would be involved. Above all I needed to earn enough to support my family. Working as a teacher felt good, and soon I began to seriously consider becoming an academic. Why not? It was respectable, and would make my dad happy. Many of my friends in ordnance had become professors. It wasn't boring, I wasn't bossed around. I was helping to nurture the next generation of intellectuals and making a decent living.

Yet I was not content. The ivory tower, while pleasant and convenient, was not where I belonged. Where I did belong was still a big unknown. I envied my colleagues, who had always known they would be physicists or musicians, authors or researchers. My own path remained hidden. Despite giving my all to academia, I never stopped hoping for something else, an omen, a pillar of fire, or some other clear signal. How it would come, when, and in what form, was anybody's guess, but come it will—as in the song from *West Side Story*: "Something's comin', something good …"

My good thing materialized in the form of the highly energetic Yehuda Faust and his laconic invitation to do some business together.

Yehuda had been a student in the Decision Theory course I taught at Technion. The idea of integrating decision-making, Games Theory, Operations Research and Utility Theory was considered bold in those days and attracted mature and original students like Yehuda. One day, in the fall of 1972, he phoned and asked me to meet him for coffee. Without beating around the bush, he said, "I've left a senior position at the Ministry of Housing and now I'm managing the offices of Dan Eitan and Eri Goshen as a partner." I had met the well-known architects during my army service. "We're swamped with projects," he said in a voice hoarse from smoking. "There's been a huge development boom since the Six-Day War, and we're short-staffed. I'm not looking for architects, we have plenty of them," he added when he noticed the quizzical look on my face. "I need people like you, who understand economics." A circle of bluish smoke drifted from his nostrils. "Tell me," he said, coughing, "Aren't you bored with all that academic stuff? Why don't you come in with us? We've got a lot of work and some really good people. Come on, let's go into business together."

Business! Was this the omen, the signal I'd been expecting for so long? It was highly unusual for an industrial engineer to be asked to join an architect's office, but Yehuda Faust's invitation sounded perfectly logical to me. It had come at just the right moment and not entirely by surprise. The knowledge-driven and high-tech industries in Israel have to rely on personal recommendations. We want to work with someone whose paths we've crossed in peacetime and with whom our sweat and blood has mingled in times of war. We know and trust each other.

Yehuda Faust had known me from our days together in ordnance and at Technion. To Dan Eitan he presented me as a valuable item of human capital that he felt would contribute to the team. Eitan trusted the personal recommendation, didn't ask too many questions, and agreed to take me on, presumably on the basis that I might be useful one day. Instead of humbly thanking him for the opportunity he was giving me, I said, "I don't want to be a hired hand. I'll work for you as a freelancer." And Dan, who should have kicked me out for my chutzpa, nodded with a smile and shook my hand. He must have been pleased to see that I was the determined kind.

That's how my career in business began. One fine day I stopped being an employee in academia and became a small subcontracted freelancer for a large firm of architects. Now I had to justify their trust and see if the gamble I'd taken was also worth the risk. I proved my ability, working at full throttle on financial planning with Yehuda Faust, and the detailed programs I wrote for the architectural projects produced handsome profits. Soon I began to feel confident in my choice and started to dream about establishing a business of my own. After looking into various prospects and launching a few trial balloons, I realized I would have to be patient and wait for the right moment.

Two years later, at the end of 1972, I took the plunge and set up my first company within the Eitan-Goshen structure and named it Einav Systems. No pillar of fire appeared, the god of business didn't whisper in my ear. I just had a feeling that this was the right time, a moment of clairvoyance. Later on, experience taught me that economic and business processes have a rhythm of their own with which you have to flow. Like seeds, they develop below the surface and burst forth at just the right time.

At first, everything stayed the same. I continued to work on joint projects for Eitan-Goshen just as before. The only change was in the invoices I submitted that now bore the new Einav Systems logo, which my wife, Matia, designed, and my proud father printed on stationery and business cards at the Achdut Press. Owning a business made me feel good, but other than an increase in volume, the now independent Einav Systems simply continued to provide financial and managerial services to the flourishing architectural firm—its one and only customer.

During 1973, people in the office began whispering about "something very big" in Iran, then still ruled by the Shah. There were various rumors, including one about the manager of a known Israeli engineering firm who was going around Teheran in a chauffeur-driven Mercedes. When some of us expressed our disapproval of such extravagance, we were told by someone in the know that the manager used this show of wealth to impress the Iranians in the hope of getting a piece of the very big "something." More to the point, success for the man with the Mercedes might lead to Eitan-Goshen, by now one of Israel's biggest architectural firms, being asked to play a major role in a huge foreign construction project.

The office was then situated at 111 Hayarkon Street, facing the sea, and close to my parents' apartment. That enabled me to pop over and see Dad frequently. Since my mother died, he had become withdrawn and quiet, detached from the world. He was still living in the same apartment at 27 Nordau, which remained exactly as Mom had left it. He continued to water the giant cacti that she had grown on the balcony but didn't know how to care for them, and most died from over-watering. He fed her fish dutifully, but they, too, had become enfeebled in my mother's absence.

My dad loved his work as manager of the printing press, but his social life, now that he was single, had dwindled considerably. My brother Uri often invited him to the kibbutz, and Matia and I had him over to our house. Amnon, when he was discharged from the army and started to study economics at Tel Aviv University, went back to live at home. But Dad remained lonely. He was reading a lot, as he had always done, but his taste had changed. Instead of Tolstoy, he immersed himself in the writings of the Talmudic scholar Maimonides—as if he'd suddenly discovered religion. I didn't ask him about it. In our family we didn't ask personal questions. Matia and I visited him with Liran as often as we could. Just seeing his grandson made him forget his sadness briefly and he'd look for ways of amusing the little darling.

On January 10, 1973, we celebrated Amnon's birthday. Matia brought a nice cake, and Dad gave a humorous speech in honor of the occasion. The party was over late, and I arrived at my office the next morning bleary-eyed. Just as I reached for the calendar to tear off the previous day's page, the phone rang. It was Amnon. "Come home, quickly," he said in an odd tone. "Why, what's happened? Are you all right?" Instead of answering, Amnon became angry: "Didn't you hear me? I said come home now."

I dropped everything and ran to the apartment. In the stairwell I almost collided with the doctor from the clinic. He was apologizing profusely for something some nurse had said. Not knowing what he was talking about, I bounded up the stairs. He, despite his age, didn't lag far behind. Amnon was sitting in the living room, pale and stunned. He pointed toward our parents' bedroom. I hurried in with the doctor. Dad was lying on his side of the bed, motionless. Next to the bed was a copy of his last project, *Fighters Talk* (Siah Lohamim, later published in English as *The Seventh Day*). His hand lay over the cover as if he had just set it down and folded his reading glasses. He looked asleep, but he wasn't breathing. That's how Amnon found him. The doctor straightened himself from leaning over my father's body. "I'm sorry. I'm very sorry." He sounded more like a friend than a doctor.

I made the necessary phone calls. I already knew the drill. The cause of death had been cardiac arrest. Death in one's sleep was merciful, the doctor said. Our father had probably not felt a thing. He looked peaceful, calm, noble. I certainly hoped he hadn't suffered. Amnon, who was in shock, managed to explain that after calling me he'd contacted the clinic, and a nurse had told him they didn't make house calls at that time of day. Raising his voice, he insisted on speaking directly to the doctor, who then rushed over to our house. Only when Dad was placed on the stretcher did my brother emerge from the shock and begin to cry. I didn't cry. I was angry, a painful, bitter anger. It had happened to each of us. I'd been with Mom. He'd been with Dad. We'd become orphaned from both of our parents.

Their lives were short and tough, but full of meaning and warmth. They'd both died relatively young: Mom at sixty-one, and Dad, who was three years younger, at sixty-two. They were a pair of idealistic urban pioneers who had lived frugal lives the likes of which it is hard for us to imagine. They brought up three sons, and made no demands on anyone. They had an absolute belief in collective responsibility as a way of life, and never once said, "I'm entitled to this" or "I deserve that." Such thoughts would never have crossed their minds. They worked hard, educated us as best they could, and helped each other and their fellow Israelis on both personal and national levels. When Dad considered it his duty to take revenge on the Nazis for murdering his family and volunteered to join the Jewish Brigade, Mom never tried to dissuade him from leaving her alone with two young children. Each man and woman had a role and she knew that it was her duty to grin and bear it.

My parents knew in their hearts and minds that the Jewish people in the land of Israel must be a collective, a community, a united team, and that solidarity was a condition for Israel's renaissance. They had fun, and despite their modest means, managed to travel the length and breadth of the country they loved. In their tiny Tel Aviv apartment they had friends over for dancing parties, the only accessory being a phonograph and a few records. They went on trips, squeezing dangerously into a friend's pickup truck. Together they sailed the Yarkon River, then relatively clean. Above all, they led a life based on their beliefs: that work is a privilege, that spiritual needs come before physical needs, that the Jewish state is a gift, that man is also a people. When Dad died, Amnon and I were already young adults—but our age didn't lessen the pain of parting from him. Amnon was sunk in sorrow, and I barricaded myself behind a wall of anger.

As I was to discover, becoming an orphan is difficult no matter what age you are. When shiva, the traditional Jewish week of mourning, was over, I went back to work, hoping that keeping busy would make my rage go away. But I couldn't stop thinking about my parents, about their lives, and their deaths. The anger gnawed at me relentlessly. When I was starting to overcome it, I went to visit Amnon at our parents' apartment. The sight of their empty room threw me back into an emotional turmoil, which lasted until the eruption of the Yom Kippur War in October of that year. Only then was my personal sorrow drowned by the worst crisis the country had had to face since the War of Independence in 1948.

The nation was in shock: how could the Arabs manage to so completely surprise us Jewish supermen? In the Sinai, the Egyptians crossed the Suez Canal and penetrated deep into the peninsula. The outbreak of war marked the downfall of Israel's lofty belief in its invincibility and in the security provided by the canal and the so-called "Bar Lev line." Like France's Maginot line before it and all other such supposedly impenetrable fortifications in history, at the moment of truth, enemy forces were able to cross it and threaten the very existence of the Jewish state. The set of core beliefs held by Israel's political and military leaders had been shattered.

At the time, Matia was working in Tel Aviv. I was a civilian waiting to be enlisted in reserve forces. But no one called. Could it possibly be that this time, experts in ordnance were not needed? That didn't make sense. I was losing patience, but Matia, who was already pregnant with our second child, begged me to stay put: When and if they need you they will find you, she reasoned. Still I was restless. I yearned to be in the thick of things again, like in the old days. How come there was a war raging and I was sitting at home?

Today we know that the crucial difference between the Six-Day War of 1967 and the Yom Kippur War in 1973 was that in '67, the reserves were called up well in advance of the outbreak of hostilities, whereas at the start of the '73 war, the General Staff Headquarters was taken by surprise. In 1967, all the fighting had taken place in enemy territory. Yet this time around, because the Egyptian attack had been so unexpected, our lines and theirs crisscrossed. The military command was simply unwilling to risk sending us onto the battlefield to photograph tanks under such chaotic circumstances.

For four or five days the war raged and we were stuck at home. Not knowing what was happening and sitting idly by was a hugely frustrating experience. Finally, on the morning of the sixth day, instead of going to Eitan-Goshen's offices, I went to the ordnance building in the IDF headquarters and asked to be mobilized. They agreed. A day or two later my whole team was called up and sent into the field to do exactly the same work we'd done in the Six-Day War.

As it happened, we began in the Golan Heights and immediately found ourselves in danger, because the road we were traveling on and the whole surrounding area was still being shelled by Syrian artillery. Though the front lines had crossed into Israel and extended into Syria, at least it wasn't the remote Sinai. We could occasionally leave the Golan Heights battlefield and go to rest, if not in our own homes then at least somewhere inside Israel. One night I slept at Kibbutz Ayelet Hashachar and in the early evening went to Kibbutz Yiftach to visit Uri and his family. We were happy to see each other and talk about Dad. I was shocked to realize how much Uri resembled him, something I hadn't noticed before.

"Maybe for Dad it's better that he died before this inglorious war," Uri said with little emotion in his voice. He no longer misses him, I thought—he's come to terms with Dad's death. When will I?

At the end of the visit, the entire Yiftach clan assembled to bid farewell to the valiant soldier Roni, who was going back to the war zone. Uri's five kids gathered around the military jeep that had come to pick me up, getting on, getting off, probing. With my gun in hand as befits a real warrior, I hopped onto the seat and then—boom—the weapon went off. The driver swore, checked to see that no one was hurt, and stepped on the gas.

I fastened the safety lock and nervously turned around to see Uri clasping his head, literally shaking with laughter, and my nephews following suit. Well, guns and me ...

This war lasted a lot longer than six days and our reserve duty was extended. We were able to survey only slightly more than half the war-damaged tanks, whereas in 1967 we spotted every one of them. But in terms of constructive conclusions, the work we did in 1973 was no less important. This time, the lessons were harsh and bitter.

Zach, our second son, whose name was a modern take on the letters in my father's name, Yitzchak, was born just before my discharge in the winter of '73, the winter in which the State of Israel embarked on a painful process of soul-searching. Along with representatives of various branches and departments of the IDF, I was invited to a meeting with Prime Minister Golda Meir. The group included pilots, armored corps personnel, infantrymen, and people from the army's intelligence unit. Golda was under daily attack by the media. She wanted to hear firsthand what had really happened from those who had been on the battlefields. "We the people are the army," she said, adding that she wanted to talk directly with "the people." I don't know if such things are done in other countries, if in other places the level of intimacy between the leader and the man in the street is great enough for such an extraordinary meeting to take place.

Golda left her desk and sat in the armchair facing us. The group was seated close to her in a semicircle, as if in a family get-together. "Tell me everything," she said in her smoker's voice. "It's just you and me talking. No minutes are being taken, and you can speak openly and freely." In her familiar American accent, she began to ask us various questions. At first, the replies were cautious, a hesitant yes followed by an equally diffident no. Then the words began to gush as if flowing from a powerful well, each story more painful than the one before. We described the shock when the Egyptian strike came like a bolt from the blue, the total lack of preparedness, the slow reaction, the blunders. Golda's face was ashen as she listened. A soldier from the armored corps said, "It pains me to hurt you, but it pains me more to think about my friends who were killed." The prime minister cried. She sobbed. I don't remember how long we sat with her. It was dreadful. We had been served drinks and cakes. No one touched them.

The state had been shaken to its foundation. The government stood accused by soldiers and civilians alike, of having been responsible for a calamity and dereliction of duty. The word mechdal (negligence of tragic proportions) entered the Hebrew lexicon as a description of the tragedy. It became impossible for the country to move on until these accusations were dealt with. The government set up a Commission of Enquiry. The Agranat Commission placed the blame on the army and the chief of staff, David Elazar, "Dado." While they were blamed for the lack of preparedness, the fact is that in no time they had turned a potentially humiliating defeat into a clear victory. The commission's limited findings led to mass demonstrations—a campaign that eventually forced the resignation of the entire government.

Despite the depth of the crisis, life gradually returned to normal—perhaps a cliché but nonetheless true. Every person in his own limited sphere has to cope, earn a living, raise children, build a home. Wars, even morally justified ones, are eventually set aside to let normal life return.

I, too, went back to my routine and to Einav Systems, and the rumor about Iran heated up again. Before long it ceased to be a rumor and transformed into an offer that Dan Eitan couldn't refuse. An unnamed Iranian contractor had been awarded a giant Defense Ministry contract for the building of three new cities for the Iranian navy. After winning the bid he turned to an Israeli company, Engineering Services, to implement the contract on his behalf. Engineering Services' manager was Nissim Barzik, the man who had been riding around Teheran in a chauffeur-driven Mercedes. His investment in opulence had evidently paid off. However, Engineering Services, a large company that was actually a group of companies specializing in almost every branch of engineering that exists, had no architectural expertise.

To fulfill the alluring Iranian contract, Engineering Services contacted Eitan-Goshen. For the three new cities they'd undertaken to build in Iran they needed programs and architectural master plans. They needed urban planning. And they needed detailed architectural work plans down to items such as air conditioners and doors. This was a gigantic project by any standard. It was any architect's dream. Eitan-Goshen jumped at the offer and I, as Einav Systems, their contracted quantification and programmatic expert, was the first person asked to begin the work. In a project as big as the Iranian one, you can't start to design anything without first having a comprehensive, detailed program. Maybe this was the opportunity I'd been waiting for? Maybe "something's comin', something good" would come out of Iran.

Chapter 6

Iran 101

Dan Eitan and his company had already designed several mega-projects in Israel and abroad. Yet when the firm was invited to build urban areas from scratch for tens of thousands of Iranian naval personnel and their families, it was an altogether new adventure. How do you go about planning entire cities?

The project was to include a large new city for 30,000 residents next to the ancient port of Bandar Abbas. Near Bandar Bushier, Iran's second main naval port after Bandar Abbas, housing for 20,000 was required. Kharg Island, a mere village, would have 5,000 new homes. Our developments were to be gated, satellite cities.

There was a lot to do. First we had to organize all the known requirements relating to housing, schools, hospitals, and other public institutions that the proposed population might require, in neat programs. These were then passed on to the team of architects, which translated them into detailed architectural plans, which in turn were handed to a firm of engineers who drafted the construction plans. Only then could the building work begin.

The Shah expected immediate implementation and his word was the law. He wanted those cities now, or else! His regime was on shaky ground, yet it was reasonably efficient. Money was no problem. Oil prices kept rising and the Shah's wealth was immense. The only thing this omnipotent ruler didn't possess was skilled technical manpower. This he found in Israel. The fact that Iran had no diplomatic relations with the Jewish state didn't bother him. We were his choice and his will was a command. Visas were issued and delivered to all of us within twenty-four hours through the good offices of the Swiss Embassy in Tel Aviv.

The whole thing was a dream come true. Go to this wasteland, we were told, and build the new Persia. We went in and designed the projects according to state-of-the-art Western standards, making allowances for local culture, the navy's requirements, Islam, and the unbelievably high local temperatures.

Feeling as if I'd chanced on a modern-day fairy tale, I got to work. I soon realized that my knowledge of Iran was scant. The only information I had about their navy, for example, was contained in one document written in poor English by the Iranian contractor. But solving new problems always appealed to me. That's what I'd built my reputation on in my ordnance days. My first assignment there involved groundbreaking research on maritime minefields. Then I helped invent the damage-assessment method we employed during the Six-Day War. To analyze the optimal design of an armored personnel carrier I combined economics, operational research, and mathematical programming. (I presented a censored version of this paper as a thesis for my master's degree.) The Iranian project offered me a great new challenge, which required imagination, initiative, and hours of research.

For each city project, I studied the population's needs in areas such as garbage collection in a modern Iranian city, municipal services, landscaping preferences, cultural institutions, shopping centers. I gathered vital information about the required mosques, schools, even cemeteries. Eventually I became something of an expert on Muslim culture. One by one, I put together the programs for Bandar Abbas, Bandar Bushier, and Kharg Island, with the help of the patient librarians at Tel Aviv's public libraries. I always kept in mind budgetary constraints because from the outset, it was clear that the Iranians had significantly underestimated the cost of the projects.

Meanwhile, my old friend from Technion, Lulu, and his company (AMAN Organizational & Management Consultants Ltd., a subsidiary of the Engineering Services group) were looking into the project's viability. In tandem, the architects and engineers, the true heroes of the story, began drafting the plans. With incredible speed, construction work on the satellite cities was underway.

The scope that we had to deal with was unlike anything Dan Eitan had ever encountered. For example, we needed 15,000 doors and 8,000 locks, which had to be imported or manufactured—fast! Some of the building components were made in Israel, some were bought in Iran, and some came from Europe. We were meticulous about quality until a local difficulty popped up. The proposal included a commitment to pre-agreed prices for various components, forcing us to use only products that the contractor had bought from merchants who had lined his pockets. This was the usual practice in Iran, and rejecting it was not an option.

In his heyday, the Shah was omnipotent. He gave orders, he provided the financing, and his instructions were promptly obeyed—even when they were impractical. It was rumored that he'd once decreed that every Persian baby must drink a glass of milk a day. All the sycophants nodded their heads except for one vizier (government officer) who dared to calculate the implications of the instruction. He figured if there were 60 million Iranians of whom five million were babies, they would need approximately ten million liters of milk per month. Iran's cow population was not large, so they would need to import hundreds of thousands of cows, build cowsheds and dairies, acquire the necessary refrigeration, set up dedicated transportation systems, and train thousands of professional dairymen. Perhaps, he suggested, it would be better just to import the milk?

The spirit of this rumored decree resembled the command to build three new satellite cities all at the same time. Yet the construction directive was practical because the Shah turned to us Israelis, world champions in working under pressure—so long as the work was in the private sector. In the public sector, Israel's record was far less impressive. My own neighborhood, Ramat Ilan, a public works housing project for only 1,000 families, took fifteen years to build. In Iran we built three cities in three years.

To be sure, mistakes were made. Problems pop up just when you think that everything is proceeding smoothly. In theory, it's the local contractor's task to anticipate them, but he is bound to miss some. Here's an example. Everyone knows that Muslims face Mecca when they pray, but not many people know that this custom affects the positioning of toilets, since it is forbidden to have a toilet facing Mecca. The navy's construction department headquarters was in Teheran and they had been involved primarily in building there and in Central Iran. Their directive was that all toilets in the projected naval cities were to be oriented east-west, bearing in mind that Mecca is southwest of Teheran. Bandar Abbas, where most of our construction was planned, is a thousand kilometers south of Teheran and almost due east of Mecca. Just before we were about to put the toilets in place according to the order—and commit a mortal sin— Dan Eitan realized the mistake and warned the naval officials. They rushed to the Muslim clerics for advice, and after stormy discussions agreed that the Israeli infidel was right. The plans were changed, the toilets of Bandar Abbas were positioned facing north-south, and the unforgivable sin was avoided.

In the end, the mistakes were negligible compared to the outstanding job we did in building these cities. The Iranians came to respect and appreciate us, and they treated us extremely well. In the Shah's Iran, Israelis were very much personae gratae, even though the two countries did not have diplomatic relations.

I did most of my work in Israel, and went to Iran only when I was needed. On June 15, 1975, I arranged to meet up after work with my old friend from Technion, Yossi Dubrowski. We were going to watch Maccabi Tel Aviv playing Red Star Belgrade in a European Cup soccer match at his place. When the game ended, he asked if my work in Iran was dangerous. I explained that although the country was a dictatorship, there was no reason for us to worry. Our biggest danger was the occasional communication problem. Once a group of us were in a coffee shop talking when a waiter came over and asked, "Coffee or tea?" No one replied because we were engrossed in the conversation, but he went on standing there until someone nodded to get rid of him. So what did the waiter do? He poured tea and coffee into the cup.

Yossi was choking with laughter when the phone rang. It was Matia. "Come home immediately!" From her tone I knew it couldn't be anything good, and was afraid that something had happened to baby Zach. When Liran was born, I'd invented a way of changing his diapers in his room, and we were still using it with Zach. It was an old drawing board, laid over his cot. It worked pretty well as a changing table, though it would sometimes slip from the railings. That didn't bother us since the babies were there only under our watch. Still, I drove home certain that Zach met with an accident.

When I opened the door, the first thing I saw was Zach, safe and sound in Matia's arms, playing with her hair. Thank God! "Where's Liran?" In the children's room I found him playing peacefully on the rug, building a Lego monster. I went back to Matia. She hadn't moved an inch.

"It's Uri," she said. "Something has happened to Uri." Uri? What could possibly have happened to him? My big brother was an athlete, and enjoyed playing hard. Did he break a leg playing basketball? Did he break both legs? I called the kibbutz. Cardiac arrest, they said. He had been swimming in the pool when it happened, and was taken to a hospital in Safed. "And what's his condition?" There was no reply. "I'm on my way. I'm getting into the car right now." I could hardly breathe. "You can come, but the kibbutz is taking care of the arrangements."

Arrangements. From that word I knew. Did I react? I remember being dumbfounded. Uri had been in the pool racing against his twelve-year old son, Gilead, the third of his five children. Gilead realized that something was wrong with his father and somehow managed to pull him out of the water and call for help.

But apparently his death wasn't quite so sudden. Uri had felt some pain in his chest that morning, and consulted an army medical officer who was then living in the kibbutz. The young doctor missed the signs, finding nothing wrong with my forty-one-year-old brother. Reassured, Uri went out to do a full day's work in landscaping, then on to Tel Hai for a rehearsal of the kibbutz's orchestra, in which he played the clarinet. Keen as always to improve his fitness, he had gotten off the bus two kilometers from the kibbutz so that he could run the rest of the way home. The competitor in him had no intention of giving Gilead the slightest advantage in the swimming race the youngster had arranged. True, he'd had a pain in the morning, but the doctor had said there was nothing to worry about. That's how it happened. At such a time, when urgent help is needed, it's not so good to be living on the border with Lebanon, quite a distance from emergency services.

I was thirty-one, with two children, and I was starting to make my way in life. As adults, Uri and I had drawn closer and become friends. When we were kids, I had been too young for him, and then he'd moved away from home. As adults the ten-year gap between us disappeared. We created a special niche of our own in which we were brothers and friends. His family welcomed me and our brother Amnon in their embrace. We spent many holidays with them at the kibbutz, and always tried to celebrate family occasions together. Our serious discussions around the holiday table about ethics, morals, and equality entered the family folklore. Uri was a man of absolute principles. Where I could see areas of gray, he saw only black and white. We loved our passionate debates, while the rest of the clan, enjoying their dessert, looked on tolerantly. Now and then, he would come to Tel Aviv on some errand, and we would meet, relishing the opportunity to spend time together. Now, suddenly, all of that was gone. Uri was gone. Dead long before his time, and in such an unexpected, unjust way. Like our father, he'd died of cardiac arrest. Two hateful words.

The anger that had possessed me after my father's death, the anger that concealed a terrible pain, became deeper and sharper. I felt as if I would explode. Why Uri? Why at his age, damn it? Is there no justice in the world? I'm not a violent man, but I felt violence within, an urge to smash, destroy, disfigure. I blamed heaven and earth. I blamed my parents. Maybe I was furious with Dad for bequeathing Uri a heart condition, maybe I was angry with Mom for abandoning us without warning. I stopped visiting their graves. I let no one calm my inner rage, which I nourished and protected—not even Matia or the children or Amnon.

On the surface, life resumed its normal course. I took responsibility for Uri's family until things settled down, and saw them often. The latest sorrow weighing me down remained hidden as I focused on looking after Bruria and their five children.

I went on working as usual, spending more time in Iran. After our success with the navy projects there, the country had become for us a land of unlimited opportunity. Offers began pouring in from business people who wanted to build hotels or yacht clubs. Our office had accumulated knowledge about the culture, the geography, the pricing system, the appropriate materials, and the local contractors. I even built an original computer model for assessing the viability of any given project, ECOMO—Economic Computer Model. Quantitative analysis had become my field of expertise, and the demand for it was growing.

Some of my work was conducted with Eitan-Goshen's employees, but in my economic calculations, I was assisted by Dr. Meron Gross, an expert on mathematical models. Meron worked for me—not Dan—and visited Iran once or twice. We co-opted a civil engineer, Racheli, and together we operated as an independent unit flying the flag of Einav Systems. Our tiny team gained a great deal of experience in the management and execution of large projects, and, for those days, made quite a lot of money. That was compensation for the living conditions we had to endure. Bandar Abbas is at about the same latitude as Sharm el-Sheikh in the Straits of Tiran. The weather can be hell—and that's putting it mildly. When parking a car, we'd leave the air conditioning on because otherwise when we came back, we wouldn't be able to touch the steering wheel without getting burned.

Though physical conditions were intolerable, the business environment offered enormous opportunities, even for the new kid on the block, Einav Systems. Many Israelis made their mark in Iran, with particular success in irrigation, oil, and the supply of military equipment and know-how. They felt at home; they brought their families and established a school where their children could follow the Israeli curriculum.

But all that glittered was not gold. Inflation had reared its ugly head by 1976, and the Shah ordered that there be no further increase in prices. To some extent the Shah's decree slowed inflation, thanks to creative thinking by a few people who, instead of raising prices, reduced the size and quantity of the goods they supplied.

Such a ploy may have been feasible in some fields, but not in real estate. One can reduce the size of a steak but in real estate the steak's dimensions are fixed and in an inflationary period, the price of the property is bound to rise. Three apartments sold at three different times are likely to get three different prices. But the Shah had decreed that there was to be no inflation, so what was one supposed to do?

One thing you definitely didn't do was to break the law. The Shah had his generous side but he was, after all, a despot whom you disobeyed only on pain of death. What you could do was to bring in foreign economic advisors, such as Einav Systems, to work out fair appreciation for the different groups of tenants who bought apartments at different times. Regardless of what anyone may say—including the Shah—prices tend to creep up while the construction has to be completed and tenants need to be moved in. At Einav Systems we took advice, analyzed the costs and price changes, defined a total of seven groups, and calculated the construction costs and other expenses for each group individually.

In the process, we found that we couldn't account for 4 percent of the project costs. No matter how we did the sums, when we added up the various costs—bricks, mortar, doors, air conditioning, and so on—the total was always about 4 percent less than the contract price. That 4 percent, it would seem, had simply evaporated. When we asked our clients about the elusive number, they replied that we would do well to keep quiet about it. If we valued our own skins, that is, and were not eager to learn more about the inside of an Iranian prison, we shouldn't ask silly questions. They urged us instead to go back to the drawing board, do the sums again, and produce a more satisfactory result. When in Rome, do as the Romans do. We did as we were told.

Iran was my fourth experience of foreign countries, and with each one I gained a greater global perspective. In 1965, as part of a student exchange program, I sailed to Athens, Genoa, and Barcelona, and then took the cheapest train to Madrid. For a month I stayed in a youth hostel and worked at a gas plant, Butano S.A. After my first day on the foul-smelling production line I asked politely if I could work in the office instead. There, on the basis of their spreadsheets, I drafted all kinds of clever graphs to help facilitate their decision-making.

After finishing my course at Technion, my classmate Dan Rosenstrum and I traveled to London, Amsterdam, Paris, and Italy until our money ran out. In 1969, Matia and I went to Europe on our honeymoon. We stayed in youth hostels and avoided restaurants and other extravagances, but we made the most of it since at the time we were sure that we wouldn't be able to afford trips abroad very often.

From my travels, I came to realize that if I wanted to succeed in the big world I needed to become familiar with it. My parents' generation almost never went abroad. My dad was in Italy during his service in the Jewish Brigade, and Matia's father, a senior defense ministry official, traveled to Europe occasionally. Neither her mother nor mine ever left Israel after they arrived there. Part of their Zionism was a belief that it was better to travel in the homeland and avoid the temptations of foreign places. After my father died, Matia and I went abroad for the third time, on a trip to the U.S. My fourth sojourn abroad was in Iran. This time, however, I wasn't a student on vacation. I was the owner of a private company and an independent businessman.

Until February 1, 1979, the day the Iranian Revolution erupted, we Israelis thought the party would never end. The revolution caught us making hay while the sun was shining, wallowing in the pleasures of Iranian hospitality, cracking jokes about our hosts, building our fortunes and theirs. There were no clouds on our horizon. Suddenly the skies opened, unleashing a violent storm. Overnight, the pampered Israeli community was running for its life. VIPs turned into refugees.

I had already returned to Israel, but my friends and partners continued to work in Teheran and at the more remote construction sites. On hearing the news of the revolution they decided to flee immediately, rather than hang around to find out the intentions of the new regime. People fought for the first available flight out. Given the numbers involved, this latter-day exodus became a complex and dangerous logistical exercise. Heads of families rushed home to get loved ones. Single men grabbed whatever possessions they could, flagged down a cab, and made a beeline for the airport. Those working in the outlying areas made a dash for once hospitable Teheran on board any available transport.

Back in Israel, we closed the office early and drove to the airport to meet the first flight coming in and find out if our colleagues and acquaintances had indeed managed to escape. Phone calls to Iran were being blocked by the Revolutionary Guards, so we had no way of knowing whether anyone had been left behind. When the aircraft touched down and the doors finally opened, there was a sigh of relief all around. Confused and shaken, everyone was nonetheless safe and sound and able to inform us that the others were on their way. Later, some of my colleagues admitted privately that if they hadn't been embarrassed they would have gone down on their hands and knees and kissed the ground.

So the Iranian dream, which began with such great fanfare, ended in a shameful retreat. Too late we learned that although Iran had enjoyed an economic boom under the Shah, he had also brutally suppressed all opposition, particularly among the Shiites. Resentment fermented into internal unrest, and crystallized into revolution. We Israelis who had lived and built freely there were totally unaware of the undercurrent. Naively we believed our work was opening a door to the Muslim world that might eventually lead to peace. Ironically, our efforts had the opposite effect.

Years later, the ship Karin A, carrying arms to Palestinian terrorists in Gaza, set sail from Kharg Island, which we had poured so much effort into developing. The vessel was intercepted by Israeli forces in the Red Sea before the deadly weaponry could be delivered. And Bandar Bushier, which we had transformed from a bleak desert into a modern city, became the site of the Ayatollah's nuclear program. Yes, we Israelis strengthened Iran. Yet the city we built was now developing the bomb designed to annihilate the Jewish State.

Young people in today's Iran know only the Ayatollah's fundamentalist Muslim regime. They know nothing of the secular Iran that preceded it, and they are unable to imagine that not so long ago things in their country were quite different. Similarly, the current generation of Israelis doesn't know the tiny hemmed-in Israel that existed before 1967. Young Israelis who were born beyond the Green Line, the pre-1967 borders, cannot conceive of giving up their homes. They don't understand why many of my generation regard the West Bank territories as a burden.

Young Palestinians, too, are trapped by the limitations of their youth. They never experienced the days before the hatred and suicide attacks and checkpoints. How tragic that history is so often dictated by the political narrow-mindedness of the current generation. The same happens in the economy, not just in politics. We worked in Iran for purely financial reasons, unaware of the political situation and ignorant of the Shiite opposition. It wasn't our business to investigate the nature of the secret military ties between the Shah and the State of Israel or consider how, at the moment of truth, those ties might affect Iranian attitudes toward Israelis. For us, Iran was a secular country where we had come to do business, but a fundamentalist religious revolution regurgitated us. It cared not for our contribution to the land's prosperity or our hope for a peaceful future between our two peoples.

The Shah and the Ayatollah Khomeini affected many lives, including that of a certain obscure Roni Einav, an industrial and management engineer and operational researcher, an Israeli who just happened to be working in Iran. Another Muslim leader who was to have a major impact on my life was Egyptian president Anwar Sadat. His historic peace flight to Jerusalem in November 1977 shattered conventional wisdom, and was as much of a surprise as had been the revolution in Iran. For me, it was to turn out to be a fortunate intervention.

Chapter 7

The Errors of Youth

Female students were scarce at the Haifa Technion. The handful of women who did enroll mostly studied architecture in the Institute's oldest building downtown, far from our main campus on Mount Carmel. I tried to make up for the scarcity in Haifa by spending weekends in Tel Aviv. My trusted pal back home, Shlomo, a man about town of the most impressive sort, had plenty of useful phone numbers (including, eventually, Matia's). Weekends in Tel Aviv were the thrilling part of the week. Only in Haifa did I find myself alone.

For the initial two years of study while still in the Reserve Officers Training Corps (ROTC), the IDF gave me a full scholarship. During the first year, I had my own room in an apartment rented with other students in Neve Sha'anan, but no girlfriend to share it with. In my second year, I decided to move into a campus dormitory that was cheaper and closer to the classrooms. I had a roommate and, together with my good friend Danny Rosenstraum, who also lived in the dorms, we formed a threesome that would share significant professional and personal involvements for years to come. The only benefit to be had from the absence of girls was perhaps the cost of living, though I in any case led a frugal existence. My only clothes were three pairs of basic pants, a pair of shoes that I polished every morning and had repaired at a local shoemaker, and a pair of sandals. I rode the train home to Tel Aviv on a discounted student ticket, and while in Haifa I ate mostly in the student cafeteria. Budgetary constraints notwithstanding, I relished every moment of my newfound freedom away from home and never ceased to yearn for female company.

A year later, my luck turned—twice. During summer vacation I sailed abroad, and met a girl who took my breath away. When we got back to Israel we continued to see each other, the only snag being that she studied and lived in Jerusalem, which made our love life difficult. Until, that is, lady luck intervened and I met another delightful girl living in Haifa. Life became a bit complicated because I now had two girlfriends in two different cities. Each knew about the other and agreed to the arrangement—don't ask me why. But then, in what must be the worst piece of timing ever, I met Matia, and this time luck was not on my side: my "Haifa girl" and Matia were roommates.

Matia concluded that I wasn't to be taken seriously. But I was serious—about her. I parted from my two attachments and embarked on wooing Matia with all the vigor I could muster. On our first date, I took her to a show that I had gone to the trouble of seeing beforehand, to make sure that my opening gambit was a hit. Still, the ghost of my reputation was after me.

During my first visit to Matia's home, her mother took me aside for a no-nonsense talk. With great solemnity, Dr. Esther Milvasky-Peleg, dental surgeon, told me that if I were truly interested in her serious-minded daughter, I'd better abandon my wicked ways. This was probably the most embarrassing moment of my life. Between stuttering and blushing, I did manage to explain that I had already mended my ways. After about an hour, Matia's father, Yaakov, joined us. He explained with great warmth that he loved his only daughter more than anything and spared no effort to ensure her well-being. "Every week I go to Haifa to make sure that everything is OK," he said, by way of a warning. A chemist by profession, he had been involved in the Haganah, Israel's pre-state defense force, and was in charge of the thousands of civilian workers in the IDF. With his mastery of labor laws and easygoing manner, it was a role he filled perfectly. I liked him from the first and I believe that the feeling was mutual, for our "negotiations" ended with my getting permission to woo Matia.

In my teens I did not appreciate the art of negotiation. When I'd completed high school with distinction, I decided to try for the army's special academic course, the Atuda. If that didn't work, I thought to myself, I'll return to the youth movement and join Nahal (Pioneer Fighting Youth, which combined army service with farming, and later community work) with my friends from the movement. As things turned out, I had no such choice. My relations with the movement had been deteriorating for quite a while. I had at first been an active member—following in the footsteps of my brother Uri. Yet over time, I dropped out of the branch council and was even thought of as something of a renegade: My Friday evenings were spent with a new girlfriend from the Scouts instead of with my peers in the movement. At the age of seventeen, the maverick in me challenged the movement's "collective will" at every opportunity, straining the boundaries until we were on a collision course.

In 1961, elections were held for the Knesset, Israel's House of Representatives. I was interested in politics and, since I had promised my parents that I would work in my spare time, I decided to combine business with pleasure and work for the Mapai Party as a recruiting officer. I was handed a list of people living in the Florentine district of Tel Aviv, and day after day, once school was over, I did the rounds of the listed families, marking each name as either "party member," "supporter," or "opponent," so that the party knew where it stood with voters. My work was due to end on Election Day, a bad fit with my youth movement's next scheduled camp, which was to start three days before the election. I explained the situation to my group leader and asked for permission to leave for the camp in the Negev slightly later. "No, absolutely not," was his angry response. "Discipline is discipline. You will go with everybody else as arranged … there can be no exceptions," and then added sarcastically: "Why do you always have to be different?" Instead of trying to negotiate a compromise, I left. The group set off for camp as planned, I continued my party work, and when that was done I joined them.

I knew that once there, I was to be grilled by the group's council, a trial by comrades. About three days after my arrival at the camp the council convened, called me in for clarification, listened to my explanation and, without mincing words, expelled me from the camp. There was a majority vote against me and that was that.

I had gone to camp absolutely sure that things would turn out fine, taking with me a suitcase full of goodies to last me a whole month. I couldn't possibly go home three days later. How would I explain it to my parents? It didn't take me long to decide that playing for time was unquestionably my best option.

I took my suitcase and set off for my uncle Zvi's house in the village of Beer Tuvia. Zvi was my mother's older brother. "Great that you're here," he exclaimed as he saw me entering. And, without bothering to ask what had prompted my unannounced visit, he set me to work in the henhouse and nearby orchard. The room I was given had once been my maternal grandfather and grandmother's bedroom. My grandfather Ahron, after whom I was named, had died two years before I was born. On entering their room, I could have sworn that my grandmother Sarah's scent lingered within its four walls. Happy with my lot, I settled into my new temporary abode and spent fourteen terrific days in Beer Tuvia. I helped my uncle "to make the desert bloom," ate well, used up the supplies I had brought, and then went home. Fortunately for me, my parents didn't seem to notice that I had come back early.

At home, I debated with myself whether I should try to return to the movement. I missed my circle of friends, but my honor had been tarnished, and so I decided not to return. Thus, by the time I was in twelfth grade, I was no longer a member of the United movement. My earlier promise to myself—that if I weren't accepted into the Atuda program I would join the Nahal Fighting Youth with my pals from the movement—had simply been nonsense. It was bravado, nothing more.

In fact, from the moment I had placed my own individual wishes above those of the group, the Atuda course had become my only option. By that point I had learned that charisma and self-confidence alone are nothing but bluster when it comes to an individual pitting himself against the masses. Anyone interested in a sure-fire path to victory would do well to invest in relations with others and in ensuring that the balance of power favors his aims. In his own interests, he would also be well-advised to pay serious attention to the views of the masses—whoever they may be.

Chapter 8

Seeds

After Uri died, his family went through some difficult times on the kibbutz. Though the communal system spared them from financial worries and their social life proceeded quite normally, the cruel fact was that with Uri gone, they were no longer a "normal" family. Bruria felt that she and the five kids had become objects of scrutiny. I suggested she think about leaving the kibbutz but she felt that was too bold a move. She did, however, want to work outside the kibbutz, and when offered a job in the health department in Kiryat Shmona, some ten kilometers north, she grabbed it with my blessing. This meant she could continue living in Yiftach but escape the constant observation.

The kibbutz ideology of equality took an emotional toll on Uri's children as well because too often it meant uniformity. Yair, Uri's youngest son, once told me he hated being asked at school about his parents and having to explain that his father was dead. May he say that he had a father in Tel Aviv? More than ever before, we tried to be together as a family, especially during the High Holidays.

By now I shared with Amnon the responsibility for the whole extended family. He had graduated successfully in economics and business administration, then went for a trip abroad and returned with a Canadian fiancée, Bonnie. Their modest wedding had taken place on October 17, 1974. It was the last family occasion Uri attended. He and I had stood at Amnon's side under the marriage canopy, in place of our parents. The bride's parents, the gracious and wealthy Gertrude and Morris, invited the whole family to a festive dinner at the Hilton hotel after the ceremony.

Amnon and Bonnie lived in our parents' old apartment on the corner of Nordau and Dizengoff with their prized possession: a color TV, one of the first in Israel. Matia and I used to invite ourselves to their place to watch programs from abroad. Amnon began working in the credit department of a bank, all set for a successful career. A highly disciplined and persistent chess player was my little brother: he made no mistakes, and almost always won. I knew I wouldn't have to worry about him. He was bright and capable and would look after himself just fine. Three years later he and Bonnie had a son, whom they named Uri.

I continued to work in partnership with Eitan-Goshen on projects in Iran and in Israel. At the same time, the small Einav Systems team worked on our own projects. We did the master planning for air force bases. The IDF's office of construction commissioned us to optimize the army's storage system and create computerized timetables for major projects. Thousands of activities had to be coordinated: data gathering, quantity estimates, and pace of execution. We were hired to do some rather complicated jobs by civilian major-league clients, and completed them successfully. We continued to rely on our partnership with Eitan-Goshen and operated from their offices. I had no good reason to change things.

The 1977 election in Israel resulted in a dramatic political upheaval, and opposition leader Menahem Begin became prime minister. The new position transformed the fiery leader of violent street rallies into a moderate and visionary statesman. Speaking at the Knesset, he invited President Sadat to come to Jerusalem and address the people of Israel from that same podium. It was a fantastic idea, which no one took seriously until six months later, in November 1977, when the Egyptian leader astonished the world and accepted the invitation. Sadat's visit fundamentally undermined the Arab boycott of the Jewish State. He spoke of an end to all war and won the world's admiration.

Most Israelis supported the peace agreement. I too welcomed these developments and joined the burgeoning Sadat fan club, without having any idea that his gesture contained the seeds of my own independence. His bold move brought peace to Egypt, released its poverty-stricken economy from the burden of a massive military budget, and dramatically improved Israel's situation in the region. A central aspect of the peace pact was Israel's agreement to return the Sinai Peninsula to Egyptian sovereignty, and remove all the IDF bases there.

One Sunday, having just returned to my office from visiting Bruria and the children at the kibbutz, I received a visit from the architect Shamai Assif, then head of Branch 10 at the IDF's Office of Construction. Branch 10 is the professional body managing the Army's infrastructure. That includes planning, maintenance, engineering support, and procedural decisions. Though managing all the real estate of the ground forces, the branch had no executive responsibility, which was exclusively the domain of the Ministry of Defense. Shamai was an ex-student of mine. He was talented and bright, and I had once given him a letter of recommendation on Eitan-Goshen letterhead, which got him into Harvard. We were just acquaintances who respected each other, so I was somewhat surprised when he showed up at my office. "Not here," he whispered. "Let's go out, find a cafe." I suppressed a smile. Was he about to disclose some top-secret information?

"Since the peace agreement," he said as we sat down for coffee, "the army has become involved in some big projects. Let's join forces." He outlined plans that were on an exceptionally large scale by our country's standards. It was nice of him to make me the offer, but I was no longer in the army.

"What's the problem? Enlist for a few years, it's worth it!" he told me. I asked him if he was joking. If this were a moment when big money was to be made, it would make no sense for me to be working on the puny salary of a major. Shamai said that he would get me promoted, but I had no intention of re-enlisting, no matter how high the rank. I wasn't going to work as a hired hand for anyone. Yet, I had a counterproposal: Einav Systems would be delighted to offer its services to the IDF.

Frankly, I don't know what gave me the audacity. Einav Systems was a small, young company, and Shamai was talking about a tremendous scope of work, preparing budgets and timetables for the evacuation of all the IDF bases in Sinai, a project that would undoubtedly cost billions. Shamai was keen on my getting it, and staked his reputation to convince the powers that be to make it happen. Still, we both knew the Ministry of Defense was a closed shop. In our heart of hearts neither of us really believed there was much chance of my being able to break in, even with my fine record and Shamai Assif's clout.

However, the political upheaval brought on by Begin's and Likud's victory at the polls turned out to be even more profound than we had at first realized. Since the birth of the state, the ruling Labor Party (Mapai) and the Trade Union Organization (Histadrut) had worked hand in glove, running the government machine like a private club. In any bid for a government contract, outsiders stood no chance. Begin's new consolidated right-wing party, Likud, brought about winds of change that removed that iron grip, and the once-firmly closed doors were now open to all capable newcomers. This is how I, who had no friends in the corridors of power, won my first big public contract.

For two weeks I told no one about my coup, for fear of jinxing it. Only after all the documents had been signed at the Ministry of Defense did I gradually begin to spill the beans.

From the office, with the contract now safely under lock and key, I phoned Matia. The only thing I told her was that all of us, children included, were going out that evening to Rusalka, a restaurant with a Russian cuisine. At the elegant place with its tables covered in fine embroidered cloth (a far cry from the simple Formica at my regular hummus place), I shared my news. Matia reacted with a broad smile and a kiss. The children asked if, now that we were rich, they could order two desserts. Matia and I raised our glasses and I prayed that this contract was a sign of things to come.

For the Ministry of Defense to hire a private company to play a major role in a billion-dollar army project was unheard of. The fact that everything (including the manpower and computer work) was to be handled by a civilian company was hard enough to swallow. Even worse, Einav Systems was located in the offices of yet another civilian company. This could create problems of security clearance and confidentiality. Despite that, the army gave us a chance, and I decided to justify their trust. First, I left Eitan-Goshen's comfortable offices and hired 90 square meters of office space in downtown Tel Aviv. The rent was $6 per square meter, not including taxes and utilities. At the entrance to the building I put up a small, tin nameplate for Einav Systems—my personal declaration of independence. Then I recruited ten new people to work on the project. Previously I had been limited to offering my own services while calling for assistance when needed, but now the relatively long-term contract with the army, scheduled to run for ten months or more, enabled me to offer my services and those of ten others for the duration.

Now I could put into practice my belief in the value of human capital, and select a workforce of proven personal excellence. Among those who came on board were economists, engineers, architects, and computer experts. Most of the new personnel were hired to work on a freelance basis. I knew from my own experience that such independence encourages entrepreneurship and creativity, and had high hopes that this approach would lead to the success of my fledgling company.

The schedules for evacuating the dozens of camps and bases scattered throughout the Sinai desert were tight, and we made them even tighter at the request of the engineers and architects at the office of construction. Gradually, we evolved into a service center, and our work relied more and more on computer programs. We dealt with construction plans, logistics, timetables, and budgets. We placed ourselves fully at the disposal of the client IDF.

About a year into the project, the air force also wanted the professional services we were supplying to the ground forces. Suddenly we had another big client. We created a computerized system for the air force that paralleled the one we had built for the army. As these projects progressed I took on more expert staff, making it possible for our still-small company to play an important role in the efficient planning of the swift evacuation of all the army's units from the Sinai Peninsula, and their transfer to new sites, either within the 1967 borders or in the West Bank territories.

Einav Systems was doing a good job, but one day the IDF realized it had become entirely dependent on the services of a civilian company. This awakening led to an abrupt change of attitude, and the army itself initiated a parallel computerized program compatible with its systems. That worried me. To lose the IDF as a client would be a disaster, so I helped the people in charge to see the light. The only way to complete the parallel project successfully was to enlist the help of Einav Systems. They were persuaded, but in my anxiety to protect the existing contract I had bitten off more than I could chew. In order to fulfill the new commitment, I urgently needed to find someone qualified to run it. Before I had time to regret my haste a chance encounter resolved this dilemma.

One evening, while carrying out the garbage, I bumped into my neighbor Motti Glazer in the elevator. Our children went to the same kindergarten, we played tennis together, and we sometimes met up on Fridays. Motti was an open, outgoing individual. Like me, he was an industrial and management engineer. He had run a TV studio, and had an extensive network of colleagues and friends. After hearing that he had just left his job and was looking for another, I said on impulse, "Come work for me." I didn't even ask him if he knew anything about computers. At that time, in the early 1980s, nobody knew about such esoteric things.

In the Israel of those years, there were only a handful of mainframe computers operating. A few had been used in the '50s and '60s but only in academia, the IDF, and a small number of governmental departments. In 1955, staff at the Weizmann Institute of Science in Rehovot (where I had paid last respects to President Weizmann years earlier with my father) built the Israeli "Weizac," now a museum piece on exhibition at the Institute. Eight years later, the "Golem A" followed. These two inventions launched Israel's high-tech industry. In 1957 Shimon Peres, then director of the Ministry of Defense and always the visionary, arranged to buy the first computer manufactured by Eliott, the 803, for the IDF's intelligence branch. At the same time, the research and planning department in his office was encouraged to build a big computer to service the country's entire defense system. These computers operated on transistors, at the time a significant innovation. Only in 1959 did the IDF purchase a Philco computer, and in 1961 the first IBM 1401 reached Israel.

I first learned programming in 1966 while at Technion. We practiced on the old Eliott 803, which, like many of its contemporaries, had become obsolete. This early British model, donated to Technion by the Jewish community of Manchester, England, didn't even have pre-punched cards. We had to punch continuous strips of paper tape. The programming language that we used, Algol, now, like the Elliot and the Weizac, is on display in a museum. Later on, while serving in the Ordnance Department, I returned to the study of programming, this time in a computer language known as Altac. The very mention of these names fills me with nostalgia.

The pinnacle of high tech for us in those days was the use of punch cards for applications and operational research. The programs themselves were written on paper and then transferred to perforated cards. We were stationed at IDF Headquarters, but our scientific squad—where the Army's mainframe, the Philco 2000, was located—was at the army's Computer Service Directorate in Ramat Gan, a distance of about five kilometers. At least once a day, we had to go to the computer with boxes of punch cards wrapped in rubber bands, hand them to the dispatcher, who gave them to the operator, who in turn transferred them to the printing supervisor, who eventually gave us back the punched product. If we made a mistake with a dot or a comma, we had to wait twenty-four hours to correct it, or even to know that such an error had occurred. We branded these back and forth runs "van processing," since the hardest thing to get at HQ was a van to cart us off to the computer center. Today, the tiny disk-on-key, a superb Israeli invention, stores information that once required thousands of cards in hundreds of boxes.

I entrusted the IDF's internal computerization project to Motti Glazer, who joined us as a subcontractor. He quickly mastered the problems and worked with the army programmers alongside me. Gradually, we began generating a new income stream by placing programmers with the army. We did this also in the civilian market so that instead of selling projects and know-how, our programmers worked in the offices of our clients. In professional jargon, this IT placement was known as "head trading." We would send a salaried Einav Systems engineer to work at Bank Hapoalim, for instance, and bill the bank for that person's work. The success of this multilayered system hinged on our employees' ability to work independently, take responsibility, and maintain loyalty to our company and the client. Our able and resourceful employees could be relied on in all these areas. The problem in the early days was that pay rates for engineers were too low for the skilled and sophisticated people we came to attract. It took a while before the market accepted that the fees for high-tech experts had to match their qualifications and allow the placement companies to make a profit.

I remained friendly with Dan Eitan, though we had almost no mutual business interests anymore. Most of my time was spent managing Einav Systems' independent projects. My routine involved shuttling back and forth four times a day between the offices of the IDF's office of construction, air force HQ, and the offices of AMAN. I now engaged this company, with which I had worked on the Iranian project, as subcontractors. Our shared experience and my long-standing friendship with the senior manager, Lulu, made communications between us efficient, quick, and virtually paperless. My clients being the army and air force, confidentiality was the foremost issue. I personally delivered client instructions and never let classified papers out of my sight. Cell phones hadn't been invented yet, and when the pager system appeared in Israel I bought one. It helped a lot, though it didn't completely eliminate the need for daily visits to my various outposts. And sometimes, when I felt overwhelmed, I would ask Matia's father, Yaakov, who had the appropriate Ministry of Defense security clearance, to help me collect the checks.

I arrived at Matia's thirtieth birthday, which was celebrated on the balcony of Dan Eitan's new office overlooking the old Jaffa harbor, exhausted after a day of running from pillar to post. I barely had had time to take a shower and change. The extent of our continued personal friendship was demonstrated by Dan's offer to throw the party. From 1977 onward, I worked exclusively and at a frantic pace at Einav Systems. So did Motti Glazer, who gave his all to the company and after a while, asked to become a partner. My heart rejected the idea, but my mind said it was the right business move. On his beautiful Jaffa balcony I told Dan that Einav Systems had developed in new directions. Our partnership had been sealed by a handshake; I'm sure we hadn't signed any formal agreement. Dan understood and we dissolved the partnership in the same way we formed it—with a friendly handshake. Now I was free to take a new partner on board.

It was a while before Motti and I had the time to draft a written agreement: Einav Systems was snowed under by work. During the three years or so of the Sinai evacuation, many new civilian clients looking for computerized solutions had approached us: banks, insurance companies, industrial plants. I didn't always know what they were asking of me, or what the solution would look like. Often, the client himself did not understand what was needed, since he was asking for something that did not exist. These situations arose quite frequently in the early days of programming. I would always say yes to the project, however vague its requirements, then hasten to recruit people who could turn my promises into programs. It sometimes took a little longer than I expected, but usually I was able to make good. And so I built my reputation. Self-confidence plays a major role in those situations, but it is never enough. It has to be backed by the managerial ability to make things happen. Following the success of the Sinai evacuation (the first stage, evacuating the bases, was completed in 1980), my credentials had paved the way for my company's entry into the civilian market.

When one of Israel's leading banks, Bank Leumi, asked if we could create a comprehensive program for savings plans, I said, "Yes, of course we can," though I hadn't the slightest idea whether it could be done. In line with a directive from the Bank of Israel, every time the bank put in place a savings plan, it had to rewrite its computer program from A to Z. The ministry of finance's love of innovation was a major hassle for the bank, which was searching for an efficient solution to this problem. Would Einav Systems be able to write a generic program for savings plans, so that when a new savings plan was being launched the bank would only need to modify and add configuration parameters to describe the new plan, while the core program remained unaltered? Such a program would obviate the need to rewrite everything from scratch every time a minor alteration took place. I said, "Yes, sure," and went back to my office.

When my talented bunch heard what the bank was demanding, they were up in arms. "Are you nuts? Give us a break! Nobody here knows anything about banking!" But I wasn't going to relent. "I don't know" and "I can't do it" were never part of my lexicon. Leaving my workers to their protest, I went into my office and started calling my contacts, determined to find someone who knew how to build this kind of program. The name Alex Schwartz, an ex-army man, kept coming up. He had served in army communications, a computerized environment similar to the bank's setup, and seemed to have the ability to cope with such a challenge. I invited him in for an interview.

Self-confident to the point of arrogance, Alex Schwartz could clearly do the job. He was about to leave the army and was fielding offers from major companies, including the software house ATL, Advanced Technology Ltd. (now part of NESS). I offered him a good position with a competitive salary. I told him, "Yes, we're a small company, but if you join a small company you can make a difference. And if after a few months you decide you made the wrong decision, you can pack up and go to ATL."

He thought for a moment, and then said: "OK, I'll join you." Together with the bank's representative, who was also called

Alex, and a team of about ten people, they created our third biggest project, the Bank Leumi "Tichon Project." Instead of selling them software, we placed with them a think tank, working with the bank's computer team to develop a specific software solution that met the bank's specific requirements. This turned out to be a highly lucrative contract that lasted for three years. The software we built survived the millennium bug and is operating at Bank Leumi to this day. Alex Schwartz and I remained good friends long after he left Einav Systems.

Chapter 9

All My Prodigies

The Bank Leumi deal was brought to the company by Meir Arnon, who had joined us in 1979. He was Motti's friend, had served in the general staff's prestigious commando unit (Sayeret Matkal), and had a degree in agricultural engineering. When he showed up at our office, all heads turned at the sight of this handsome young man, well dressed, well spoken, with the grace of a nobleman—most unusual in our neck of the woods. He had grown up in a wealthy home and was as talented as he was good-looking, a person of integrity, energy, and creativity. His father had held a senior position at Bank Leumi and Meir inherited a network of well-placed connections there. Motti and I made a verbal agreement that gave him a 1 percent stake in Einav Systems for every $150,000 of business he brought in. Over time, he was to become our partner.

Meir's first contribution, the Bank Leumi project, was a big one. From then on, the company was able to cover its overhead comfortably and pay salaries, not just to our employees, but to Motti and me. We had a business that provided a livelihood for several families. I was able to move us to a bigger apartment, go abroad twice a year, and buy my wife a brand new car. The budget was balanced, and we were secure. That surely was as much as anybody could hope for.

Now that we had a larger staff, the company had the capacity to increase the number of billable hours it supplied to customers, but we were still just a service provider. I still had to sell as many projects as possible. Dependency on customers staying with us still troubled me. My apprehension, possibly an intuition, or perhaps a mixture of the two, propelled me to search for new challenges, to look beyond the horizon and not simply settle for what I had already achieved. It wasn't wealth or the dream of a global business that spurred me on. What drove me was an urge to do more than just make a living, to be involved in something that would lead to personal growth that would be innovative. To achieve that, I would have to develop a totally different kind of business, one that was risky, terra incognita.

Too much of the company's activity still revolved around me and I had virtually no time to spare for creative thinking. Nor did I have the spare cash. All I had were my achievements. I began to play with the idea of duplicating Einav Systems but with different partners and a different range of products. My fantasy was a company that would not only develop software in response to specific requirements, but also possibly sell technology, first in Israel, and later abroad.

It was conceivable to sell a finished software product without my direct involvement, without production lines, warehousing, transportation, customs problems, and, just as important, with a simple payment system. "The optimum is the maximum," became my motto. Motti laughed at my fantasies. As far as he was concerned, the only feasible thing was what we were already doing—selling computer services. That had indeed been the reality for a long time.

Digital computers had first appeared in 1943, a year before I was born, and operated on the basis of a simple machine language. Programming them was a task of writing code in numbers. IBM computer models 1401 and 1620, which were capable of translating a higher level programming language into machine language (Fortran for formula translation), appeared only in

1960 and came with operating programs that were supplied by the manufacturer free of charge with the sale of the hardware. Manufacturers bundled their software into the hardware as if that were the only possibility. Everyone was so excited about the appearance of this incredible piece of equipment, that no one imagined the possibility of splitting the packaged deal. Nor did anyone foresee the enormous number of potential applications awaiting development just beyond the horizon. Computers were regarded as being simply a sophisticated piece of machinery: punch-card machines, tabulation machines, card-reading machines. As the usage of computers increased and as hardware developments raised users' expectations, manufacturers began to add basic software applications in mathematics, statistics, and the likes. Only a handful of visionaries thought about creating brand new programs with commercial applications in such fields as accounting, salary administration, or engineering—programs that could be produced and distributed independently of the hardware.

The idea was so revolutionary that in the U.S., the world's leader in the field, only three commercial software companies were formed in the 1950s. In 1955, two former IBM employees founded the Computer Usage Corporation (CUC), the first company that attempted to develop programs for users. Its modus operandi was similar to that of Einav Systems: CUC sold computer services and specially designed programs created to suit the unique requirements of clients. The trailblazing company Applied Data Research (ADR) was formed in 1959 by seven graduates of the American space program. It was the first to develop and sell a computer flow chart program, Autoflow, as an independent product not bundled with the hardware. ADR set a precedent when they won a court battle against IBM and shattered the Blue Giant's monopoly in this field. There was a third company to be established in the U.S. during the 1950s, but it came and went in the blink of an eye.

In the 1960s, Americans already understood the potential of such products and about thirty new software companies appeared. A few of them supplied software services, like Electronic Data Systems (EDS), which later was to become one of our clients. Some, like Boole & Babbage, whose subsidiary Boole & Babbage Europe (B&BE) would eventually become our European distributors, focused on the development and distribution of the software products themselves.

The pioneer in developing Israel's civilian software industry was Amiram Shor. In 1963, a few years after such companies began being formed in the United States, Shor and Arie Shemesh formed the first Israeli software company, Institute of Statistics and Office Mechanization. For many years it was one of the leading companies in the Israeli private sector, operating computing centers for data processing. (The government ran its own center, known as the Computer Service Directorate or CSD.) Israel Local Authorities Data Processing Center, the next such company to be founded in the country, supplied software services to municipal authorities.

During the 1960s, a number of other similar businesses operated in the private sector. These included service agencies belonging to IBM and others run by the Mittwoch family—the representatives in Israel of NCR through a franchise obtained in pre-1948 Palestine. Nikuv and Data Mechun, both long defunct, were also formed in those early days, as were Yael, Contahal, Dagesh, and Mittwoch. ATL was established in 1969 by six visionaries, among them Yosi Vardi and my former teacher at Technion, Professor Shleifer. The company was subsequently purchased by Tadiran, in those days one of the largest Israeli companies in the field of electronics and electrical engineering.

The concept of software houses emerged during the 1970s and caught on in the 1980s. The Israeli Union of Software Houses was not founded until 1982, and I must admit that in the early 1980s, when my partner Motti Glazer was knocking down my dreams, he was being realistic and I was the fantasist. The software industry, which was later to become the driving force of Israel's economy, was still swaddled in nappies.

In our own home that year, 1981, the only nappies that mattered were those of our newly born third son. We named him Ramon, a fusion of my name and Matia's as well as having been the code name for the evacuation of Sinai, the project that had given me financial independence. Our growing family moved to a more spacious apartment in Ramat Ilan, and Amnon moved with his family to our now vacant apartment, so that we could be near each other. That year we experienced grief as well as joy. Matia's father, Yaakov Peleg, an honorable man, died of a heart attack. Our children were left with only one grandparent, Matia's mother, Esther, who filled the void by devoting many extra hours to her grandchildren.

That year, Einav Systems landed its fourth big project from the Ministry of Defense, this time in the area of air force logistics. We hired excellent new people. Among them, a young man named Arik Kilman, an expert in communication and programming, was particularly noteworthy. We met when he was a major in the army and worked with us as a representative of our client. We valued his abilities, and when he returned to civilian life offered him a decent salary, a small car, and the prospect of promotion. At the same time, Motti stopped managing the ground forces project so that he could run the new air force contract together with Arik.

In April 1981, Motti and I finally had time to sign a formal partnership agreement. The fondness I felt for him before he started working for me had begun to dissipate. The two of us were not a match made in heaven. In truth, Motti was too extravagant for my taste, a bit of a fibber—even when we played squash he used to "bend the truth"—and he always over-dressed. We were complete opposites. From the outset there had been an underlying strain between us. I felt it important to fulfill my commitments. To Motti, promises mattered less. Of course he had some excellent qualities. He was second to none in making a quick presentation or in conducting a speedy system analysis. He made friends rapidly and was able to draft the more talented among them into our company. It's just that he always made me feel jumpy. With most people I am at ease. With him I could never relax. At first we worked side by side, but I found it difficult. Eventually, we found ourselves working for a joint cause—but separately.

The partnership came about as a gradual process. Beginning as a subcontractor for an agreed fee, he was paid the money the company charged for his work, plus percentages from the income of the workers he managed. I was usually the one who brought in the projects, but once he took charge of them he dived in, developing, extending, and taking control. The truth is that before becoming a partner, Motti did not bring a single project to the company. In the partnership agreement, it was accepted that he would get a 30 percent shareholding and after six months he would get a further 20 percent, thereby making us equal partners. At the last minute I caught myself thinking: there's a limit to generosity. It's enough that I'm giving him half my company for free and he's making no financial investment of his own. The IL (Israeli lira, currency in use between 1948 and 1980) 400,000 already in the kitty surely has nothing to do with him. But we were afraid to put it on paper in case the IRS would tax us on the notional profit, and it was our only reserve. We made a handwritten notation in the margin in the partnership agreement: "If in the future the partnership is dissolved, the first IL 400,000 will go to Roni."

Was the partnership with Motti worth it for me? Yes, I needed a partner. It's very hard to operate alone in business, to attend to clients, and to be able to have proper time away. A partner can provide moral support, someone to consult with who ostensibly shares the same interests and goals as you. When these interests don't overlap, things turn sour. Initially, we didn't experience this problem. Work was divided efficiently between us in a manner that allowed for the expansion of the company. That was until our first direct conflict. It happened over Meir Arnon.

Meir, who kept his word and brought in work on the promised scale, such as the Bank Leumi Project, now wanted the 1 percent ownership pledged to him as a return. But Motti decided to back out of our commitment, being, as was his wont, too clever by half: "We said 'projects—plural,'" he quibbled. Meir was deeply hurt and I was not prepared to lose him.

To this day, I do not fully understand Motti's attitude. Maybe he wanted an exclusive relationship with me, or thought that three partners were too many. Maybe he was afraid that this minor shareholding would give Meir the casting vote in the management of the company. Whatever his reasons, he tried to block him, while I felt bound by the commitment we'd made. This was the first bone of contention between us. At the time I did not realize what it foreshadowed.

In entering into a partnership Motti and I were both being naïve, because in business, as in marriage, one never knows how things will develop. Nowadays, when young people setting up a business partnership ask my advice, I tell them: "The chances are overwhelming that you'll have a fight within the first five years. You change. Conditions change. Stuff happens. And money rears its ugly head." That test case with Meir revealed the gap in our respective approaches to business. Motti wanted the company to maintain the status quo. I wanted it to explore new directions.

In order not to lose the talented and original Meir Arnon, I suggested that we form a subsidiary company in which he would be the main partner and own 60 percent of the shares, with Einav Systems owning the balance. This way, he would be free to manage projects that he initiated. To my great delight he agreed, and in February 1982 we formed Einav Computer Systems. As Einav Systems, I thus became a partner in a second independent company, and a new set of opportunities beckoned. Meir insisted that "Einav" be part of the new company's name so that it could benefit from our reputation. As a result, in many instances, clients failed to distinguish between the two. Early on in the new partnership, Meir developed an architectural program that became a company called ACA. It typified his daring and broke new ground as one of the first ever architectural software programs.

ACA did pretty well, yet somehow it was never able to keep up with market demands. Something was always off—either their computer was too big, or another company got there first—and ACA's founders ended up in bankruptcy. Today, though, AutoCAD is used by architects the world over, unaware that a farsighted Israeli named Meir Arnon was among the first to develop the idea.

Indeed, numerous fascinating and at times odd innovations flourished and declined around me in those days. So I repeat: when something good happens, don't become too excited because in the end it might fail. On the other hand, don't lose heart over every flop, because something good might come of it. In any event, Meir Arnon, like me, possessed sufficient vision to believe that one could do things that had not been tried before. Motti was never willing to accept such an approach. If others wanted to take risks, it was their affair; if there was a profit at the end of it he was quite happy to get his share.

Meir experimented with a few more business ventures, among them the founding of The Fourth Dimension, which I will discuss in depth later on, before he decided to cut and run. In 1984 he went off to study Business Management at INSEAD in Fontainebleau, France, and asked me to take over the management of Einav Computer Systems. The company continued to generate an income from the Bank Leumi project and with Meir's pay now reduced during his leave of absence, I was able to gradually put the bank account in balance and the company back on its feet. Now that Meir was gone no one actually worked there. It had all along been a one-man entrepreneurial band. Still, the subsidiary opened up new possibilities and enabled me to work independently of Motti.

These were the early days of the software industry in Israel, and a whole host of bright new faces started to join Einav Systems. I built my relationship with these new recruits calmly and deliberately. When applicants came to me with an interesting idea, my response would almost invariably be to invite them to work with me for a year or so and then decide if there was something solid we could build on together. Highly gifted people always aim for the sky—and fast. I knew that their hope was to climb to the peak under my wing. More than one eyebrow was raised at my turning the company into a virtual test lab. But I was convinced that investing in human capital was the right thing to do. My hope was that this would be my path to glory. Since we were expanding fast, I rented an additional 300 square meters at the same address. In no time at all we had taken possession of half the floor and I was able to provide each of the inventive newcomers and their projects (later to be called "start-ups") with their own tiny workspace. Though not always easy, working with original talent was at least great fun.

One of the most prominent among my recruits was Dr. Meron Gross, who worked with me in the 1970s, mainly on the Iranian project. He and Matia had been high school classmates, and he had gone on to earn a degree in physics. On my recommendation, he had joined the army's ordnance unit and in the course of his service obtained his Ph.D. in operations research and physics. Outstandingly brilliant, he later studied law so he could run his family's construction business.

In 1982, when we secured the air force construction contract, the company recruited Arik Kilman, who joined Motti Glazer in the management of that project. A year after he began working with us, the gifted Arik brought in his friend Zeev Yanai, who had a similar background. "Together," Arik told us, brimming with self-confidence, "we will do something big." Motti and I agreed to form a company in partnership with them. They had all sorts of ambitions, but nothing in the way of a business plan or any clear notion of where they fit within Einav Systems. Their thinking was: If Roni is around, we'll eventually be OK. Why invest in scores of pages of legalese when no one knows if there is going to be a successful outcome? Under some circumstances a formal agreement can be helpful, but it can just as easily be a hindrance and none of us had the time, the money, or the patience to bother with formalities.

So we joined forces in the hope that fate would be kind to us. In March of that year, together with Arik and Zeev, we formed our second subsidiary, Liraz Systems (with Arik getting 25 percent, Zeev 25 percent, and Einav Systems retaining 50 percent), almost a mirror image of the parent company. The link between the two companies allowed me to hold on to Liraz's two excellent founding members while expanding and varying my activities.

The difference between Einav Systems and its new subsidiary was in the type of mainframe used in developing their respective programs. Einav Systems specialized in the use of Digital's Vax computers and the IBM mainframe. Liraz acquired a particular expertise in working with IBM's 34/36 and AS 400. The era of PCs had not yet dawned, and all programs were written for the various sizes of mainframe computers. Between them, our own two companies covered almost all the available options.

Arik and Zeev fully justified my confidence in them. Liraz did extremely well and during the 1980s was ranked just below Einav Systems in the list of the ten largest software companies in Israel. This displeased Motti and before long the talented duo, offended by his attitude, packed their bags and moved to an office of their own. Within four years, Liraz became bigger than its parent company, and in 1987 Motti and I made our exit by selling our holdings in Liraz and putting the money into Einav Systems, which was struggling. Liraz (today Blue Phoenix) was later traded on the Tel Aviv Stock Exchange, and dominated the NASDAQ Level 8 listing. Arik and Zeev became rich, their partnership was dissolved, and now each of them manages his own prosperous company.

We formed a few more subsidiary companies, using a similar model. The reputation we'd established attracted an increasing number of talented people with dreams to sell. They were able to dip their feet in the water under our tutelage and later, with our encouragement, would branch out on their own. We, Einav Systems, maintained a stake in each of those subsidiaries—sometimes 50 percent, sometimes 40 percent.

Between 1980 and 1988 we launched Einav Computer Systems with Meir Arnon, Liraz with Arik and Zeev, as well as ComDa, Vega Tools, and Modulog. Liraz and ComDa, like Einav Systems, supplied computer services and acted as consultants in communications but did not consider selling technology, nor did exports comprise any portion of their business plan.

The founders of ComDa were two colorful characters, Yisrael Grice and Zeev Shetach. Yisrael was an outstanding engineer with a boyish look and a sunny disposition. Self-discipline, however, was not his strong suit. Zeev, who looked like a boxer, was highly disciplined, organized, and wrote extremely well. They were not an ideal pair and I had to be their handler for as long as they were together. In the end, Yisrael grew tired of the relentless bickering and left the partnership. Motti was against it, but I nonetheless insisted on supporting Zeev, financially as well, until at last he was on the right path.

Vega Tools was considerably more audacious than the others. Its founders were two gifted Russian immigrants, Vadim Lebedev and Gennadi Pilkovsky. Gennadi had worked as a savings plan analyst in Bank Leumi and hated every minute of it. He had a razor-sharp, original mind. His inventive thinking led him to the idea of forming Vega Tools and focusing on PC software such as finite elements software, a program for complex architectural and engineering planning. Both Gennadi and Vadim were highly intelligent programmers who worked in our subsidiary company for three years. They developed sophisticated programs, and the company's future seemed bright. Then one day, Vadim simply disappeared without a trace, and Gennadi decided to pack up and go to the U.S. There he made good money from finite elements software, retired, moved to Long Island, and turned his hobby—deep-sea diving—into his life's pursuit.

David Shlasky, the founder of Modulog, was the complete opposite of these two odd geniuses. I met Shlasky at the IDF's construction center, where he served under Shamai Assif. I liked him and gave him my business card. The bespectacled, scholarly-looking redhead came to see me soon after leaving the army and in hushed tones said, "Roni ... I think it is possible to develop an architectural planning office using the ACA software. Are you interested?" "OK," I said, and I gave him a space to work in. Straight as an arrow, sensitive, and at the same time as stubborn as a mule, David excelled at what he did.

Looking back, I'm proud of the prodigies I nurtured. My investment in human capital always paid off, whether or not the ventured succeeded. The founders of our subsidiary companies injected the parent company with new blood and new ideas, and we gave them the guidance and support they needed to spread their wings. Einav Systems, though it lacked funds, acted as a kind of hothouse for start-ups, supporting new, raw talent. The cross-fertilization was of great benefit to all. That is why, when a particularly daring software idea was presented, I decided to form one more subsidiary company. I was eager to avoid further argument from Motti, who was never going to accept that developing software could be profitable. So after consulting with Meir Arnon, I decided that the next such company should be a subsidiary of Einav Computer Systems, which he would manage. The young stranger, at the time, who came to me with a new idea was Benny Weinberger.

Chapter 10
The Birth of Software

Benny Weinberger, bespectacled, skinny, already balding, plainly dressed, had just finished his army service in an elite intelligence unit, which he had been attached to after suffering an injury in combat training. Why hadn't he joined the brainy unit from the outset? "Because that isn't the real army." How about academic studies? "Unnecessary." He spoke at breakneck speed, and thought even faster. Motti Glazer had recruited this particular find to handle a project that needed a savior. We didn't ask him for certificates or degrees, which in any case he didn't have. Since he had served in an illustrious IDF unit, references were also unnecessary. We simply relied on our intuition, and the scrawny sabra from Ra'anana made a good impression. Who could have known that he was destined to change our lives?

The project had been commissioned by a firm called Nature Beauty, which ran a door-to-door pyramid marketing operation. Organizing the payment system for it was complex. The owner of the firm, a suave Belgian, had already been turned down by a number of software companies. The challenge appealed to me and I told him we'd do it, though I had no one on the staff capable of dealing with the particular complexities involved. Motti consulted Itzik Eldar, a neighbor who was an expert on information systems. Eldar said that he would be happy to program a payments system himself but that we would need a system analysis of Nature Beauty. Motti scanned his mental Rolodex and came up with Benny.

Quickly and easily Benny analyzed the system and Itzik Eldar wrote an effective program, to the client's complete satisfaction. Benny, who possessed a truly exceptional mind, had limitless self-confidence. A short time after he joined, we chatted about his future plans. "I've already talked to Meir," he said. "What I really want to do is to set up my own company. I have an idea."

The idea that fired Benny up was to develop a futuristic database, which, according to him, would be significantly more efficient than the existing database products, DB2 or ADABAS.

Most computer projects or applications rely on an organized database. The material is arranged by the database program in an automated way so that it can be stored and so that sections, views, queries can be retrieved from the computer efficiently, cheaply, and speedily. Information banks, which, since the appearance of the Internet are used worldwide, are stored on databases.

During the 1980s, giant corporations like IBM or Digital developed and produced such programs. Oracle tested the waters, as did a few others, including some universities. In 1967, an independent group working at the Weizmann Institute produced an outstanding product named DB1 that didn't achieve the commercial success it deserved. Imagine how people at IBM must have felt when they discovered that the name DB1 was taken and they must resign themselves to naming their invention DB2. Benny was not intimidated by the mighty names, and was tickled by the thought of competing in the big league. In all innocence, he believed that in our minuscule Tel Aviv office he could develop a better database program than any of those developed to date.

Benny was in his late twenties, had boundless ambition and, given his age, a big ego. After he dealt with Motti's negative response to the idea of software developing, he turned to Meir, as manager of Einav Computer Systems. His entrepreneurship impressed and worried me at the same time, but Benny possessed great powers of persuasion, and my fears were quickly allayed. We looked for a "futuristic" name for the company we now set about forming. We toyed with "Shop 2000" (the year 2000 still seemed a long way off) and others, settling finally for The Fourth Dimension Software LTD, which sounded both futuristic and intriguing, and which we could also refer to as 4D. Ownership of the company was equally divided between Benny and Einav Computer Systems. It was now up to us to nurture the sapling and hope that a profitable software program would indeed begin to grow.

These critical moments of decision-making—the primary responsibility of a CEO—are often accompanied by feelings of impending doom. Decisions taken at the idea stage are especially tricky because unlike traditional industries, software is a field in which one gropes in the dark. The odds were no more than even that we made the right decision in developing a database rather than going for specific applications such as word processing, graphics, or accountancy. One of the reasons we were confident in our choice—aside from Benny's ambition—was that progress in the area of mainframe computers was slow, which was good for us as beginners. In fast-moving areas, one has to race against time. That is tough today, and was ten times more so back then. On the other hand, when you're young you wonder if an "old" field such as mainframes won't soon be obsolete. In spite of my youth, I enjoyed the challenge of exploring business opportunities in areas that were regarded as old. Things that developed slowly might also die out slowly, or live on. And in fact, when we looked back later, we knew we'd made the right decision. Fortunately, even after the PC had made its appearance, the mainframe surprised its detractors and held on. To this very day, organizations continue to invest in the big computer and entrust it with their most valuable asset—information.

Benny's confidence was contagious and he persuaded Dr Arie Lavi, chief scientist at the Ministry of Trade and Industry, that he could succeed. Dr Lavi, who had worked with me in ordnance during the Six-Day War, authorized a budget of five thousand dollars. Though tiny in relation to our real needs, the funding made us deliriously happy. At last there was a reason for The Fourth Dimension to open a bank account of its own.

At this stage, The Fourth Dimension was nothing more than a name recorded with the Registrar of Companies. Its headquarters was a tiny cubicle within the offices of Einav Systems. 4D had not a bean to its name, let alone a computer suitable for the development of the program. Even the photocopying machine and word processor were shared with the mother company. We set off on our adventure without financial backing other than the aforementioned five thousand dollars. What this would cover, if anything at all, was one of many unknowns. With characteristic generosity, our partner, Meir Arnon, suggested that Benny work on ACA's computer. ACA's pioneering computerized architectural planning had been developed on one of IBM's 4300 series, which were relatively large machines. In exchange for a modest monthly payment, Benny was provided access to it.

Stage A was complete—we had found a place in which to develop the idea. For more than a year we spent and spent without a penny of income and with growing doubts. The database development was slow and new ideas would pop up, like producing something simpler to finance its continuing development. To no avail. Not for a moment did we consider quitting, nor did we at any time lose hope. We simply admitted failure, and halted the development until things got better. It wasn't easy; for me it was a setback, for Benny a bitter pill. But we were like the little engine that could. We'd do better next time, we told ourselves. And next time came pretty quickly.

Our new idea was also intended for mainframes: the design of Easy Programming Tools that would significantly improve the efficiency of the programmer in Cobol and in other computing environments. If we could complete the work quickly, we'd be able to finance our database project. Benny's unrivaled talent as a programmer brought us to the brink of success; the product was almost ready to be marketed. But again the process was too slow and the signs were mounting that we were about to face our second business failure. Our denial lasted a while but I knew the game was up. We had failed again. Despite Benny's confidence and my faith in him, The Fourth Dimension's first two attempts at developing a viable product had ended in dismal failure.

A second failure hurts a good deal more than a first, and is therefore also more dangerous. A first failure one can write off as an experiment and a lesson to be learned. What doesn't kill you makes you stronger. But with a second failure that sparkle in the eye vanishes. You begin to question your decisions, reassess your options. Why not become a lecturer at a university? Why subject yourself to these tensions and seemingly pointless struggles? Perhaps we had been too hasty in setting up a subsidiary. Perhaps a brilliant mind is not enough. Perhaps our working methods weren't right. Perhaps trusting the mainframe had been our fundamental error.

It was a dark time. I couldn't spot even a flicker of light at the end of the tunnel. Taking stock had become a painful ordeal. How sad it would have been if Motti Glazer were proven right and our attempt at developing software was nothing but vanity and folly.

Sunk in these thoughts one morning, I looked up to see Benny entering my office. The twinkle in his eye had returned. Cynically I said: "What price salvation now?" Benny had attended a lecture at Bar Ilan University—our second failure made him consider studies—where he heard from an acquaintance about a very interesting software program being used in the air force. Overnight, this program was scheduling and submitting the hundreds of jobs being run, so that by the next morning, the nightly batch run was done automatically without the need for operators.

Benny's acquaintance was a young soldier, Avi Cohen. Avi was one of the masterminds of the minimalistic scheduling program he'd described, called the GS Daily. GS Daily contained approximately ten thousand coded lines in the computer language known as Assembler. At the start of every day, the GS Daily managed the workload. It was an organizational management program that automatically activated jobs. In effect, the program managed the life of the entire organization. The air force was worried about the vacuum that was about to be created when Avi and his friends ended their active duty.

Benny was excited about the potential for the GS Daily in the civilian market. If the software was capable of automating military processes, why shouldn't that apply to business activities? "Only he who dares wins," I said. "Invite Avi Cohen in for a chat."

Avi was a stocky, precise, broad-minded young man with a wicked sense of humor. "You eat Kosher, Avi?" I asked him. "Also," was his response as we sat down in the restaurant. He explained in great detail the potential he saw for the civilian use of GS Daily. What he told us fueled my curiosity and I offered him a job as soon as he was released from the army. In the meantime, could he arrange a meeting for Benny and me with his superiors? Thanks to the successful projects Einav Systems had carried out for the air force, my name there was good. We were invited to meet Lieutenant Colonel Sheula Heytner, deputy to the head of the Infrastructure branch. The branch head, Jacobi "Yambi," was also in the loop. Sheula didn't beat about the bush. "We must increase the life span and output of a very important program. Once Avi Cohen and others in his year are released, it's unlikely that we'll have the capability to do that."

Sheula was touching on a bigger quandary in the software field, the problem of in-house software. If somebody develops an important piece of software as an employee in an organization and then leaves, the result is a loss of know-how likely to cause the whole system serious damage. As the world of software advanced, so did the recognition that buying products is preferable to investing in in-house software and becoming dependent on experts who might leave or leverage their power if they stay. In the military, damage can result merely by an officer or soldier coming to the end of his or her duty.

Still, many large organizations continued to rely on in-house software. In all, there were at the time some 15,000 organizations in the world that used or could have been interested in using a management program such as GS Daily run on an IBM mainframe. The software programs they employed provided only partial solutions to their range of needs. In 1982, Israel's air force was among those using a software program that would, in due course, cease to be viable, unless, as Sheula told us in the meeting, its ongoing development and maintenance were handed over to a company in the private sector. This was a wise and farsighted conclusion. From the air force's perspective, the issue was restricted to its own future interests. Whether such a project would benefit the private company formed no part of the calculation. What mattered to the air force was that from those private hands it would get back an advanced, state-of-the-art, updated technological product with a far longer shelf life.

Based on this line of reasoning, the air force handed over to us the ten thousand coded lines written by Avi Cohen and his friends. In return, we undertook to update and maintain the program for the air force for as long as it remained in use. I believe that this was possibly the only occasion that the army struck such a deal. In consideration of our commitment, and our pledge that all future versions—if and when they materialized—would also become available to the army, we obtained the GS Daily free of charge. At the end of that amazingly productive meeting, Lieutenant Colonel Sheula Heytner handed us the program in the form of a tape.

The Fourth Dimension's encounter with the GS Daily could hardly have come at a more opportune time. IBM's first PC computer had made its debut in the market only a year earlier, in 1981, and whether it had a commercial use was anybody's guess. On the other hand, in large organizations whose computerization was founded on mainframes, there was a growing appetite for applications that would raise productivity and save on manpower and time. In Benny's view, ours was going to be an uncomplicated project. "Based on the GS Daily, we'll quickly develop a system for automated production management, which will be better than any of those currently on the market. The income from its sales will finance the development of the database." He described a program that would automatically manage a computer unit's production system, decide what jobs to submit, when and under what circumstances they should be submitted, and what should be done in problem situations. The new system would allow close surveillance over work in progress, proper division of the workload, and practically transfer the entire production management to the computer. In Benny's opinion, commercial and industrial firms would leap at such an opportunity.

Then two things happened: we set to work on developing the program, and soon thereafter realized that the army had had no right to strike its deal with us, or any deal whatsoever. The moment we were alerted to the problem, we understood that we had taken a huge risk. The deal wasn't in our pocket. We hurried back to Sheula Heytner and were told "no worries," the go-ahead would arrive shortly. We waited a week—nothing.

Another week passed by and still nothing. We were already midway through the process of developing GS Daily, and in Benny's view we would very soon have an excellent product. The development continued unhindered, parallel to my unrelenting pursuit of the Ministry's letter of confirmation.

After two failures that had cost us dearly, we were on our knees, teetering on the edge of bankruptcy. Access to a computer with the required capacity to improve the basic program we'd received—one development station including the software development tools, communications, and everything else that was needed—cost approximately three thousand dollars a month. Benny wanted to add a programmer to reach the finish line more quickly. Assuming we could somehow scrape together the money for one, where would he work? Who had a mainframe for hire? Benny did some research and discovered that a university close by had the development stations we needed. The administrators were happy to rent them to us and make a bit of a profit on the deal. The only snag was that we didn't have the money.

In an act of either naïveté or stupidity—depending on who's telling the story—Benny told the university that we couldn't pay, but that if the development succeeded they too could benefit, and offered them 3 percent of any income derived from work done on their premises. He even wrote them a letter to that effect and they in turn agreed to the arrangement. What had they to lose? The stations were idle. Benny conducted the negotiations and it was he who decided on the percentages. I didn't object. I think I could even have agreed, I don't really remember. In any event, it was the wrong decision, but at this early stage we still didn't know the true value of our product. What we did know was that we were broke, and ready to do anything just to make some progress. As for Benny's letter of agreement—we would cross that bridge when we came to it. Conceivably, at that point, as my lawyer friend Spigelman liked to say, we'd have to make eggs from the omelet we had cooked. And sure enough, when the time came, that is exactly what I did.

During 1984, a year in which the company moved ahead at a frantic pace, the new software finally saw the light of day. In December 1983, Matia had given birth to our fourth son—the first time that I had dared enter the delivery room. I was so overwhelmed that I retain only hazy fragments of what went on in there. We named the little ginger baby Yoav Yaakov, after Matia's father. How fortunate we were to be able to balance the frenzy of our working lives with the delights of family. Yoav's birth was followed in 1984 by our eldest son Liran's Bar Mitzvah, and my own fortieth birthday. I don't recall having to struggle with a mid-life crisis as such, but I did reach some conclusions as I crossed into middle age. One of them was that each of my four sons would learn to know the world, and a trip to the U.S. with one's father would do nicely for starters. The first to get there was Liran, and his rite of passage inaugurated the Bar Mitzvah voyages that became a family tradition.

Meanwhile I continued to pursue the Ministry of Defense. It had already been two years, during which time we'd been working feverishly in the university's basement, and we'd reached 100,000 coded lines instead of the original 10,000. We still didn't have a saleable product. During those first two years, we had only two programmers working on the project, Benny and Ariel Gordon, another ex-serviceman drawn from Benny's prestigious unit and a real genius. Later on, there were to be four programmers, one of whom was Avi Cohen. He was the fourth or fifth to join the group and advanced the product a step farther. Avi, a rare breed, grew up in a Yeke (German Jewish) household known for its tradition of discipline and precision. In the easygoing, carefree (some would say sloppy) Israel of those years, Avi was an invaluable asset. Step by step, he taught us how to proofread a manual, the importance of technical support, and how to give numbers to bugs.

Control M—this was the new name we gave the GS Daily—began to take shape. Our belief in it was greatly strengthened when CGA, a large American vendor, wanted the software, along with the services of Ariel Gordon, to transfer the knowledge and oversee the operation for six months. They offered us a handsome fee for the package deal. Things seemed to be looking up, but then CGA was bought by the giant software company CA. Ariel remained at home and The Fourth Dimension remained strapped for cash. This was the first time that CA was destined to interfere with our plans.

For two years we worked, progressed, and fully expected that our dedication and effort would deliver its rewards. The only fly in the ointment, or so we thought, was the ongoing absence of the letter of confirmation from the Ministry of Defense. In fact, what had arrived instead was a new type of bother. One evening I stood waiting for the elevator, clutching three sack-loads of office trash. Benny constantly worried about industrial espionage and I had volunteered to be the company's garbage collector. As twilight descended and everyone else was off doing the pub round, I would be off doing the Tel Aviv trash bin round. To confuse the enemy I would chuck a sackful into one remote bin, and then the next in another randomly available dumpster, and so on until every item of garbage had been disposed of. As far as I knew nobody followed me, and our precious waste reached its final resting places intact. If somebody were trying to spy on us it certainly wouldn't have occurred to them that the CEO was also the collector and disposer of refuse and that he was the man to watch.

That evening, the elevator doors opened and I saw Benny and Avi Cohen, their faces white as sheets. "You're not going home yet," they told me in no uncertain terms, and dragged me back into the office along with the trash bags. Benny made sure the door was closed and whispered angrily, "One of our codes has been stolen." He had employed a variety of stratagems to avoid such industrial espionage and now, despite all his subterfuges, his worst fear had come true.

"Explain," I said quietly, my heart racing.

"An Israeli branch of a German company called Software AG with a product named ADABAS NATURAL is also working on the university's computer," said Avi, "and it appears that they've started to use our concepts." His tone was uncharacteristically agitated.

That was alarming. ADABAS was already in the market where we planned to introduce our product. Its manufacturer would find it far easier to add a second product than we would to launch our first. That night none of us slept. In the morning, we began to look into the incident as thoroughly as we could, and became convinced that concepts, material, and codes had indeed been stolen from us via the university's computer. We had no idea how this could be proven, nor did we have the resources to fight for our rights. At the end of the day, and despite the scare, it turned out that we had suffered no real damage. The lessons to be drawn were clear: we couldn't afford to take any further risks. Our location and our luck had to change.

We left the university and transferred to the Histadrut's pension company, Mivtachim, which had a large computer operating in Tel Aviv. With them we also struck a barter deal. In exchange for our using their equipment, we provided them with the product, which by then had reached an advanced stage of development. After a while, we left Mivtachim and went to Scitex, where Amnon Neubach, who held a senior position, agreed to do me a favor. Thanks to my friendship with him, I was able to secure four development stations in exchange for our product. By my reckoning, Amnon's gesture was worth a quarter of a million dollars—four stations at $2,500 each per month times 24 months—a huge favor for which we remained eternally grateful.

During 1984, when we began to see the product emerge and the need for finance became pressing, the Ministry of Defense's writ was still mired in bureaucracy. Desperate, we went looking for partners to back us financially. The first was Galia Streiker, who came on board in May of that year. A formal agreement with her wasn't signed until several months later, at which point the corporate structure had to be redrawn. Einav Systems via Einav Computer Systems had a 50 percent holding in The Fourth Dimension. After Galia joined as a partner, the shares in The Fourth Dimension were redivided between Meir Arnon, Einav Systems, Galia, and me. (Galia, unlike Motti Glazer, paid for her stake in the partnership.) She flew frequently between Israel and the U.S. and our hope was that in future this would be helpful to the company.

As mentioned, Meir Arnon stopped working in the jointly owned company but maintained his share and from time to time drew money. After Meir's departure, we resumed our search for new partners in The Fourth Dimension and found ATL, managed by my friend Yechezkel Zaira, from Technion days. Owned by Tadiran, ATL was one of the earliest software companies in Israel. It distributed the software products of large foreign companies such as CA and Legent.

We gave a detailed description of our emerging product to Yechezkel and to Amos Magor, another top executive at ATL and a shrewd marketing man. They were all ears, and obviously impressed by Benny's professionalism and the high motivation we all demonstrated. At the end of our presentation, they expressed their strong interest in encouraging an Israeli company in this field, and proposed a fifty-fifty partnership. "We decided to join you before you become our competitors," was how Yechezkel put it. According to their estimate, 4D was then worth about $100,000. The proposed deal was that ATL would provide us with a programmer they figured to be worth three thousand dollars a month. I told Yechezkel that Benny was also worth three thousand dollars a month and that we were using two development stations. ATL agreed to transfer to us $6,000 a month. This helped to finance the rest of 4D's outgoings such as technical writing, printing up of manuals, telephone, telex, fax, maintenance of Einav System's office, and a bit of secretarial work.

In spite of this progress, there still lurked in the background a menacing shadow: the non-arrival of the Ministry's letter approving the project. At the time of our partnership agreement with ATL, the letter was still in bureaucratic limbo. Since we had assured our new partners that the problem would be sorted out within a month or two at most, we had to agree to an escape clause.

ATL was a big company that had dealings with the army. Israel, on the other hand, is a small country where everybody knows everybody. Someone in the army said something to ATL and Yechezkel Zaira received a warning from his lawyer. I reassured Yechezkel that the authorization was a mere formality. It was far too late for the army to backpedal. But a big company has its own bureaucratic imperatives and Yechezkel had to cave in.

Benny brought me the "divorce" papers they had sent. In an apologetic tone, ATL informed us that should we fail to produce the authorization within the allotted time frame, then, in accordance with the aforementioned clause in the agreement, they would sever their connection with us, i.e., exit the partnership. At the same time, they reasserted ATL's interest in distributing Control M when its development was complete—notwithstanding the fact that the product was deemed illegal. They wanted to have their cake and eat it. Benny was beside himself. "How are we going to manage without their financing?" I had a little tête-à-tête with my usually reliable intuition and told him: "This is the best letter you've ever received. Don't answer it. Don't even ask them to reconsider … just sit tight and do nothing."

ATL ended their partnership with us in March 1985. It had lasted just six months. We got back the 50 percent they had been holding and their letter was to become part of 4D's folklore.

My unremitting pursuit of the letter of permission continued. At least once a month I showed up at the office of Ezra Cohen at the Ministry of Defense to plead my case. He didn't know what to do, for he had never before been confronted with a similar situation. Ultimately, attrition was our savior. After two years of harassment in which he'd sent me from pillar to post, on the 22nd of October, 1985, he'd had his fill. And this was the letter he gave us:

The State of Israel, Ministry of Defense
Department of Acquisition and Production
Air Force
Attention: Mr. Roni Einav
Re: The Product Control M

We hereby authorize your usage of the above product as you see fit and proper based on the duly referenced letters.

Signed Ezra Cohen

The fog of military bureaucracy had lifted and daylight emerged. We were free to be on the market and find out whether our efforts had been worth it.

Chapter 11

The Wizards

Before describing the first sale of Control M, a momentous event, I want to dedicate a chapter to the company's trailblazers—the men and women who turned theory into practice, the dream into reality.

In every department we had first-rate people, but the members of the product development team were truly outstanding. They were extraordinarily gifted computer wizards and thanks to them, 4D had acquired a reputation as an unconventional company where it was fun to work. Because of that 4D was able to attract interesting people who relished a challenge. The first to come on board reached important and lucrative positions. Our workers' successful recruiting of new hires was rewarded by an all-expense- paid weekend retreat. Benny, Galia, and I agreed on a policy of choosing new staff from among people recommended by our employees. Their camaraderie ensured that the development team as a whole would be an organic group based on mutual trust, able to work together in pursuit of a common goal. Moreover, some 30 percent of the workforce was comprised of women. During the first few years they were all so loyal that everyone stuck with us. People joined, nobody quit. The commitment to one another, to the company, to success, was rock solid.

Initially, we did not divide up our staff into teams. Everyone worked on the various tasks at hand. When a problem arose it was dealt with. From ten in the morning until eight at night, workers would come and go. They didn't clock in and out, and we didn't count the hours. Avi Cohen and Ariel Gordon formulated a development program, and everyone was responsible for carrying out the tasks assigned to them. If an urgent job had to be completed—a common occurrence—everybody stayed until it was done. Anyone who was hungry simply had to open the fridge, which we kept stocked with goodies. The weary could nap in the cafeteria and return, rested, to their workstations. Within the team, responsibility was shared equally. The overriding objective was uninterrupted progress, and an absentee's tasks were taken on by colleagues.

In order for it to be successful, our work model required that everyone be well-informed on most of the subjects at hand and accept assistance from teammates without hesitation. Natural ambition and competitiveness were channeled into teamwork. Benny, who was head of development, interviewed most of the applicants. Those cases that called for a more refined questioning were referred to me. On rare occasions, it was Galia who took charge. Eyal Diskin was one of her first interviewees.

Eyal's story:

In 1989 I came home from a trip abroad after discharge from my army service and immediately went into the reserves for thirty days, rejoining the navy's computer unit, in which I had previously served. I had that month to find a job. A friend in the unit told me that The Fourth Dimension, a serious company, was now recruiting. I got in touch and was asked to come for an interview. Somebody by the name of Galia Streiker introduced herself as a manager and briefly interviewed me. Then she called in Avi Cohen from Development to quiz me on my professional qualifications. When that was over, Avi and Galia talked for five minutes, at the end of which she got back to me. "We want you," she announced. "What salary do you expect?" Wow! I had expected to be sent off for a series of suitability tests—nothing of the sort. I scanned my memory to recall what my contact said he was making and threw a number into the air. "OK," Galia said. "You start tomorrow." I explained that I was still in the reserves. "Fine," she replied. "Start on Sunday, then." I had already twigged that this was no ordinary place. Whether I should be happy or worried about it, only time would tell. When on Sunday morning at eight o'clock I turned up for work, the entire office floor was deserted. The only sound was the drone of the cleaner's vacuum machine blending uneasily with the still chirping birds outside. I sat and waited, until, toward midday, somebody from the development team arrived, introduced himself, turned on the computer, and started to clue me in. He also explained what I had already seen for myself —the workers were night owls, quite unlike my own habit of rising with the lark.

Eyal turned out to be an intelligent, responsible, affable young man, who quickly rose to a senior position in development. At first he was trained by Avi Cohen and later on, Benny took Eyal under his wing.

Eyal's story continues:

I loved working with Avi. He doesn't work quickly, but rather thoroughly. In those days, we in development and technical support worked mostly via telex. Customers would send us telexes describing problems that had arisen during use of the software. We prepared reports and passed them on to the person in charge of fixing job errors. This system was confusing until Avi, the stickler for order, worked out a method of numbering the bugs. Thanks to him, we were able to deal with customers quickly, in real time, and avoid repetition.

Benny was a very different type. He was brilliant and charismatic, a great motivator, but at the same time temperamental and unpredictable. Sometimes he would sneak up from behind with his catchphrase, "What are you spoiling now," making me jump in alarm. Benny was also a bit of a meddler, poking his nose in where it was not really wanted. He'd take over my computer, then get up and leave, muttering, "Get on with it, what are you waiting for?" In my first year with him, my nerves were sorely tested. My ability to withstand the pressure was due in no small measure to Roni in his role as global pacifier. He would wait for Benny to be out of the way, and then come over with a word of encouragement in his soothing tones.

The company owed its distinctive character to a motley group of individuals. There were those like Eyal, Israelis who had done their service in army intelligence and other such elite units, and had had significant experience working under pressure. And then there were immigrants from Anglo-Saxon countries. They had good command of English—a must in the field of software—and the sort of cultural background and marketing savvy in their countries of origin that helped our fledgling company a great deal. Some were religiously observant, and when we moved to new offices in Kiryat Attidim we set up a makeshift synagogue especially for them.

In the melting pot that was The Fourth Dimension, Israelis met up with Australian and American programmers, a writer of technical literature from South America, and an American lawyer. Our technical writer was an accomplished philologist who earned his living writing technical manuals but spent his leisure time researching the sources of English. He located about 1,700 words originating in Hebrew. We also recruited two Russians who had immigrated to Israel during the 1970s. As they tried to integrate, the newcomers faced difficulties ranging from learning Hebrew to adjusting to the prickly Israeli temperament. They found our directness nothing short of brutal and our creativity, well—chaotic. This was a winning team made up of all sorts, a kaleidoscopic mix of the well mannered and the blunt, the levelheaded and the impetuous, foreigners and locals.

Later on, our distributors abroad were also included in our social bonding. This contributed tremendously to the professional links. If some problem arose in Amsterdam or Madrid, they didn't hesitate to call Eyal or Tamir's home phones (before the age of cell phones), as one would a friend. The Europeans greatly appreciated our open door and the rapid, high-quality responses to every inquiry.

Seeing as we were constantly working under pressure—"constructive chaos," as Eli Mashiah, one of the developers, called it—staff loyalty was every bit as important as talent. The new version of Control M that we were due to begin distributing after the first Gulf War (1991) was behind schedule. To help ensure completion at the eleventh hour, we asked Eyal Diskin to postpone a planned trip to the U.S. He didn't hesitate and rescheduled the vacation twice, working around the clock with the whole team until four a.m. of the day on which the new version was due to be released.

Eli Mashiah had specialized in data-security programs during his military service. His role with us was to develop an interface for our company's products, enabling them to operate seamlessly with data-security products already on the market. This required him to do his job in environments where products we wanted to interface with were already in place—in other words, in the offices of our customers. As he did the rounds, the various tests he conducted sometimes led to the client's computer crashing. Eli's popularity quickly plummeted and he offered to develop just the skins—imitations of the data-security programs—himself, so he could work in our offices. The ever-pragmatic Avi wanted to know how long that would take. "Two weeks," replied Eli. Avi knew this was an unachievable goal. He never believed in fairy tales, but in people he trusted.

Eli takes up the story …

He [Avi] agreed to let me try to develop the imitation programs and gave me three weeks to do it. After four days of intense effort, 4D had the capacity to develop and debug every interface operating in conjunction with all the known and accepted data-security programs then on the market. I made this effort both because I had been assigned a task and out of a desire to prove that if you set your mind to something, even the impossible is achievable. Obviously, the security API stubs included only a subset, aspects of the original security program, but it was sufficient to develop the support we needed in the product. There was something about the way The Fourth Dimension was managed that brought out the best in people, egging them on to try to reach beyond themselves to succeed.

Within less than six months, our products' interface with data-security programs was better than that of all our competitors, giving us a significant edge in the market. Years later, when Eli set up his own company, Memco, I was happy to reward him by allowing him and his partner Israel Mazin to develop their company's products on our computers.

More than once, I went out of my way to hold on to an outstandingly brilliant staff member. Yossi Aloni was one such person. He lived in a small community in Northern Israel and was reluctant to make the daily journey to Tel Aviv. I struck a special deal with the Haifa Oil Refinery, customers of ours. Yossi would work for us out of their offices, testing on their computers new versions of programs we had developed, and at the same time provide the refinery with technical support for the software they had bought from us. Yossi's hosts were extremely happy with the arrangement. Ironically, this same man in due course willingly moved to our office in the United States. California, unlike Tel Aviv, wasn't too far away for Yossi.

A new breed of outstandingly well-educated people, quite different from anything we had encountered, flocked to Israel with the wave of immigration from the former Soviet Union in 1991. Given their assimilation challenges in their new environment, many of them were forced to make do with menial jobs just to survive. Only a fortunate few managed to join Israel's high-tech industry. The Fourth Dimension succeeded in recruiting two of them, Alex Goldblatt and Leonid Nishtat. Alex, an experienced programmer, had been working for Coca-Cola as an unskilled laborer. In an interview with me, he said that he would be satisfied with a salary of five hundred dollars a month so long as he could work in his chosen profession. I retorted that in the event that we were to employ him, his starting salary would be the same as that of anybody else taken on by our company—seven times the figure he had mentioned. He was hired, paid three thousand five hundred dollars a month to begin with, and stayed on for seven productive years.

Leonid's tale is a real Cinderella story. Somebody recommended him and I invited him in for an exploratory talk. He had only just arrived in the country, lived in Acre and spoke broken English. To test him out, I told him about Control R, a program we were having difficulties with. It was designed to deal with a bug in any given program in the most optimal way possible. The ingenuity lay in re-starting the subject program without having to revert to the beginning of the job, and instead go back as little as necessary, and fix the bug from the point at which the program had begun to malfunction. The problem was that the development of Control R had not proceeded at the pace we had hoped for.

As I explained all of this in plain language, the young man began to smile until the smile became a laugh. There he was, sitting in my office, laughing at me. What impudence, I thought. Leonid sensed my annoyance, apologized, and told me who and what he was: none other than the former manager of the computerized ticketing system of the Soviet railway network. In the event of a breakdown, it was up to Leonid and his team to get the gigantic system back to normal in as little time as possible, and to make sure that ticket sales didn't grind to a halt. Leonid's men became experts not only in software and its applications but also in hardware, operating systems, program architecture, and even in doing technician's work. We happily engaged Leonid and were not exactly shy in asking where we could find similar talents. In Moscow, he replied. Within two years, his entire team had arrived and joined our company.

A place in which people of excellence work attracts other such people. Measured by international standards, the quality achieved by Benny Weinberger's team was second to none. The coming together of minds from such differing backgrounds increased creativity, and the feedback from the field clearly indicated that the quality of our developments was indeed much higher than the norm. Customers reported back that our products were preferred not only because of the quality but also because they used a smaller proportion of the host computer's resources. This was something we didn't know, couldn't have known, and it was undoubtedly due to the superiority of our development team.

My appreciation was expressed in a number of ways. First, I made sure that my wizards enjoyed first-class working conditions: fridges full of everything the heart and stomach could possibly desire, a true home away from home. Then there were trips to conferences around the world, dinners, parties, and pleasurable breaks. I marked every Jewish High Holiday with a handwritten note sent to each employee. At least once a year, I would sit down with each one individually to discuss raising their salary. They appreciated the fact that the initiative came from management. In addition, all kinds of incentives, such as bonuses, stock options, and other fringe benefits, were offered. We nurtured and respected our dream team until it became recognized the world over as a winner. We believed that with such a team, we were up to any challenge thrown at us, and time would prove us right.

Chapter 12
Moving On

ATL had "divorced" us in March 1985 because we didn't have the Ministry of Defense's written authorization to develop Control M, and six months later we got it. Meanwhile we had completed Control M's development. We now had our first finished product ready for use plus the precious letter of authorization. We offered it magnanimously to none other than our ex, ATL, who said yes and immediately sold it on to Tadiran, its parent company. Perhaps in hindsight they regretted their decision to bow out of the partnership with us. I never asked. My attention was focused on selling the new product.

Our track record as 4D had included two failures and zero success. For two long years we had worked frantically on the development of a product that wasn't officially ours. Despite the Ministry's equivocation, we gave it our all and forged ahead. For two years we had twisted and turned to reach this moment. Now we were there, on the brink of making our first sale of an authorized and legitimate product—4D's maiden software package. It was a great drama.

As time went by and our sales volume increased such moments became more routine. But landing that first sale in January 1986 was critical and our excitement was overwhelming.

Benny and the dream team continued the development work at full throttle, with the knowledge that good software can always be improved on. The success we had with Tadiran was encouraging and we could only pray that it was a sign of things to come. Indeed, potential new customers such as Mehish (Bank Mizrahi's computer services arm), Bank Hapoalim, Bezek, El-Al, Israel Aerospace Industries, and the Israeli air force were all interested.

Ariel takes up the story:

Mehish wanted to buy Control M and asked Benny if it supported "started task." Benny said it did, promised that we would give them a demonstration within two days, and rushed back to the office to ask me what on earth "started task" was, and how long it would take to program it. I told him at least a month, but for him we'd do it in two days. We worked non-stop for forty-eight hours, producing an improved version of Control M with the required feature, and demonstrated it to the customer. A similar situation occurred with Raphael (Advanced Defense Systems). Again we promised to deliver a feature we didn't actually have and custom programmed it for them alone. This was our way of working. Flexibility was our trump card.

Our client list in Israel continued to grow: Bituah Leumi (Israel's Social Security), then the Treasury. Galia put out early feelers in the U.S. There, an American we hired by the name of Bill Drews had written a superb technical marketing manual for Control M. In Israel, a good proportion of the staff of Einav Systems and 4D's team (Benny, Dorit Dor, and sometimes the programmers) continued to squeeze into the limited space at 7 Derech Hashalom.

Motti complained of not being sufficiently involved in the work of 4D and that nobody ever consulted him. But then when somebody did, he would invariably say that he wasn't interested because in any case nothing would come of it. His grumbling about Benny wasting electricity, or paper, and other such trivialities, never ceased. Not a day passed without some new allegation by Motti: why doesn't Benny pay rent or, when he did, why doesn't he pay more. Perhaps this was concealing a much deeper concern. Motti may have been jealous of the ever-closer relations developing between Benny and me. I told Motti to calm down. We would move out as soon as we possibly could and 4D will be out of his way. Until then, please let's try and be civilized. It's going to be my second son's Bar Mitzvah soon, why spoil my mood?

In November 1986 we made our first sale in the U.S., unfortunately without Bill Drews' impressive technical manuals. Most of the booklets arrived in the U.S. waterlogged. We hadn't been able to afford to send them by special courier and had them shipped by sea instead, in a container that got badly damaged en route. I kept my promise to Motti and the minute a bit of money started to come in from Israeli and European customers, I went in search of new offices for 4D. Galia had approached a friend of her father's. As luck would have it, he had 300 square meters for rent in Kiryat Attidim. We only needed 180 square meters so it was agreed that we would get the whole floor but pay only for the space we used. We packed what few portable belongings we had and moved from the overpopulated eight square meters we had shared with Einav Systems to the one hundred and eighty that we now had all to ourselves in Kiryat Attidim. What luxury! For the first time in 4D's history we had room to breathe.

In business, every development has its own rhythm that one should pay attention to. The move to new offices stemmed not only from the squabbles between Motti and me but signaled also a natural and inevitable process of parting; 4D had simply ceased to need the sponsorship of Einav Systems. During that very same period questions arose in Scitex about our free use of their computer. We reviewed our new situation and concluded that instead of paying the ten thousand dollars Scitex was starting to demand for the four development stations, we could buy a computer of our own. A company by the name of 2D, owned by David Rubin and my tennis partner, Baruch Palai, was selling used computers at ridiculously low prices. The only snag was that in those days buying second-hand equipment was not done. In Israel the purchase of mainframes was then restricted to large organizations such as the army, banks, or Technion, who bought their equipment directly from the manufacturer at a set price. Firms were afraid not to buy from the manufacturer—a fear that I shared. Avi Cohen and Ariel Gordon, our experts, told me to stop worrying; the used equipment could be easily checked before purchase to ensure it was all up to scratch. Having thoroughly examined the main components and allaying my fears, they sent me off to 2D, where I struck a very good deal, and 4D bought the computer from 2D at one tenth of the manufacturer's price.

Now we had to purchase an operating system from IBM, who had the sole rights to the expensive Multi Virtual Storage (MVS) program. At the time, rights ran to about $20,000 a month, a fee we were naturally reluctant to pay until we began actual use. In the course of negotiations I had suggested that the payments should start on January 1, 1989, regardless of the actual situation, and no one objected. Now, all of a sudden, that mutual consent was being ignored. I reread the contract and to my pleasant surprise discovered that IBM had only gotten around to adding their signature on December 31. Still, only a fool would engage in a dispute with the Blue Giant; 4D agreed to pay a debt it didn't owe in minuscule installments over a long period of time, and we had a truce.

The new old computer was hauled to Kiryat Attidim, its operational system already installed, and started to purr. Because of its size we were forced to place it in the center of the floor with the development teams seated around it. This improvisation solved one problem but there were others, mainly this giant's annoying tendency to crash without prior warning when its temperature rose to 38 degrees. We tried everything we could think of to prevent it from overheating. We had the air conditioning blow right at it. We placed fans in all four corners of the room, took its temperature every two hours as if it were a sick baby. It's an amusing memory but not so funny at the time. Despite the occasional bitter pill we were happy with our lot.

One of my most important principles in 4D was that no matter for what purpose a customer wanted a scheduling program, I could pledge to them that ours would outdo any other. Control M would work better and faster and practically without human intervention. We were selling automation, a system for automated production management—if you will, robotics without a robot. With our program the computer doubled as a robot.

Another principle, no less important, was to behave and perform like the big players even when we were still relatively small. That extended to our customer service. We had, from the outset, set up a support center operating 24/7. Local and overseas customers regularly contacted us with problems their distributor couldn't deal with. They got in touch by telex and telephone—later on by fax—and the staff member on duty would physically pass on the inquiry to the support team. But we grew at an exponential rate and what had begun as a small pile became a veritable mountain of paper. Avi understood that the manual system no longer sufficed and searched for a better way. He readily accepted Jacob Steinmitz's suggestion of writing a basic program for managing faults, and the speedy programmer completed it in just four days. The new program enabled the support team to receive an inquiry, classify and number it according to date, product, customer's and distributor's name, and the seriousness of the problem. Within twenty-four hours confirmation of registration would be issued. If there was a ready solution, based on a previous identical glitch, it was sent to the client immediately. If not, it was rapidly dealt with.

On Saturdays and Jewish holidays, there were always people on duty to respond to clients abroad. Staff members who were religious were asked to swap watch with those who were not, without involving management. The duty officers responded to inquiries from home and, if necessary, went to the office computer. The exception was Ariel Gordon. Ariel knew all the code lines by heart and was always in a position to supply a perfect answer from memory (overseas customers had no doubt that he was sitting in front of a computer). At the end of each month Avi assembled an updated maintenance disc of the repairs that had been carried out and confirmed by the customer. The disc was sent out to all our distributors. There were, of course, those that forgot to confirm because, having had the bug dealt with, they simply carried on working. For this too, Avi found a practical solution: verification. At the end of a three-month period a solution was regarded as having been verified whether or not the client had confirmed it. We gained the reputation of supermen, a team capable of solving any problem that came our way.

It would be misleading to say that we had a clear idea of Control M's golden future. It was a good product that filled a need, but 4D at that stage was just one more subsidiary, though a promising one. As time went by I became less and less involved in Einav Systems and devoted more of my time to 4D. Despite the successful development of Control M and its impressive sales, difficulties, not dividends, were still the order of the day for me. Through all those years the disagreements between me and Motti Glazer continued. He insisted that the development of software was a dangerous and foolish enterprise and that Einav Systems must focus on supplying computer services. He also managed to infuriate me by launching a number of initiatives from which I was excluded. The mutual feelings of discontent festered until finally in 1988, I decided that enough was enough.

Chapter 13

Friends in Need

Doing business with friends may be unwise but who hasn't succumbed? Israelis, especially those of my generation, are more prone to this sin than later generations, who grew up in the global village. We were raised in a newly founded small country where everybody knew everybody. Together from kindergarten to conscription and university, we even married within the group. Government and business in our little Israel were run on a handshake. Did a greenhorn like me, who some thirty years ago needed a business partner, put an ad in the paper or interview strangers? Never. The done thing was to inquire among friends or acquaintances with similar interests. Why not the jovial neighbor I used to meet in the elevator? When he told me he had quit his job I invited him to join me. It was that simple. That complicated.

I have already described my first serious dispute with Motti. He had refused to honor our agreement with Meir Arnon, and I bypassed him by setting up Einav Computer Systems, a partnership just between me and Meir. Over time, as disagreements with Motti escalated, I was glad to be a partner in a company where I could pursue projects he rejected. As 1987 approached, the rift deepened and we were in fact working separately. As so often happens in a failing marriage we were both unhappy and wary of parting. Perhaps we would overcome our difficulties, one or the other will see the error of his ways. It's not easy to dissolve a company and a partnership without damaging clients, reputation, and financial stability. We kept going, together yet apart, while beneath the surface a slow process of disengagement eroded what was left of the union.

In the course of 1987, Einav Systems ran into real financial difficulties. As the result of a major deal being canceled, the company nearly ground to a halt. The slowdown led to a serious budgetary deficit and we needed a loan for which the bank demanded guarantees. Motti refused to provide any form of personal pledge. In his view the responsibility for all existing and future debts rested with me. These financial problems further clouded our already wobbly relationship. After many a sour discussion, we agreed to cover the deficit by selling our shares in our subsidiary company, Liraz. Einav Systems exited Liraz during a crisis, ditching the shares at a relatively low price. From a business perspective, that was a mistake, since Liraz had been a good investment. The company continued to prosper and when it went public, its value rose. But at the time we were in no position to weigh Liraz's prospects. We just needed breathing space.

During this bad patch my younger brother, Amnon, was a tower of strength. He lived a stone's throw away, and every day I dropped in to cry on his shoulder. Patiently, wisely, and with great affection, he always knew how to encourage me. Occasionally we'd meet near the school that our children attended. At one stage six of our offspring, three of his and three of mine, were being taught there by Motti's wife, Ruthie Glazer. To her credit it must be said that if she was aware of the tensions, she never let on to me or to my children.

"It never rains but it pours," proved to be painfully true in our case. At approximately the same time as Einav Systems was in deficit, 4D got into trouble. While our European distributors made good progress, the revenues were slow in coming. To make matters worse, revenues were halted completely when a dispute arose over another product we had developed, Control D. We were also at odds over the same product with our American distributor. This left 4D with promising products in various stages of development and no money to complete the work. I proposed to various businessmen that they invest in the company, and all but my old friend Meron showed me the door. Meron agreed to a loan because of our friendship, but refused shares in 4D as collateral. I had hoped that Motti would help, but he wanted nothing to do with it, feeling, he said, that the entire enterprise was financial suicide.

For 4D, 1983 to 1987 were years of trial and error, a time in which we took many risks, often faltered, and often failed. Motti stayed well clear, not willing to provide any form of financial guarantees for this nebulous thing called software. A friend of his, the founder of Nikuv Software, failed spectacularly, lost the company, and ended up in debt and crying on Motti's shoulder. Up against the wall, Galia, Benny, and I decided to give the bank personal guarantees to keep 4D afloat.

Motti and I didn't quarrel openly; at least I wouldn't say so. However, we had a fundamental disagreement at a critical moment in business. Added to the creeping process of disengagement it marked the beginning of the end of the partnership. The crises at Einav Systems and 4D were ostensibly unrelated and yet both involved the same set of people.

Trouble, it is said, always comes in threes. As we were dealing with the two problems, a third reared its head. Meir Arnon, my partner in Einav Computer Systems, decided to bow out of the business and sell his shares. This came about gradually. Before he left we agreed that while he was studying I would transfer to him company funds to which he was entitled in line with a pre-agreed calculation. For his part, Meir would continue to work for the company from abroad. Then in phase two, in May 1984, when Meir wanted to develop some of his own initiatives, he suggested selling part of his holdings in the company. Angrily, Motti agreed to the new structure.

Phase three came in December 1987. His studying days over, Meir wanted to go off in an entirely new direction and to sell his remaining stock in Einav Computer Systems. Galia and I had a thirty-day option to buy. Meir scribbled his proposal in a handwritten note and the formal agreement was signed later. Galia and I bought the remainder of his stock, and Meir left Einav Computer Systems for good. Galia now held 40 percent of the stock, my share was 44 percent and Einav Systems maintained the 16 percent it already had. Meir got the funds due to him from Galia and me, and said his farewells. The last receipt he gave me was signed, "in true friendship."

With Motti Glazer it was a different story. The difficult 1987 signaled a turning point for us both. While he became more and more involved with his own private affairs, I spent half of my time working for 4D without any form of remuneration. If we are to continue as partners, I thought, these facts should at least be acknowledged in a new agreement. Our original partnership agreement precluded us from an involvement in private business.

In July 1988, we drew up a handwritten "summary of understandings" in which we redefined our respective duties, adding that each of us was entitled to pursue private business interests. At Motti's insistence we also agreed to change the company's name. Motti made all sorts of suggestions and in the end we settled for "Einav M.G Systems." I proposed that we draw up a new handwritten agreement that included the new name, just as we had done previously. But Motti decided to bring in a lawyer, so the agreement we made in April 1989 was drafted by his legal representative.

Just as we were about to sign, Motti had the gall to demand shares in "Einav Computer Systems/4D." I told him that Galia and I paid a fair price for what we got. Motti, of course, was unwilling to offer either cash or financial guarantees. Once that gambit had failed, I insisted that I would not sign the new contract until he first signed a declaration that he was fully cognizant of the relevant facts. I didn't want him coming to me later, saying that there were things he didn't know about or that were done against his wishes.

And so it was written: "The parties hereby declare that there are no further disagreements between them and/or any outstanding claims and/or any complaint with respect to the management of the company or partnership … and that in the event of some outstanding disagreement the sides hereby waive all such complaints and or claims." We also included a clause covering the eventuality that we would one day want to dissolve the partnership. If so, we agreed that the dissolution would be overseen by an arbitrator acceptable to both sides. In the event it was Motti who chose the arbitrator, it would be his good friend Danny Abarbanel. That was fine with me. So we put pen to paper, and henceforth each of us would have leeway to follow his heart's desires with the full knowledge of the other.

Ostensibly, we had turned a page. The paperwork had been re-ordered and there was agreement on all the key issues. As we were to discover, rather than patching things up we had simply given the rift between us an official stamp of approval. A business partnership really does bear a great resemblance to marriage—easy to enter, difficult to exit. In practice, we barely connected. Communication between us was via the arbitrator, Danny Abarbanel, whom Motti nominated in 1990 to Einav Systems' board of directors. I expected a lull, a period of relative tranquility. But things remained unsettled, as did Motti, who continued to be unhappy with his lot.

Chapter 14

Childhood Promises

It was the summer of 1953 and I was nine-and-a-half years old. After Amnon was born and Mom stopped working, our home life changed. Every member of the family was assigned various duties in addition to the already established house rules that had been set by my parents, to teach their sons responsibility and sharing. Most of the new tasks had at first fallen on Uri's shoulders but before that summer he had joined the army and I, all of a sudden, replaced him as the big brother. I would have gladly forgone the honor if it had kept him at home.

Mom cooked only for Amnon. Dad had lunch at work. My job was to go every day after school to the dining hall on the corner of Nordau and Hayarkon Street, to eat and then bring food home for Mom's lunch. "Wash your hands, Ronile," she said in her Polish accent as she gave me a three-tiered aluminum mess tin (the bottom part for soup, the middle for the main dish, and the top for dessert). "Go straight to dining hall, Ronile, no dawdling on way, or you'll be given all leftovers." Just as I opened the door the sound of the iceman's bell heralding his arrival on his horse-driven wagon stopped me. "Should I first bring up the ice, Mom?" I volunteered. I loved licking the bits that scattered as the blocks were hacked. "No, no, ice I will get. Go to dining hall," was her disappointing reply.

The dining hall was part of the workers' housing estate that had been built on Nahum Street. Several such projects, intended for urban laborers, had been put up in Tel Aviv, which at the beginning of the 1920s had become the hub of the country's Labor movement. Since people like my parents had no chance of owning homes, the Histadruth (trade unions) organized a collective building project. The idea of a people's architecture developed in Europe between the two world wars, when several countries decided to build housing for the working class. In pre-state Israel it was adopted for the benefit of the Hebrew worker, and in Tel Aviv these estates became known as "workers' lodgings." Their design was intelligent, simple, and uniform, and they've remained little oases of beauty and charm to this day. Every unit consisted of four Bauhaus-style buildings with columns, each three or four stories high, built as a rectangle surrounding a green lawn.

Ironically, there was a gulf between the original egalitarian vision and the final outcome. Preference was given to the upper echelons of the Histadruth, people in power or their sidekicks, those who had the appropriate party affiliation. In fact, the occupants ended up being a highly select circle of "worthies" rather than "workers," luminaries such as the chairman of the Histadruth Joseph Shprinzak, the future mayor of Tel Aviv Mordechai Namir, literati such as the poet Avraham Shlonsky, and stars of the theater. My parents, the archetypal workers, were not among the select few. The best they could get was the privilege of paying rent for half of one apartment with a shared kitchen and toilet, so as to benefit from the excellent institutions included in the grand design.

From stories I've been told, my father was at home only occasionally during those years because he had volunteered to join the Jewish brigade to fight alongside the British army against the Nazis. His family, which had stayed behind in Poland, had been exterminated and he, the sole survivor, felt guilty and needed to atone. At first he served in Israel—at least long enough for me to be born. He was then posted to Italy where he remained until the end of the war. On the eve of Israel's War of Independence, we moved to a slightly bigger apartment on Shimon Hatarsi Street, but we continued to use the facilities of the estate: the cooperative store, the library, and the dining hall. Dad had managed to acquire a holding in the store and we were still regarded as members.

At noon on that summer day, I took the three-tiered mess tin as usual. The neighborhood's streets formed a series of squares with public gardens in the middle, closed off to all but pedestrian traffic, part of an original master plan for Tel Aviv to be a "garden city." On that little patch of green, my friends and I set up an improvised soccer field. When I arrived, carrying the three-tiered mess tin, my classmates were already waiting with the ball. The assembled group included a future chairman of the Israel Football Association, Itche Menahem; Ilan Kutz, who in later years became a psychiatrist and well-known painter; and Mickey Hirschprung, now Mickey Eitan, the politician and orator. That day we were also joined by Gad Flom, also known as Schatz, who was to be murdered after a short reign as king of the Israeli underworld. They had already had lunch at home and were ready to play. None of them had been saddled with my kind of grown-up tasks. Ilan kicked the ball toward me, and I passed it on to Mickey. The goalkeeper on that day was Schatz. Mom had said that I mustn't dawdle. But surely, I thought as I put the mess tin to one side, a few minutes of football, the love of my life, wouldn't hurt. There would still be plenty of food left at the dining hall. Come on, let's play!

One goal and one offside later I began to have pangs of conscience. How long had it been? It was hard to tell since none of us had a watch. We'd have to wait till our Bar Mitzvahs. It had been a while, that I knew, and Mom was at home waiting for lunch. This was not the way for a responsible child to behave. But how could I possibly leave without at least one victory? In the end, duty prevailed. I stayed just to score a second goal, and then went on to the dining hall in high spirits. The only thing that bothered me a little was the sweat trickling into my eyes and soaking my shirt. I had reached the corner of Nordau and Dizengoff. I remember thinking that if I hurried I'd be able to play a bit more on my way home and win again ... and that was the last I remembered.

"Aaron, can you hear me? Look at my finger. Can you see it moving, Aaron?" Who's this person calling me Aaron, and what's this nonsense he's talking? Next to this man in a long white robe is my father, even paler than the gown, and Uri in uniform. "Uri, Uri, how I've missed you," I say. "Give me a hug." But instead of hugging me he repeats the same nonsense. "Roni, do you hear me?" What's the matter with them? Of course I can hear, I tell them. "What did you say, Ronile? Say it again." This is my father. Poor man. "When did this happen to him? He can't hear a thing." I despair of the grown-ups and turn to my big brother. "Uri, is Dad deaf?" Now he hugs me and laughs. "No, no, Dad can hear you, believe me. He can hear you, and how!" The faces all around me smile. All except my father who tries to smile but manages only to weep. "Don't cry, Daddy. Please don't cry ..."

Later on I was told that I'd been hit by a taxi as I was crossing the road, and they read me a story from the newspaper with the headline, "Four Road Accidents in Tel Aviv in One Day." The paper reported, "Roni Einav, aged nine-and-a-half, who lives on Shimon Hatarsi Street, Tel Aviv, was badly injured by a taxi while trying to cross Dizengoff Street. The child was taken to the city's Hadassah Hospital in critical condition. The taxi driver, David Shaltiel, was arrested and released on bail."

It is said that on the brink of death your whole life flashes before you. Nothing flashed before me. I know only what I was told: that during the entire episode despite having been hit by a car I never once let go of the three-tiered mess tin. I held on to it all the way to the emergency room and during all the checks and treatments. Only several hours later did someone succeed in prying it out of my hand. For three days I lay unconscious in Hadassah Hospital—the very same hospital in which I had been born. It was thought I would surely die; or, if by some miracle I survived, it was unclear what shape I'd be in. I listened spellbound, as if this was a story about somebody else's hair-raising adventure. I could recall nothing, not the moment of impact or even being knocked out. I remembered only the football game and the sweat dripping into my eyes. One thought stuck and never let go: my mother. I hadn't brought my mother her lunch.

On the day Dad brought me home my mother came into the room from the balcony. She took one look at me, and without a word took me straight to my bedroom. "Rest. Doctor said you have to." Undressing obediently I got into bed even though it was still very early. I expected her to say something about the lost lunch and my irresponsibility, but she was silent. She must be terribly angry with me, I thought. She pulled the sheet to cover me up and asked dispassionately if I was hungry. I said I wasn't and sheepishly asked where the mess tin was. If it too had been saved perhaps some time in the future I would be allowed to make amends for my crime. She stood up and gave me a withering look. "In the attic," she said fiercely, "and you not going there any more, not crossing any road until I say you are allowed." I hadn't yet learned that attack is the best form of defense and that this reprimand was the maximum level of tenderness that my mother permitted herself to display toward her child who had so nearly died. I was far too young to understand that she was angry with herself and not with me, that she was consumed by guilt for having sent me on an errand that almost killed me. What I did come to understand was that the near catastrophe had been a blessing in disguise. Henceforth, I was given an honorable discharge, absolved of lunchtime and/or other such duties.

Chapter 15

Discovering America

In 1984, Tel Aviv and California were separated by more than an ocean. The real gulf between them was psychological. It was not just a matter of crossing oceans and continents, but also of bridging a chasm of fear and insecurity. Indeed this gulf was too much for us. We had neither the means nor the know-how to negotiate it. So we sat in Tel Aviv and fantasized. What if America came to us? Dreams are cheap, but our dream was so intense that lo and behold it materialized. It was Galia who made it a reality.

Galia Streiker had served in the Israel air force (IAF) as a programmer, had worked briefly for IBM, and was familiar with the field. When she was not with her husband in the U.S. (he had a position at UCIC), she was hovering somewhere in midair on her way to or from Israel. When she came to see me in 1983 about the distribution in Israel of some U.S. software programs, I agreed to help. Because she understood programming and I wanted a foothold across the Atlantic, I proposed a partnership. In May 1984, I sold to Galia a 26 percent share of Einav Computer Systems (also representing a 13 percent stake in 4D) for $13,000. I remember the number. The amount was transferred to 4D's bank account. For us that was a great deal of money, given that 4D was then valued at only $100,000.

Galia became our chief of competitive intelligence, our woman in the U.S. We didn't have the money to send her there. She went on family business and while there didn't forget our shared dream of the conquest of America. The majority view was that this was a mission impossible. Who did we think we were, anyway? Objectively speaking, our program was more efficient than that of the giants. It was more flexible and required fewer resources from the host computer it was managing. Our human capital was superb. Separately and as a team we were more talented than our competitors. And above all, what became clear to us as we competed in the marketplace was that we were more determined and more industrious than the biggies and ready to take more risks than they were. Arrogance? Not necessarily. Unqualified belief in our own ability? Definitely. And that was what we needed to conquer America. That, a bit of luck, and of course, Galia.

As it turned out, Galia's neighbors in Irvine were the owners of a family software company called Tone. Based in Anaheim, Tone Software engaged in automation, like us. They had developed a program that wasn't exceptional but was certainly adequate for medium- and large-sized organizations. They were also in the business of marketing products that complemented their own, and had hundreds of customers in the U.S., Europe, and the rest of the world. When Galia met the owners of Tone Software, Don and Barbara Harrison, they were looking to distribute complementary, up-to-date programs, to increase their pulling power in the market and take better advantage of the infrastructure they had built.

One weekend during the summer of 1986, Galia invited them to a barbecue and began to sing the praises of 4D. They showed immediate interest and the conversation continued the following day. Galia canceled her other engagements and spent that weekend in talks about our company. On Monday evening—Tuesday morning Israel time—she phoned to say that Tone was seriously interested in distributing our software and that we should come over as soon as possible to discuss terms. The idea was certainly worth investigating.

Don Harrison was a programmer, a skilled professional who had developed the company's software products. Barbara's background was in real estate and she didn't have a clue about programming. Out of plain ignorance, she stuck her nose into every detail, damaging everything around her. Even though Galia had become fond of the couple, I didn't like them. In general, I don't like family businesses. They bring along all sorts of irrelevant problems. Not my cup of tea, that's for sure.

Perversely, we were exactly their cup of tea. They were taken with 4D and seriously interested in negotiating with us. I decided to give this opportunity that my partners so clearly believed in a chance. Benny flew over and he and Galia conducted the negotiations while Matia and I went off for a trip to Spain, keeping tabs on the talks from a distance. The talks proceeded at a snail's pace.

Meanwhile, our trip was wonderful. While in the Alhambra Royal Palace in Granada, just as Matia and I were having our photographs taken in the famous Sala de Dos Hermanas (Hall of the Two Sisters), we got the news that Amnon's wife had had twins. Two daughters, good reason for our male-dominated family to celebrate. When we returned from our trip we went straight from the airport to my brother's to enjoy the newborns. Only after that did I make time to ask the office what had transpired in California. Had they sent me something to sign? The pregnancy there should also by now have ended happily. Not yet, I was told.

When my brother's twins got to be two months old, Benny and Galia were still indulging the couple from Tone. I lost my patience. My initial doubts about our attempting to penetrate the U.S. market returned with a vengeance. Perhaps it would be best to back off and wait? In October 1986, Benny and

Galia at long last signed a contract with the Harrisons, and my hesitation went into cold storage. Tone started to market the product immediately and ten months after we had first sold Control M to Tadiran we sold it in the U.S. When I saw our U.S. published advertising package, I even allowed myself to be thrilled. But that didn't mean my worries were over.

From the moment that our operations in the U.S. became a reality it was Benny who took center stage and Galia moved to the sidelines. Or perhaps I should say, "was moved," depending on who is telling the story. After her vital contribution in locating the distributors and connecting with them, Galia was a bit out of it. Other than occasional meetings, she had little to do and was mainly a funnel transmitting Tone's complaints to us, not exactly the world's most exciting job. But she had done her part. Our woman across the Atlantic had traversed the ocean and got us a foothold in business America.

The first customer Tone found for Control M was a company called Burlington Air Express (BAX). As per the distribution agreement, we immediately received an advance of $25,000. For us, who were used to negotiating with Israelis who bargain interminably and then pay in installments, this was a windfall. BAX turned out to be a magnificent first customer. An international freight shipping company, it operated 500 terminals in close to one hundred countries and was shipping cargo, dealing with customs, excise, and logistics all over the world. It operated a huge fleet of trucks, planes, and ships and its annual sales were in billions of dollars. In November 1986, supervised by Benny Weinberger, Tone's personnel installed Control M in the BAX computer system. Our sales and marketing in the U.S. were on the road in more senses than one.

On the day Benny informed me that the program had been installed, the IDF was at long last withdrawing from Southern Lebanon (after a nearly twenty-year war). I rejoiced about our boys finally coming home, but my heart was across the ocean.

Would Control M bring us honor or shame? Will BAX's trucks reach their correct destinations? Or would the plane heading for Dallas land in Saudi Arabia? An American satellite had just been lost in space due to a program error. Why should we be immune? If we succeeded with the first client, then the game was won. If not, it was back to the drawing board.

At the end of the week the phone woke me with a jolt at five a.m. Israel time. Just then the skies opened up with the season's first rainfall and woke up the rest of the household. It was Galia calling. Without a pause for commas, full stops, or breath, she told me their managing director's response had been positive and encouraging. Everything had worked like clockwork. The program had functioned smoothly, BAX's trucks left from and arrived at the right terminals, ditto the planes and ships. Everything was hunky-dory.

I turned to Matia and with as much restraint as my Israeliness could muster told her, "Our first customer in the U.S. is satisfied. Very, very satisfied." A joyous cry escaped me. After that we couldn't go back to sleep. Matia went to check on the children. I got up and hurried to the office earlier than usual. I phoned Benny to hear the details. Sounding happy but utterly worn out, he confirmed what Galia had told me.

In our conversation we also managed to come back down to earth and remind ourselves not to tempt fate by celebrating prematurely. Perhaps this was just beginner's luck. We needed another customer to prove otherwise. The second customer Tone found was a university hospital in the town of Loma Linda—a huge, church-owned institution. The hospital had an intake of about thirty thousand patients a year and an annual income of some two billion dollars. To my pleasant surprise the hospital administrator told Benny and Galia that thanks to us life at the hospital had improved beyond measure. And just like that, we were on the map.

The man on the street may think that the exceptional businessman must be made of some special stuff. A transaction involving fantastic sums reinforces the notion that behind the deal are people who quite literally move mountains. Most of us are ordinary mortals with a dream. The business world is dynamic and chaotic, and chance plays a leading role. The first quality a businessperson needs is the belief in dreams, the second is the courage to improvise, and the third is the willingness to lose. He who waits for ideal conditions before taking the first step will never take that step. It may be that he won't lose but he also won't gain.

The issue of the balance between doubts and dreams is a recurring one in business life. The universal impulse for self-preservation leads to skepticism. I tended to take the road less traveled, as did Benny and Galia, and follow the dream.

The phase in which our American dream was realized, compared to the struggle of getting there, was anticlimactic. In the financial arrangement between us and Tone it was stipulated that the Harrisons would get 70 percent of the final payment from the customer, and that we would get the rest. On the face of it this did not seem fair. And indeed at our son Zach's Bar Mitzvah party you could see what colleagues in the know thought of this arrangement. Some of them, after wishing me Mazal Tov, told me in no uncertain terms that I was an idiot. I tried to explain that in the initial stages of our collaboration, Tone had had to invest in setting up a system dedicated to our products, and train technical support and marketing teams. Their 70 percent was intended to cover these costs and at the same time give them a profit. My good friends didn't realize that if the distributor doesn't make money, we don't either. Our excellent software was an unknown quantity in the U.S. There is no doubt that we paid Tone a great deal, but they gave us our money's worth. We encouraged them to sell more and they responded enthusiastically, opening branches in Washington, Chicago, Dallas, and in Toronto. We expanded to meet the demand, none of us aware of our company's full potential.

Tone Software was our representative in North America from October 1986 to just after the first Gulf War in March 1991. Despite their investment and our relative success, there was always tension between us. The relations between a distributor and the software owner are rarely harmonious, even if they start off well. The distributor always thinks he's the reason for the product's success and deserves more than he's getting. The owner tends to suspect that the distributor is cheating him or that his efforts are not equal to the superb product entrusted him. That's human nature. Among the three of us partners, it was Benny who was always angry with Tone, like a doting father who can never be satisfied with his daughter's intended. They annoyed him with demands for modifications, and they nagged incessantly about packaging and technical support having to be exactly as they ordered.

In many ways Tone was justified. They taught us how to operate in the U.S. market correctly. They educated us about packaging a product for the American customer, who was the polar opposite of the Israeli counterpart. If an Israeli company is selling a first-rate software program, and some document happens to be missing, it's no big deal. You explain to the customer, borrow a similar document from somewhere else. You don't delay a sale because of a piece of paper. Not so in America. If an American salesperson or customer isn't handed a perfect set of instructions for installing and activating a program, there is no deal. Tone was strict with us on this issue. Even though Benny will never give them the credit, it was nevertheless thanks to the Harrisons that we learned how to operate as an international company.

We presented them with our own demands. We insisted that our name be on the advertising material so that people would begin to recognize our brand in the U.S. They didn't always agree. Distributors sometimes prefer that only their name appear, to protect themselves from being circumvented or to boost their own market image. At the beginning, we insisted on having our name appear just because we were the new kids on the block. Sometimes we backed off, thinking that there was a fair chance we would encounter anti-Semitism down the line. Only around 1990, after Israel had already acquired an international reputation in high tech, did we consistently demand that our name appear, everywhere, and in bold type. By then Tone was only too happy to oblige.

When we discovered America, Europe discovered us. Tone Software's distributors in Europe, a company named Boole & Babbage Europe (B&BE), heard from the Harrisons about the Israeli software they were distributing successfully in the U.S. In March 1987 we signed an agreement with B&BE for Control M to be distributed on the Continent.

Because I devote a separate chapter to B&BE and its superb manager, Han Bruggeling, I will add only a few words here. Since we were short of cash we didn't thoroughly investigate our distributors. Research of this kind requires resources, time, alternatives, everything taught in MBA programs and lacking in real life at moments of decision-making. The distributors, from their point of view, became interested in us because on paper 4D's future looked rosy. But the agreements with them didn't immediately direct money into our empty bank account. From the time that a distribution agreement is signed, some months pass before the distributor is ready to sell. We signed with B&BE in March and by July they began selling our product in Europe. Even with all speed, we didn't see the money until December at the earliest. On the one hand success had certainly put smiles on our faces. We had a distributor in the U.S., a distributor in Europe, and six foreign customers about to purchase our product. On the other hand everything was at our expense. And what if at the end of the day the customers didn't buy? That too was not an insubstantial probability. Ironically, just as we were beginning to grow and the first buds of success were making their tentative appearance, we had to endure long periods of time without any money. It was a kind of built-in paradox.

Chapter 16

The Year of the Paradox

In December 1987, the first Intifada erupted. It shattered the hope for peace and the sense of calm and security we had begun to embrace, individually and as a country. I knew that I would soon be called up to do my reserves duty in the West Bank, escorting children from the Jewish settlements to school and to various extracurricular activities. How was I going to explain to our international clientele why, in a non-emergency situation, a senior manager should be summoned to serve his country at the expense of the country's economy?

I packed my uniform (and all my troubles, as the song goes, into my old kit bag) and calmed the fears of our anxious overseas representatives: "No worries, Israel isn't closing down. It's business as usual."

I was given a rifle and off I went to escort children from their hilltop settlements to basketball, music, ballet, karate, and crafts classes. During rest periods, I contacted distributors all over the world and repeated the party line: "No worries … business as usual." I was stressed, tired and, as a result, a bit disorganized.

One day after lunch I set off on an assignment and thirty kilometers or so down the road discovered that I had forgotten my rifle in the Beit El dining hall. My comrades dropped me by the roadside and I hitched a ride back. The settlers who picked me up, on hearing my story, contacted somebody in Beit El to get my rifle. The army tapped into the conversation and a menacing voice asked, "Who forgot his rifle?" The settlers smiled and kept silent.

At Beit El, I was handed the rifle while across the crackling airwaves the inquiry continued. Once I was shamefully exposed, there would be a complaint, and a court-martial would surely follow—just what I needed. But then the "guardian of holy fools" came to my rescue. It turned out that the weapon I had forgotten wasn't mine. It belonged to someone named Giora, who had taken my gun by mistake. Giora underwent intense cross-examination and I wasn't questioned at all. We both agreed it would be best for me to keep quiet, until finally the security people gave up and dropped the whole thing. Fortunately no criminal or terrorist act had been committed with the weapon. Had that not been the case, our conduct would have been far less lighthearted.

Throughout that period I barely slept a wink at night and dozed off during the day. I would watch my sleeping children, full of regret, and ask myself what on earth I was doing to them. In the second apartment we bought in Ramat Ilan the children each had a room of his own, Matia had a study, and the views from the building's ninth floor were of open spaces for as far as the eye could see. What would happen if the next day I had to decide between selling the apartment to pay peoples' salaries and closing down 4D altogether? The future of my children and that of the company were pitted against each other.

Galia, Benny, and I were forced to approach the Society of Foreign Trade Risk Insurance Ltd. and give them personal guarantees of more than one million dollars. The company had been set up to provide insurance to Israeli corporations exporting to so-called problematic countries and elsewhere. One department guaranteed bank loans to companies in need of credit. The three of us signed up with them, they became the bank's guarantor, and only then did the bank agree to lend us the money we needed in order to continue.

Today no sane entrepreneur would do such a thing, but at the time we had no alternative. Venture capital funds and their various offshoots that have sprouted in more recent years had yet to be thought up. We put ourselves, our own money, and our families in jeopardy by gambling on the success of the company. If the gamble didn't pay we stood to lose everything. The bank, in the event of such a failure, would get its money back from the insurance company. We, the guarantors, would be required to repay the full amount that we'd signed for. They might not shoot us, but they would undoubtedly dig deep into our pockets for many years to come and hound us to our graves. It had happened to others.

The year 1987, was one of the most difficult I had known. The investment in Europe began to bear fruit only toward the end of the year, even though the distribution agreement had been signed in March. In the intervening time Motti and I had been forced to sell our holdings in Liraz to raise cash for the payroll. I continued to guarantee my own holding in 4D as well as Einav Systems' stake in the company. Motti maintained his policy of non-intervention; my personal difficulties did not concern him in the slightest.

The internal paradox that became apparent during that period nearly drove me crazy. Precisely when we were on the brink of success we found ourselves facing a protracted hiatus of uncertainty in the affairs of Einav Systems and 4D. I hoped that most of what we'd started would mature but I couldn't be sure. There was always the possibility that despite our best effort we wouldn't succeed and wouldn't earn enough to cover what still needed to be done. Moreover we couldn't let out that we had a cash flow problem for fear that we would lose credibility and prospective clients. In business you're trapped by crises that fray your nerves and sap your energy. Motti saw in our hardships a justification of his skepticism vis-à-vis 4D and kept his distance.

In the meantime, 4D developed a second product called Control D, a program designed to manage printing operations, and we invited the Harrisons to Israel to check it out. Together with their chief engineer Garry Cooper, they turned up on our doorstep in July 1987, earlier than planned, putting us under a good deal of pressure. The product was still in its initial phase of development and not yet linked up. It wasn't at all clear whether the program would function. Ariel Gordon, who was in charge, told us that he was working full out on the completion of critical components and that we'd better play for time, since every hour counted.

I kept our guests in the office for as long as I could with refreshments and small talk, then instructed the taxi driver to take them to Scitex in Herzliya via the scenic route. Just moments before Garry Cooper opened the door, the product began to respond. By the time the guests sat at the computer, our new baby was performing nicely. "Is this live or just a presentation?" Benny whispered to Ariel, who was by that time exhausted. "It's live," Ariel replied. Benny chuckled. "So tomorrow you'll be installing this in Bank Leumi."

The enormous potential of Control D was apparent to anyone with eyes in their heads. But Garry and the Harrisons seemed less impressed than we had hoped. We went on being the perfect hosts, taking them on the mandatory trip to Jerusalem. Normally it was I who escorted important guests but this time I had forgone the pleasure.

At the end of the visit we gave them the distribution rights for Control D in the U.S. and they flew home. The plan was that we would then sign a distribution agreement for Control D in Europe with B&BE. In December 1987, as we were getting ready to close the two agreements, Tone announced that they themselves had developed a product similar to Control D, called Reports Distribution System (RDS), and that B&BE had just signed an agreement with them for its exclusive distribution in Europe. Control D and RDS were rival products, and when B&BE was ready to sign a distribution agreement with us, Tone drew their attention to the clause in their agreement that denied B&BE the right to distribute a competing product. In effect Tone was blocking Control D's distribution in Europe.

This was a bombshell. Our product was undeniably superior. We were sure that in the U.S. Tone would market it successfully, because 90 percent of the potential clients there would never consider the competing program. They were already using Control M, and Control D was its natural extension.

It quickly became apparent that Tone was indeed interested in distributing D in the U.S., while preventing B&BE from selling it in Europe. I had the feeling that when they saw during their visit to us that their product was inferior to ours, Tone had slyly maneuvered Han Bruggeling to sign with them. We were all upset. But feelings and business had to be kept apart. The impasse served no one's interests. We had to find a way out of this imbroglio and set an example by calming down. I persuaded Han to invite the sides to a neutral place and in January 1988 a meeting was arranged in Dusseldorf.

Tone was represented by the Harrisons and Garry Cooper. On our side Galia arrived from the U.S. and I from Israel. The quick-tempered Benny was not the man for delicate situations and stayed behind in Tel Aviv. I was sure that Han would act as a mediator but to my utter surprise all he did was to give us his office and disappear. Perhaps he felt responsible for having gotten us into this morass in the first place.

We stayed in one hotel, the Tone group in another. Every morning we met in Han's office and talked into the wee hours of the night. Our encounters were like those of two enemies forced to negotiate a truce. Barbara was, as usual, negative and aggressive. Don took his cue from her and Garry did his utmost not to get caught in the crossfire. Because time was of the essence we didn't leave the room even to get fresh air. We ordered takeout and ate in silence. On average I got three hours' sleep at night during the whole time we were there.

Eventually, I hit on a way out of the quagmire. I proposed a formula for the sale of Control D in Europe by B&BE and in North America by Tone that would include compensation to Tone on sales in the European market. To get things moving, I suggested that in return for their dropping their objection to B&BE distributing Control D in Europe, we would pay them a commission. Admittedly this was an expensive and unusual solution but it broke the deadlock. A few hours later I was on my way home. Between takeoff and landing I did nothing but sleep. I got home on Friday evening and the next day the whole family went to the Bar Mitzvah of my good friend Shmuel Lahman's son. Everyone said I looked full of vim and vigor. I had every reason to feel happy and proud.

In the course of 1988 we began to see results in Europe as well, and at the end of that year we decided that 4D could move to its own offices. We moved to offices in Kiryat Attidim, relieving Motti Glazer of our presence. Though Galia had promised the landlords that we would only use the space allotted to us, we found it difficult to keep that promise and gradually started a creeping annexation of the rest of the 300 square meters.

At the end of 1989 the sales in Europe of Control D via B&BE's agency far outstripped Tone's sales in the U.S. When Tone was made aware of the annual results they appointed two expert accountants to check our books in Tel Aviv. Everything was found to be in order, whereupon Tone paid the auditor's fee and transferred $100,000 to us "on account" as a gesture of good will. Benny was not content. He feared that our accepting the funds could be interpreted as a concession or a compromise.

While Iraqi Scud missiles were falling on a blacked-out Tel Aviv—the first Gulf War had begun—and the population of Israel was sitting anxiously in sealed rooms, our business carried on almost as usual, including the issuing of daily demands to Tone regarding the funds they owed, which they dodged with weird and wonderful excuses.

A month later the Gulf War was over and Israel, thanks to the restraint shown by Prime Minister Shamir, emerged from the conflict with only minor bruises. The battle against Tone, on the other hand, now moved into high gear. We were sick and tired of their excuses and decided to take the bull by the horns and sever our relations with them. Benny, Galia, and I were unanimous in that decision. The distribution agreement had nominated London as the venue for the settlement of disputes. In March 1991 we lodged a petition in London's High Court to terminate our agreement with Tone. We had to serve it personally to the defendants. Under California law, until notice of proceedings is handed to the respondent with the statement "You have been served" (just like they do in the movies), the petition lacks legal standing.

As soon as the Harrisons found out about the petition, they began to play a frustrating game of hide-and-seek to avoid having it served. We consulted friends in the U.S. and were told that there were bikers who chased slippery customers until they pinned them down and served them with the papers. We hired one of these, a Schwarzenegger look-alike in a black leather jacket and dark glasses who, to my surprise and delight, had fine manners and a good mastery of legal jargon. This guy on his Harley Davidson lay in wait for the evasive couple outside their house. The moment they got into their car he rode up alongside them and attached the petition to their vehicle while uttering the sacred words. They had indeed been served. And that was that. Message delivered.

End of story? Yes and no. Though we had severed relations with Tone and had taken the legal steps required, the relations had not been actually cut. Tone played for time and claimed that we had no right to operate in their country because the marketing rights for 4D in the U.S. were theirs. We had to carry on with our business in the shadow of a huge crisis. We couldn't simply wait for the judicial process to play itself out because from the moment the papers had been served, we had to prove that business was indeed "as usual," sell the software, and give technical support to existing customers. The mere hint of a vacuum could scare them away. Our concern was that Tone's deliberate delaying tactics would lead to just such a result. So instead of sitting around waiting for the court's decision, we set up a parallel organization of our own while the crisis was still in full swing.

A major problem was that we didn't have a reservoir of skilled personnel at our disposal because they still worked for Tone. We nevertheless went ahead and opened an office in California. Benny Weinberger moved there quickly, ahead of his family, to join Galia and her son, who was now working for us. Reinforcements in the form of a team of three came from Israel, among them Eyal Diskin, who at the time was in the middle of a trip to the U.S. and responded to our urgent call. Three was the absolute minimum we needed and the maximum that we were able to allocate at that time. We simply didn't have ten spare experts in Tel Aviv who we could ship off to the U.S. We desperately wanted Tone's trained staff. What if instead of going for a solution based on common sense the Harrisons became more and more vindictive? In spite of having established our own organization, and the impression we'd created that the agreement with Tone had been dissolved notwithstanding, we continued to look for ways to persuade the couple to release at least some of our people.

An odd detail from those transition days is the fact that even though 4D had customers across the U.S. it had no financial standing whatsoever. With no credit history, even a small transaction—renting an office, ordering a telephone—was beyond our reach. What we had to do we did with Galia's personal credit card.

Tone didn't budge and we remained deadlocked. By April 1991, I had concluded that we had to try to reach a settlement, regardless of our feelings. We suggested conducting negotiations in Los Angeles, a mere two-hour journey for both parties, instead of dragging us all to a London court. The meeting took place in the offices of Tone's lawyer, Barry Lawrence. Mickey Spigelman, our lawyer, joined Galia and Benny as our representatives while I stayed in Israel. When they returned, they told me that it had been a most unpleasant encounter conducted in an atmosphere of unbearable tension. Benny was looking for blood while Barbara Harrison, by now nothing but skin and bones, threatened to commit suicide. "Please yourself," was Spigelman's response as he opened the window. It was the stuff of soap opera, to be sure.

Apparently Tone was hard up for cash, but we were at the point of no return. The Harrisons had to make a choice: either destroy all they had built up in the U.S., bringing the temple down around our ears, or reach a compromise with us. We certainly had no wish to see their client base and support mechanism destroyed. Quite the contrary. It was obvious that they were at the end of their rope, yearning for a lifeline. So we proposed a face-saving plan. We would pay them a million dollars in cash—scratching the very bottom of our tiny barrel—and 50 percent of the profits derived from the maintenance work among existing customers for three more years. In exchange we would be given the choice of the employees we wanted, plus Tone's list of clients, technical support, accounts, pending sales, and their registration at the Pentagon. Within four days we had closed the deal and agreed to put our final signatures to it two weeks later.

Immediately after the agreement had been signed we plucked fifteen of their most able employees, who joined our trio from Israel. We opened a business account at Bank Leumi in Los Angeles, where we deposited a symbolic sum. Much relieved, we made a public announcement that 4D was now representing itself in North America. In the new setup Benny was CEO in the U.S., Galia his deputy and president of the U.S. company, and her son the administrative general manager. In Israel, I took Benny's place in the day-to-day management of 4D, which had been the case since March, and I continued in my role as chairman of the board. From then on Benny's office was in California and mine in Kiryat Attidim.

When we found the time to have our books audited we realized that over the years Tone had received more dollars from us than we had from them. But we had no regrets. They had played their part, launched our product in the American market and introduced us to B&BE. The price of the split—our freedom—had also been high but we believed that the independence we had won would prove to be worth every cent.

Our outgoings at the dawn of independence were between one hundred and two hundred thousand per month. This was the sum required to operate 4D in the U.S. during the transition period. All our dollar reserves had been drawn on for this purpose and it wasn't clear who, if anybody, would step into the breach to help us finance our independent operation there. The second unknown was how long it would take us to get organized, start selling, move into the black, and then into profit. The third and most significant unknown was whether we would achieve any of these objectives. Even though we'd sketched out the blueprint for a U.S. operation at the beginning of 1991, the real plan was developed with no financial backing. It is very possible that advance planning and a more conservative approach would have averted such a risky move. In retrospect we were right to do what we did. We dived into deep waters with the hope that we could keep afloat until we found our mooring. I knew that the first thing I had to do was to look for such a mooring in Israel—money, some kind of interim finance.

All the company decisions in the Tone affair were made by Benny, Galia, and me unanimously. We were a well-integrated team that worked together harmoniously. I said it then and I still say it today: it was this trio's combination of talents that was responsible for the success of 4D. Benny's professionalism and ambition, Galia's shrewdness and connections, and my managerial skills combined to produce the magic formula. We dreamed of conquering America, and we damn well did.

Chapter 17

Throes of Independence

We celebrated the separation from Tone with merriment tempered by apprehension: only the future would tell whether we had acted wisely. In the meantime we had to cough up one million dollars. Not only that, we also had to find funding for 4D's ongoing operations in the United States. Having courageously launched an American division, our very limited monetary reserves could keep it afloat for a few months at best. Our shaky financial situation was management's most closely guarded secret.

Now the truth can be revealed: we lived from hand to mouth. Our coffers were empty and we had nothing to fall back on. In the first half of 1991 we had a negative cash flow. Even when, by the sweat of our brow, we managed to put together one hundred thousand U.S. dollars, Israel's cumbersome foreign exchange regulations didn't allow us to send it to 4D in America without a mountain of bureaucracy, which took forever. We felt choked. Every move we attempted was complicated. Even the branch of Bank Hapoalim, where we had banked over the years, kept us on a tight leash. Earlier, in light of our 1990 figures, they had promised us credit of up to a million dollars. Our plans to go it alone in the U.S. were based on that. Yet when we approached them in April 1991, following our dispute with Tone and the subsequent temporary halt in sales, the bank was only prepared to offer us $250,000. Eighteen months later 4D's worth would be $120 million, but during spring and summer of 1991 we were on the brink of collapse. In the U.S., Benny and Galia pushed ahead at full steam, while in Israel I went from pillar to post in search of alternate funding. Surely I could find someone out there who could be persuaded to believe in us.

I turned to my old friend Lulu, who showed interest and said that he would look seriously into the matter. He contacted our mutual friend Shmuel Lahaman, who told him that IBM had a competing product of high quality being developed by a large team in Stockholm. Lulu backed off. Though fond of me, he found it hard to believe that our small company could successfully compete with IBM. His argument was logical but wrong. IBM's development teams were isolated from each other, and their products were incompatible. We, on the other hand, had developed a system known as IOA, which turned all our software into a wholly harmonized system. This gave us a marketing edge and enabled us to challenge the big corporations.

After Lulu's change of heart, the name Alex Eldor from Bank Leumi popped into my mind. I had first gotten to know him in 1988 when we installed Control D at the bank. At the time the workers' committee had opposed him because the program was bound to cut jobs, shorten working hours, and reduce management levels. The committee fought tooth and nail against Control D and brought the workers out on strike. Alex mounted a smart campaign in its favor and won. Like me he was an industrial engineer, a bit younger, and had been the manager of the bank's computer center. He took a training course in banking and moved up the ranks until he was appointed to manage a group of about thirty branches. By 1991 he held a senior position.

"Just look at how they're screwing me at Bank Hapoalim," I cried on his shoulder. Alex sympathized and did everything he could to help. He approached the relevant committees of the bank, begged and bullied but was turned down everywhere. They insisted on guarantees that were not within my power to give. A computer program is an ethereal commodity; a software house possesses no material assets. I couldn't mortgage a building, because I didn't own one. I couldn't raise money against the machinery because that too didn't exist. Intelligence, our skills, our collective hope—human capital—could not be translated into bankable guarantees.

As I was doing my rounds, Galia phoned me from the U.S. to tell me she couldn't wait any longer. The next day salaries had to be paid and she had no money. Our new U.S. venture, established overnight, included a number of branches that had begun marketing and servicing our products. As yet, there was no significant income stream. With products such as ours the sales cycle can extend over many months, sometimes even a year. The company was not sufficiently credit- worthy to get a loan at an American bank. I decided not to tell Galia about my own via dolorosa from hard-nosed investors to unyielding bankers. Why depress her? She needed to keep forging ahead in the U.S. I told her I was dealing with it. "Continue working. It will be OK. The paychecks will be there. I promise."

Once again I traveled from Attidim to Bank Leumi in Herzliya, wearing my best poker face to hide my true feelings. I told Alex I came to him because there's no one left for me to go to.

"How much do you need?" he asked. "I'm going to sort this out for you."

"I need $100,000 now."

"What security can you give me?"

"We're back to that?" I was livid.

"I need something for the bank, not for myself. Just give me something."

Convinced that he had really crossed over to my side, and was prepared to put himself at risk for my sake, I offered him a personal check for NIS (New Israeli Shekel) 100,000, payable in six weeks. "If you want it—please take it." And he agreed. He agreed! I gave him the check and he gave me the money. That is how $100,000 found its way to the U.S. Galia paid the salaries and the company continued to operate.

With all the personal guarantees we had given, Benny, Galia, and I were teetering on the edge of an abyss. Benny provided 50 percent of the guarantees, Galia 20 percent, and I was responsible for 30 percent. In total our personal pledges amounted to nearly two million dollars. Terrifying. Not all the guarantees were to the banks. Some were given to the company that insured against foreign trade risks. We guaranteed them and they in turn gave promises to the bank, so the risk was divided between them and us. Still, I had small children, and I could be jeopardizing their future. Another real danger was that our life's work—our innovations, our wonderful plans to sell software to American organizations, banks, and big corporations—would all go up in smoke the moment a rumor surfaced that we were bankrupt.

In effect we were trapped. Our heads told us not to take the risks, but our hearts said to have faith. To the world I continued to give the impression that I was a brilliant businessman, making proposals, and promoting sales. Inside, I felt like a juggler throwing balls into the air, catching a few, dropping many.

After receiving the $100,000 from Alex at Bank Leumi, my banking connections were exhausted. Though we had found a temporary solution to the payroll problem we were still hanging by a thread. I approached additional private investors, and tested the gray market. Everybody's response was negative. The company was rickety, sales weren't going up. No one wanted to invest in us. In March 1991, I decided to give priority to the Israeli branch of 4D and to manage it on a full-time basis. While we were in the throes of setting up 4D in the U.S. and during the prolonged birth pangs of that process, it dawned on me that I must work day and night exclusively for 4D. To achieve that, I had to take my leave of Einav Systems.

In June 1991 I convened an emergency meeting of the board of directors of Einav Systems, where there had also been serious liquidity problems. We agreed on reducing expenses and increasing efficiency and waited for an improvement, but none came. The already lousy relationship between me and Motti got even worse. In a second emergency meeting in July, I informed the board in unambiguous terms that I was unable to work with him any longer. I suggested that we part and that Einav Systems' operations be frozen. Motti objected to that idea. He wanted us to part for good and for the company to be his and his alone. I thought, if only not to see you ever again, and agreed. Despite the fact that it was my company, I had lost all interest in continuing with our deeply flawed romance. Motti drafted a handwritten document that gave us an option to implement the separation within two months. We each signed the proposal, as did Danny Abarbanel, Motti's friend who had tried to bridge differences between us in the past and was now again acting as an intermediary.

Less than a week later Motti decided to exercise the option. What he checked on, if anything at all, I don't know. We could have frozen Einav Systems in March 1991, and kept the holdings each one of us had in the subsidiaries as they were at the time. But when we began negotiating the dissolution of the partnership, it transpired that if I were to withdraw I would owe him money, a sum of NIS 500,000. And he coveted the check. He demanded—and got without a fight—my entire holding in the subsidiaries, apart from Einav Computer Systems-4D, in spite of the fact that this was not included in the option that we had agreed on. I had reached the end of the road. I didn't care how much I was losing as long as I was rid of him for good.

In a meeting on August 1991 in the offices of Mickey Spigelman, who had prepared the separation agreement, the question arose as to the value of Einav Computer Systems' shares in 4D software. Spigelman said that if the move to set up an independent company in the U.S. should fail, the value of the shares would probably be zero. If on the other hand it succeeded, the company was likely to be worth millions. That is what he had already told Motti in a previous meeting when Motti had asked if he was being deceived about 4D. Motti's response had been, "4D is of no interest to me. Roni is welcome to it." He didn't want to have any tax liability if and when the company was floated on the stock exchange. I undertook to pay any taxes that might be levied and he was reassured.

We signed the agreement to dissolve the partnership and turned the mediator into an arbitrator of future disagreements, should they arise in the course of implementing the separation agreement. Spigelman began to prepare the detailed documentation and I heaved a sigh of relief.

That evening I said to Matia. "I am not at all sure that I'm doing the right thing. On the one hand I am paying Motti a great deal of money, the maximum that I can afford. On the other hand I am putting all my eggs in one basket. Even Galia is hesitant about being part of it. I have no doubt that with Motti gone I will live longer. From a business point of view, who knows if this is the right move or not." Matia heard me out, expressed no opinion one way or another, and simply supported me. "You've made a decision—and that's that. I'm with you." It was good to get the strong support of someone who loves me and believes in me. It has also to be said that, to her credit, she had identified Motti Glazer as an oddball years earlier.

All these things—independence in the U.S., our financial difficulties, and the dissolution of the partnership with Motti—occurred simultaneously. And as if I hadn't already had my hands full running between banks to inject money into Tone and 4D, I now had to pay Motti five hundred thousand shekels from my own pocket. I managed to mobilize the money by mortgaging a second apartment I owned, took another loan, and paid.

There wasn't a single moment of relief. In the U.S. the dispute with Tone dragged on while in Israel the arguments with Motti Glazer continued. Very shortly after we had signed the agreement to dissolve the partnership, he popped up again and once more demanded arbitration: "I'm owed more. You didn't tell me everything about the position of Einav Systems." He had "discovered" a liability amounting to some tens of thousands of shekels. I tried very hard to keep my cool but my blood pressure climbed to dangerously high levels. In November 1991, after another nerve-racking round of arbitration, the arbitrator issued a partial finding. In December 1991, Motti received from me an additional sum amounting to tens of thousands of shekels and all my shares in Einav Systems and its subsidiaries. In exchange he transferred to me his holding in Einav Computer Systems-4D. Each gave to the other what had been fixed in the agreement. In order to be able to pay him the additional sum I took a second loan from the bank, and Matia took a deep breath and signed a mortgage on our apartment as a guarantee.

On April 21, 1992, the arbitrator Danny Abarbanel issued his final report, with the following comment: "The purpose of this arbitration is not to bring the sides closer or reconcile them but rather to put an end to what have been irreconcilable differences." In essence "Roni and Motti will sign all the required documents as presented to them by the attorney Mickey Spigelman so as to finish the process of dissolving their partnership. This must be done within thirty days of the issuance of these arbitration findings."

A set of documents was sent to Motti for his signature. This time the whole affair had really come to an end. It wasn't the beginning of the end, nor the end of the beginning. At long last it was all over. A final finding of an arbitrator is the same as the final verdict of a judge. What a relief. I was now mentally and emotionally free to join Matia in accompanying our son Zach to his army recruitment center. I was happy that he had been mobilized to serve in an intelligence unit, and wished him as interesting and productive a service as mine had been.

Such was the turbulent year 1991. In March I began working time-and-a-half for 4D. In April came the severance from Tone and the setting up of 4D in the U.S. My formal withdrawal from Einav Systems came in June. The separation from Motti dragged on from June till August. In October our independent business in the U.S. began to stabilize. And internationally, Koichi San, our Japanese distributor, continued to do well with his sales, as did our Australian and European distributors. 4D had representation in thirty countries, including Brazil, Argentina, Venezuela, and Chile. We had also reached South Korea, South Africa and Singapore. There was a light at the end of the tunnel, yet the financial difficulties continued to overshadow the hopes we had of surmounting them. The year was not yet done with either its curses or its blessings.

Chapter 18

A European Friend

Don't mix business with pleasure. Everyone knows that. Yet every rule has its exception, and the European chapter in the history of 4D was indeed exceptional. Here is the story of a business that was also a pleasure, a tale of friendship.

Around October 1986, 4D began distributing its products in the United States via Tone Software. Our financial position bordered on the catastrophic. We were hard-pressed to find additional channels of distribution, knowing that it would be a while before we'd see revenues from U.S. sales. And it was dangerous to put all our eggs in one basket. We were able to find a distributor in Brazil and urgently searched for suitable contacts in Europe. A Jewish-owned French group was interested in distributing Control M and paying us 45 percent of the proceeds—more than we were getting in the United States. Even Benny was impressed.

The French saw it as a done deal and called a press conference to announce the agreement. The contract had not yet been signed but negotiations were almost complete, and distribution in Europe was to begin in January 1987. Around that time, a Belgian company, Dolman, discovered us. Dolman was the owner of a big chain of supermarkets. Lulu, who had passed up the opportunity to invest in 4D, had found them. When I mentioned to him that we were looking for European distributors, he immediately put his best contacts at our disposal.

In March 1987 our family began to prepare a surprise party to celebrate Matia's fortieth birthday. Since her appointment to a senior position as traffic supervisor in the Tel Aviv metropolis, her workload had increased, and we decided to organize a party without her involvement. Regrettably, I wasn't able to contribute much because I had to go to Brazil with Benny. The baton was passed to the children and I scheduled my flights to ensure that I was back in time for the happy event.

The trip to Brazil was important. There we helped 4D's first distributor, Thornix Informatica, to get set up, hire workers, participate in exhibitions, and prepare presentations. Moments before we left the hotel in Rio for the airport, our office in Israel called to tell me that the Belgian company had requested I stop there on the way home. It was important, they said, that we conclude the agreement.

The contact with the Belgians had been handled by me but this sudden request didn't fit with my already tight schedule. Making progress in Europe was a matter of urgency, though, so I decided to squeeze in a short meeting in Brussels.

I didn't tell the Belgians that for personal reasons I had very little time to spare. In negotiations it's not a good idea to admit that you're in a hurry, so I played it cool. Fortunately the draft contract was signed, sealed, and delivered in the course of that one brief meeting. I politely turned down my hosts' offer of dinner, making do with a celebratory toast in their office.

I was pleased to hear that in Europe the sales cycle was a bit shorter than in the U.S., meaning we might see money in the bank in this lifetime. It made me even happier to know that I could catch a flight home that night. I sent a fax to the office in Tel Aviv, reporting the signing of the contract and returned to the hotel to pack my bags. Even before I had opened the door I heard the phone ringing. It was Tel Aviv on the line. Another European distributor, by the name of The European Software Company (TESC), which was Tone's distributor, had heard about us. Could I hop over to Amsterdam for a quick visit? Usually I would have jumped at the opportunity, but this time I had to stand firm and say no. If they were serious, they would wait until I could speak to them from the office on my return.

I arrived home just in time to participate in the final arrangements for the party. We happily celebrated the occasion in the penthouse of my best friend, Danny Rosenstrum. The birthday party in the bosom of my family and the love shown by our close friends was for me a precious time-out from the rat race, a reminder of what life's priorities ought to be.

TESC-B&BE, as they were renamed after being bought by a California software company, Boole & Babbage USA, was serious, it turned out. The only snag in the business proposition was that the commission, 37.5 percent, was lower than the offer made by the French, but the caller had made a good impression. We weighed the pros and cons and concluded that on her way back to New York, Galia would stop over in Amsterdam and give TESC-B&BE a copy of Control M to check out. That wouldn't cost any money and, depending on their reaction, we'd decide how to proceed.

What had started as a trickle was now a stream of distributors' interest, with an increasingly powerful current. In sending Galia off with a copy of Control M we were going with the flow, casting our bread upon the waters. Galia landed in Amsterdam, met up with Jan Ofschoor, one of B&BE's managers, and gave him the tape of Control M. These were the pre-disk-on-key days of heavy magnetic tapes, and Galia complained that they were curbing her style.

In the few weeks required by B&BE to check the program we tried to keep the Belgians and French on hold. At the end of March B&BE called. They had finished their tests of Control M and sounded enthusiastic. It had reached them at exactly the right moment because they had recently lost the distribution rights to another software program, and Control M was the perfect product for their marketing resources in Europe. It seemed that this was their chance as well as ours. We discussed basic terms, following which they sent a letter summarizing the conversation and raising twenty issues for further discussion. To ten we consented immediately, five others took a little longer, and on the balance of five we were unable to agree.

We began to conduct daily negotiations by phone and fax with B&BE via Mickey Spigelman's office—we didn't have a fax machine of our own. When we had reached agreement on basic principles we arranged for a conference call. On their side was a man who introduced himself as Han Bruggeling. Ian White, Han's right-hand man, was also on the line. They told us that Jan Ofschoor, the manager to whom Galia had given Control M, thought that it fit in with the capabilities of the company, and that its sales potential in Europe was very big. They sounded serious, well informed, and interested. It was decided that Han would come to Israel at the earliest possible opportunity to continue the dialogue.

Benny and I went to meet Han at the airport. Introducing himself to us was a tall, gray-haired, handsome gentleman accompanied by an astonishingly beautiful dark-skinned woman named Joan. He had brought his assistant along to celebrate her thirty-fourth birthday. We dropped Joan at the Hilton, and went straight to the office. As we sat down in my room he announced: "I am Europe. You sell to me, and in effect you are selling to sixteen countries." It took us a while to digest the implications.

TESC-B&BE made a commitment to sell twelve franchises of Control M annually—that was the quota they undertook in the contract—and pay us at least $196,000. For us that was a phenomenal sum. All of this Han Bruggeling explained to us on the first day of his visit, in my overcrowded office on Derech Hashalom Street No. 7. He spoke quietly, politely, and with a slight Dutch accent.

Of course we grabbed the deal. We didn't have the money to find out more about who and what they were, but we didn't care. We were captivated by the man. Communications with him were excellent, and he and I "clicked" from the get-go. One of our secretaries joked, "Watch out, Roni, you sound like a man in love ..." I said to Benny. "We've stumbled on a treasure. I can feel it. Let's celebrate. The Dutch are Christians, let's take Han to Jerusalem." We felt optimistic and we wanted to gladden the heart of our guests as well.

In the evening, we organized a birthday party for Joan at a Brazilian restaurant in Jaffa's harbor. We were joined by Matia and by Benny Weinberger and his wife. Our relaxed style, openness, and lighthearted manner always seem surprising to Europeans. He and Joan enjoyed themselves so much it was a pleasure for us to watch them. Toward the end of the evening Han changed places so he could sit next to me, asking my permission to order a wine of his choice. The wine he selected was indeed subtle—I didn't even know wines like that existed. He saw me reading the label and said, "If you're interested in wine come and visit me in Dusseldorf." I could see that it was the beginning of a special friendship.

On the following day, a dispute arose over one of the clauses in the agreement and we made a huge effort to overcome the obstacle. As we were discussing the problem, I received a call from my eldest son, Liran: he had broken his leg in a football game. I made my excuses, explaining that I had to rush off to take the boy to the emergency room. Han said. "Go to your son and don't worry, we'll close the deal." I could tell he meant it, that he really intended to make it happen.

I took Liran to Sheba Hospital, where they put his right leg in a cast, and then I drove him home. My next task was to phone the office to find out what had transpired. Han had indeed tied up all the loose ends, and we had a signed agreement. Before leaving Israel he called to inquire after Liran's health. I knew

I had been right about him. Now the question arose as to what to do about the other European distributors with whom we had also reached agreement.

The contract we'd signed with Belgium was already in effect, the one with France not yet. In the course of our telephone negotiations with B&BE we told them about the other agreements. They said that if France wasn't included in their distribution agreement there was no deal. France, England, and Germany each accounted for about 25 percent of the whole market, Spain was about 8 percent, Italy 6 percent, Sweden about 2 percent, and Belgium 2 percent. It was clear that B&BE couldn't afford to forego France.

We notified the French that things had changed, and we would not be able to sign. With the Belgians it was more difficult because we had already signed a distribution agreement with them. They were angry and even threatened to take legal action but in the end did not, so we decided to accommodate them by offering a compromise: they would distribute Control M in Belgium but not in Luxemburg. B&BE agreed to this and the agreement was signed. Now all we could do was cross our fingers.

We didn't expose our financial difficulties to Han. It's poor practice to appear weak or needy while working to forge a new business relationship. But behind the scenes these difficulties continued to bear down on us throughout 1987. Particularly worrying was the deficit in Einav Systems that forced us to sell Liraz and deepened the split between Motti and me.

Work was an essential part of me but the family always came first. Despite my gloomy mood Matia, Liran, Zach, and I went to Europe in July 1987, for a summer holiday as planned. I also planned to visit the offices of B&BE. Matia had already explained to me that their funny-sounding name honored two highly distinguished personalities: George Boole, the inventor of Boolean algebra, and Charles Babbage, the inventor of the computer.

In Dusseldorf we were welcomed warmly, all my queries were answered, and we were treated like VIPs. The visit marked my initiation into the good life, the beginning of a voyage during which my new Dutch friend acted as my guide, teaching me what I didn't know about food, wine, and various other pleasures I had never heard of and learned to enjoy under his expert tutelage. From Dusseldorf we went to Paris and there too I visited the B&BE offices. I began to understand the structure of their system and their methods. Everything I saw led me to the conclusion that this time we hadn't erred. Despite the hurried courtship the bride appeared to be a real find.

In October 1987 B&BE invited us to their international kickoff in Alexandria. We still had no revenues and we simply weren't in the mood to socialize. Instead, we sent our senior staff members, Avi Cohen and Ariel Gordon, to give an initial presentation of our company's products to B&B's sales personnel. Galia also stopped over there on her way from the U.S. to Israel. Benny and I were too troubled to go. When our new friends heard that we weren't coming they stopped off on their way to Egypt to visit us in Israel. We then made the acquaintance of Edward Williamson, the third partner, a cultured and amusing man, who lifted our spirits somewhat by telling us that he had high expectations for the forth quarter sales.

In January or February 1988 we at long last received the first payment and only then did we emerge from our long dark tunnel. After that our sales were steady. B&BE sold our products at a dizzying pace, substantially more than Tone, and they paid on time.

This was a creative and exciting time for 4D. On average, 60 percent of our bids were accepted, an achievement we had good reason to be proud of. There were hurdles in our relations with B&BE, differences that needed to be sorted out, of course, but thanks to the good relationship we had with Han, most of these issues were resolved easily. There were a few serious hitches, such as their contract with Tone that blocked Control D's distribution in Europe. I suspect that this was carelessness on the part of Han, but I believed it to be a mistake rather than deceit. Nonetheless, it was damaging to us. Then there was the occasion in 1989 when we decided to pay them a bonus for sales above the quota as an added incentive. Except that the actual sales bordered on the agreed minimum. According to Han's interpretation of the figures they had exceeded that target and were owed 250,000 Dutch florins. According to Benny no such sum was due to them. Somehow I managed to make my own calculation and reach a compromise.

In addition to our solid business relationship, Han and I became good friends. I began to invite him to private functions and he invited me to his astounding house in Majorca, where I got to know his good taste. He kept his promise and taught me—with characteristic grace—which wine went with which course, what to chill and what not to chill, as well as some of life's other pleasures. Curious about the origin of his special approach to life, his consistent avoidance of pettiness, his ability always to find an elegant solution, I decided to ask him about it. His answer surprised me. "When you're on the verge of death at the age of twenty, you gain a proper perspective on what is important and what is not."

In 1965, Han was hospitalized with TB while serving in the Dutch army. The doctors didn't expect him to recover, but to everyone's surprise he did. Once restored to health his character and outlook on life changed. "Before the illness, time for me was of no consequence," he told me. "After it, I understood that time is the most precious commodity we possess. I knew that I had to go for only those things that suited me, rely only on my inner voice and to hell with what is and is not acceptable." He then decided to be his own boss, never a hired hand. His originality, as well as his fine human relations and command of several languages, made B&BE the success that it was.

Once when I phoned Dusseldorf, I was told that he was ill. A week passed and he didn't get back to me. I began to worry, but restrained my urge to make inquiries. In Europe such intrusions into the private lives of others are regarded as ill-mannered. After another week had passed I decided to make the call. Ian took it. Guardedly, I inquired after his boss's health and asked when he was expected back. Ian told me it would not be soon. A blood clot had been discovered in Han's brain and that he was recovering from an operation. His condition was good, Ian reassured me, there had been no consequential damage, but it would be a few months before he was back to normal. Though Han hadn't told people around him about his illness, he had permitted Ian to fill me in.

At the peak of our love affair with B&BE they accounted for 60 to 70 percent of our revenues. At the beginning of 1988 the proportion was even greater. From their perspective, when success smiled upon us, we represented about 35 percent of their sales in Europe. The software produced in the U.S. by B&BE's parent company Boole & Babbage accounted for about 30 percent of the distributor's European sales, sometimes even less, something that often irritated B&B's financial officers and its managing director, Paul Newton. Tone, on the other hand, accounted for a mere 7 percent or so of B&BE's European business. Their products were in no way outstanding, certainly not when compared to ours. And, surprise, surprise: Han, Ian, and Edward were also no great fans of Barbara and Don Harrison.

With the active support of my friend Han, our success in Europe was meteoric. We established friendly relations with the entire group of B&BE companies that made a lot of money from us, receiving some 60 percent of the turnover in sales. The American distributors got between 70 percent and 75 percent. In Europe we got 40 percent, in America 30 percent and sometimes even less. I used to explain to those who thought I was a fool to allow the sales agents to get twice as much as me, the manufacturer of the software, that my concern was not how much the agents were making but ensuring that we made enough. The marketing drive was the key to success. That impetus could only be maintained if the distributors thought the effort was worthwhile. Profit fires human motivation, that's a fact.

In addition to being represented in Europe and in the U.S., we were, thanks to B&BE, soon also represented in forty-five other countries. They introduced us to their people in Australia, New Zealand, and Japan. That is also how we landed in Argentina and Mexico. We reached South Africa, Singapore, Hong Kong, and South Korea under our own steam, by being creative and making use of various promotional techniques. The main thing is that we had established a global presence.

As for Han Bruggeling, his record in Europe so impressed B&BE's bosses in California that they invited him to manage the parent company. He arrived in the U.S. in 1988 and worked there until 1991. Edward Williamson then took over the management of the European operation.

Han's transfer to the U.S. did not end his relationship with us. In his new role he was responsible for overseeing the activities of their subsidiary companies that included B&BE. At that time, B&B began to propose that we merge. David Dury, an accountant working for B&B, was sent to put out feelers as to whether there was a chance for a takeover. I suggested we first meet at Mickey Spigelman's office, see what he had up his sleeve, and then decide whether he should come to our office. After an hour with Spigelman it was clear to me that there was nothing of substance for us to talk about.

Ariel Gordon was worried that behind the scenes Han was supporting David Dury's initiative. Ariel's reasoning was that Han had correctly understood the difficulties that had arisen between us and Tone and that as B&B's managing director, he was himself interested in taking over 4D. Whatever the case, once Han saw that our launch as an independent company in the U.S. had succeeded, he set himself firmly on our side.

At the end of 1991, a critical moment for 4D, Han's presence in the U.S. really saved us. The contract we'd signed with B&BE for the period 1987-1991 was about to expire. We thought that Benny and Galia would capitalize on their presence in California and renew the contract without difficulty. But then, precisely at that moment, we decided to part from Tone and became embroiled in a crisis. Fortunately for us Han was around and in October 1991, he personally closed the deal to renew the distribution contract in Europe for an additional three years. Signing the extension gave us stability in Europe just when our position in the U.S. was being undermined.

We extended the contract without telling Han about our decision to part from Tone. It was something we couldn't tell him while the story was unfolding, but the need to do so weighed heavily on me. A few months earlier I had flown to Paris and saw Han while I was there. I couldn't tell him about our proceedings against Tone but I didn't want to lie to him either. I told him that there were big changes in the offing but that I couldn't specify what they were. He'd find out in a few days. I knew that the petition would soon be presented to the court in London.

After that our financial difficulties got worse because of our quarrel with Tone and the banks in Israel refusing to give us credit facilities. I turned to Han in California and updated him with respect to our separation from Tone and the financial squeeze we were in. And he, big man that he was, didn't disappoint. He offered a lifeline by giving us—as part of the distribution agreement extended in October 1991—a number of back-to-back letters of credit to the value of $800,000 per quarter. Based on these, my friend Alex at Bank Leumi gave us a credit line of a million dollars, a sum big enough to relieve the pressure. Finally, finally, we were liquid, independent, and 100 percent owners of the company we had set up. The liberated 4D was free to sail on in the U.S.

Chapter 19

Uri, a Passion

My big brother Uri doesn't belong to this story, since he wasn't there during most of it. Yet he belongs in my life in the essential sense of that word. I loved him deeply, and was deprived of him too early. A sense of bitter loss lingers with me. I will forever live with my sadness. Today I am aware of how big Uri's influence was on the man I was to become.

When I was little my big brother was God to me. Because he was ten years older, we had only a few years together in the family home. I admired him as only a child can. Every minute of those years is etched in my memory as a perfect tableau against the backdrop of the small room we shared. The way I clung to him, the way I followed his every move, the way I watched him shaving, and loved the white spot he often graced my nose with. How I enjoyed it when he woke me every morning toward seven with a tickle and we exercised together to the voice of radio's "Mr Gymnastics," and how best of all I loved it when he took me with him to his various activities, most of which were related to sports.

My perfect brother Uri was an enthusiastic sports fan and an active athlete. I remember sitting on the floor of Hapoel's gym watching him in Ping-Pong tournaments, most of which he won. I think he tried his hand at practically every popular sport. He competed in pole vault, then new in Israel, and did very well at it. I tagged along wherever he permitted me to go, and sometimes even without his OK. For me just being with him was the ultimate joy, worth any price. No friend or game had an earthly chance of competing with my big brother's "Wanna tag along?"

When I grew up we drew closer and even became friends, especially after the deaths of our parents. Thinking back about our shared past I realized that I knew nothing of what he was like as a child. My brother Amnon then gave me a treasure trove that I had no idea existed, correspondence between my parents, dating back to WWII. It contained letters that my father had written to "Urik" as he liked to call his eldest son, all in beautifully stylized script with diacritical marks for the more difficult words. Amnon, who had continued to live in our parents' apartment after our father's death, discovered them by chance, organized them in a file, and kept them safe.

In one of the letters Dad pleaded with Mom and Uri to write to him more often. "Your letters and your solecisms are like vitamins for my soul," he wrote. In her letters to him, on the other hand, Mom complained about day-to-day difficulties and in particular Uri's obstinate refusal to obey her. "He take bike, cycle in mud down Ben Yehuda Street, showing off. It is dangerous. He not look where he is going." From these letters I learned that Uri was mischievous and very much in need of a father to discipline him. Apparently our father was able to contribute to his firstborn's education even from afar, because a while later Mom wrote, "Uri now helping a lot with 'small menace,'" my parents' nickname for me. Uri was dubbed "the big menace."

When Dad returned from his tour of duty in Italy he brought Uri a decorated enameled harmonica. According to family legend, when Uri was ten and already an accomplished flutist, he picked up the harmonica one day, having never played it before, drew it close to his lips, blew into it once or twice, and to everyone's amazement was able within no time to play recognizable tunes. A year on he was also strumming a mandolin and later on added the alto flute and clarinet to his repertoire. By that time both of us were already adults.

In 1953, when I was exactly ten, Uri left home and joined Nahal with his close group of friends from the youth movement. Settlement and agriculture were the core of the ideology on which all children born in Israel were raised then, including those brought up in cities. As a result, the best of the youth of those days joined Nahal. It was taken for granted that our duty was to turn the movement's motto, "rise and realize," into a living reality. Uri and his friends were sent to Kibbutz Yiftach to put that promise into practice.

While eager to fulfill their commitment, they were far less enthusiastic about Yiftach. The members were mired in a dreadful dispute as a result of the Kibbutz movement having split into two rival factions, a division that tore many kibbutzim apart and broke up families. This made a very bad impression on the Tel Avivians who decided that they didn't want to join a kibbutz where ideological disputes were settled by force. But that decision was not theirs to make. The United movement which had already dispatched a succession of Nahal groups to Yiftach insisted that Uri and his friends be sent there. After the split the kibbutz was left with only 45 members and badly needed reinforcements. "We are forced to accept the decision of the movement," Uri wrote in one of his letters. "In a few months time this place will become my home. I shall rise and realize, with enthusiasm. For me Yiftach is a passion."

Our mother was less enthusiastic. Uri's mobilization so traumatized her that she needed to recuperate in a rest house near Jerusalem. She wrote to Dad that their eldest son's call to arms reminded her of him joining the Jewish Brigade. She was comforted by "Roni who is one of two outstanding pupils in his class and is also learning to play the flute."

After Uri joined the kibbutz I nagged my father to take me there until he finally relented. He took a day off from work and we spent an entire day traveling in the antiquated buses of those times, finally reaching the kibbutz at around six in the evening. When I was a bit older I was able to go on my own and I tried to spend as much of my vacation time in Yiftach as I possibly could. During summer vacation when I was in fourth or fifth grade, I was on the kibbutz with Uri for almost an entire month. Some of that time was spent picking apples and some of it gathering grapes. If I was lucky we would go out together to collect bundles of hay. Uri drove a tractor towing a wagon while another kibbutz member pitched the bundles onto it. Sometimes he would let me drive the tractor through the wide-open valley while he got off to help his workmate. They worked and sang patriotic songs loudly and with real enthusiasm, not just to drown out the loud rattle of the tractor's engine. This was an experience second to none, accompanied by a strong sense of adventure, tension, and danger. A mere 150 meters away was the Lebanese border with the nearby village of Balida watching us.

Uri and his friends continued to protect their kibbutz and the state with passion, repelling nonstop attempts by terrorists to infiltrate, murder, and rob. In 1953 the guards at Yiftach killed an infiltrator who got into the cowshed, in 1965 terrorists detonated an explosive device close to the residential area, and in 1969, following the Six-Day War and the painful experience of seeing houses in nearby Kibbutz Gadot being erased by Syrian shelling, Yiftach's members decided to fortify the childrens' dorms and dig tunnels between those buildings and the shelters. It never occurred to them to abandon their hilltop, their home facing Lebanon. In the words of a poem written by one of the kibbutz members, "Of all the magical places on earth, this hill is our choice," a sentiment entirely in keeping with Uri's own feelings.

Despite the fact that he spent all his adult life on the kibbutz it never became a matter of routine for him. The romantic ideal never left him. That is why every role assigned to him was fulfilled with the same degree of seriousness and dedication. Taking on the tasks of landscaping or being a lifeguard at the pool were no less important roles for him than being the community's treasurer. Idealists, as we all know, are not easy people. What they demand of themselves, they also demand of others. Friends got angry with him on more than one occasion especially when he insisted that they cut back on expenditure so as to achieve the kibbutz goal: return debts on time and progress toward financial independence. At an early stage he was appointed to be the kibbutz's treasurer, then its overall coordinator, and then its secretary. Until, at a certain stage, after he had understood that fulfilling these managerial roles conscientiously cost him too much in terms of personal relations, he decided to take on more pleasant tasks such as landscaping.

Before that he had been able to develop the orchards, the fishery area, and the industrial sector. It was Uri who set up a packaging plant, a state-of-the-art refrigeration unit, and pushed hard for investment in a particularly good variety of apples. As early as 1962 their orchards yielded an outstandingly large crop—five hundred tons—and within less than four years that number had been doubled. There is no doubt that in management roles Uri was very effective. And sports were also something he never neglected. He made sure there were facilities in the kibbutz for basketball, football, and swimming, and would take the children of the kibbutz to regional and national competitions. He practiced what he preached.

And then, suddenly, his life was cut short. He was buried in the cemetery that he himself had planned with such wisdom and foresight.

Over the past years, with Uri long gone, my own ego already satisfied, and with time on my hands to sit back and reflect, I have begun to feel that he is once again present—not faded, not extinguished, but rather, gathering strength and growing within my heart. As his friend Amnon Zakob said at the stone-setting thirty days after his death: "His bounty was boundless. The more he gave, the more he had." My big brother Uri.

Chapter 20

Obstacles

When 4D was established we tried to attract investors, and everyone sent us packing. When our fortunes turned in 1992 after a series of crises, setbacks, and successes, they did so with no outside help. Every professional and commercial move we made was a first. Every gamble we took—today it's called development—was paid for out of our own pockets. We developed infrastructure software when software was not considered a viable, profitable business. Since then, things have changed and Israel has become a major player in the world of high tech. At one of the many conventions hosted here we were described as the "wilderness generation," one that paved its own way. We were preceded by the "dinosaur generation" of Uziah Galil and his friends, who founded the industry. Those who followed us were named the "bubble generation" and the "peace generation" because Israel's centrality in the field had in the meantime become linked to political and international developments.

Nobody wanted to invest in the wilderness generation of the 1980s. Once in a while we would make a pilgrimage to potential investors but we'd draw a blank. Some were nice people who wined and dined us in their offices, and listened attentively—but offered nothing. We approached Fred Adler's Athena Fund. We turned to Mickey Federmann, owner of the Dan Hotels chain and an investment fund managed by Aharon Bet Halami. We appealed to private individuals. There weren't that many doors to knock on and those we did manage to enter held nothing for us. We were like nomads in the wilderness, digging for water and finding only stones. The concept of venture capitalism didn't exist in Israel until the 1990s. Because our distribution in the U.S. was in the hands of local distributors and not under our own control, investors turned us down. Only after we had severed all links with our American distributors and begun selling on our own were we able to present ourselves as an independent U.S. company and attempt to raise local funding.

When at long last we did set up our own operation in the U.S., the revenue from B&BE's sales of our product in Europe became proportionately smaller. There were two reasons for this. First, we did well in the U.S. Second, our accounts there recorded 100 percent revenue for every sale instead of the 30 percent or so in royalties we had been receiving from Tone Software. Moreover, other foreign clients frequently asked their offices in the U.S. to contact us directly. Our overall position had changed.

So far as new sales were concerned, B&BE became less important, though the number of customers in Europe was twice our client base in the U.S. Our U.S. clients, on the other hand, were big corporations. They included MasterCard, EDS (Electronic Data Systems, founded by H. Ross Perot), with whom we had a huge deal, and AT&T. While Tone had never reached such heights, our Benny had courage in spades. "AT&T is a giant? OK, big deal, let's go for AT&T!" That was his approach, and we followed his lead. Our confidence and faith in ourselves pushed us ahead rapidly not only in the U.S., but also in Switzerland, where Credit Suisse, one of the world's biggest banks, became a client, and in France, where we struck a deal with the highly respected Credit Agricole. We were not daunted by the challenges posed by these grand customers. They just speeded up the development of our products. Needless to say we didn't go straight from Bank Leumi to Credit Suisse, or from Tadiran to AT&T. The ascent was as gradual as it was steep. We made station stops. In time the product improved, took shape, was perfected. And we learned how to operate in America like Americans and in Switzerland like the Swiss.

At the beginning of 1992 we were nearly out of the woods. Benny said, "After the bitter experience with private investment sources why don't we turn to the public, float the company on the stock exchange?" Why not indeed? He and Galia held exploratory talks with various financial institutions, which checked us out and concluded that such a move was premature. Though we were on the right track, we would have to wait until 4D produced the hoped-for results in the U.S. before considering a public offering.

During 1992 we redoubled our efforts. That summer Benny invited Amnon Shoham, a lawyer friend of his from New York, to visit our offices in California, to assess whether the business was now more likely to interest the NASDAQ investor. If so, we could raise the money we needed from the public and reduce our dependence on the banks and their capricious ways.

The purpose of a listing on the exchange is financial. The accumulated debt of a business, whether it's a law firm or a software house, can amount to up to five or six monthly salaries. For a kibbutz, as I learned from Uri, the sum can total as much as three years of operations. But we were not a kibbutz. In normal circumstances we had enough financial cover to keep us going for five months. We never had significant amounts of money in the till, the sort of sums that enable a company to spread its wings, to be bold as a matter of choice, not because it has to. We decided to try for an IPO (initial public offering) and Benny enlisted Amnon Shoham to help us with the initial steps. He had worked at the prestigious law firm Skadden, Arps & Co. and we asked him to write a first draft describing the company, so it could be presented to potential American underwriters.

Galia and I gave our full consent to the examination into our business affairs, though we never really asked ourselves what becoming a public company would actually mean.

The overview of the company was sent to three underwriters Shohan knew: Lehman Brothers, Kidder Peabody & Co., and Oppenheimer & Co. That summer everyone showed interest and wanted to talk. A meeting was arranged in New York between David Fox, the lawyer representing us, and their lawyers. At its conclusion the three legal advisors representing the would-be underwriters declared that they believed in us and were prepared to get together and try us out. I cannot exaggerate the importance of this backing. Those banks had a reputation for having successfully floated hundreds of well-known companies, and here they were, ready to lend their name to us, a relatively unknown Israeli company. They took quite a risk because if the flotation flopped, they'd be stuck with us. We kept supplying as much information as we could, enabling them to present us to potential investors—above all American investors—as a business worthy of their investment.

A word about David Fox. I had already met him in July 1990 when I went to the U.S. with Mickey Spigelman to deal with our separation from Tone. To avoid mistakes we wanted to consult an America lawyer and Amnon Shoham recommended David, his boss, an Israeli American who had studied law at Hebrew University. Not surprisingly, we discovered at our very first meeting that we had a number of mutual acquaintances. During his childhood in Israel he had been a classmate of our marketing manager Itai Ben Dor. An impressive figure by any standards, David was a board member at Skadden, Arps, which employed about 2,000 lawyers. He was considered one of America's most outstanding business lawyers, a much sought-after expert in crisis management. He also found time to volunteer in a project to develop the Palestinian village of Issawyah and contribute to the education of disadvantaged Israeli children. At our first meeting in July 1990, David explained our legal position in the U.S. vis-à-vis Tone. When that difficult situation turned into a full-blown crisis, he participated in planning the legal steps required to dissolve the relationship. In effect David became our lawyer in the U.S. He called the shots.

In July 1992 the underwriters' representatives arrived in Tel Aviv, where we arranged a formal presentation for them. The two most prominent members of the delegation were Adi Raviv, who worked under Ron Lubbash at Lehman Brothers, and Stanley Stern from Oppenheimer, who played a particularly dominant role in the proceedings. Following the presentation, the group visited our offices in Kiryat Attidim and saw for the first time what it was that they were selling to U.S. investors. As it turned out this was the first and last time they visited. What our software actually did was of no interest to them. Their principal objective was to confirm that ours was a sound business proposition and that the paperwork complied with the regulations for a public offering.

The company's position appeared to be good—indeed considerably better than we ourselves realized at the time. Based on their estimates and financial calculations, we tried to understand how much we were worth in the judgment of an objective external appraiser. From their point of view we were a boutique Israeli company with a range of high-quality products that were in great demand and competing well with those of much bigger, better-known companies.

Our two major rivals in the U.S., CA and IBM, are, to this day, among the largest manufacturers of software in the world, with sales running into the billions. Platinum was another big U.S. competitor. Then there were medium-sized competitors—companies with a more limited range of products such as Mobius from New York, and the Berlin-based Beta Systems, which years later also became reputable, listed companies. The three underwriters compared our performance to those competitors and, satisfied with the results, continued organizing the listing—a procedure that spanned about four months and two continents.

The most important stage in the preparatory work was deciding what price the shares should be offered. You cannot possibly know in advance what the exact price will be on the day the shares are issued to the public. All you can do is estimate. Amnon Shoham and the underwriters thought that the share value would be set at between $10 and $12. Multiplying the price of each share by the number of shares to be issued valued the company at between 100 and 120 million dollars. From that moment on these figures indicated 4D's official value and at long last we too knew how much we were really worth. Let it not be forgotten that a year and a half earlier our bank manager in Israel thought that it would be risky to give us a loan of $250,000.

We received further confirmation of the accuracy of the underwriters' valuation when EDS bought 2 percent of 4D's shares for two million dollars. This particular deal more or less ended the speculation about what the company's value would be once it was floated, as well as greatly enhanced our prestige in the U.S. EDS was a large and well-known company out of Texas that had been bought by General Motors in 1984. Perot, who had run for the presidency of the U.S. twice in the 1990s, was regarded as a tough, no-nonsense businessman.

Every day that passed brought us closer to D-Day. In our mind's eye we could already see DDDDF, our symbol in its English translation, flashing on the NASDAQ big board, four Ds followed by an F to indicate that it was a foreign company. Now we had to check and recheck every move, and in the interim keep our mouths shut (that by the way, was an official demand). Being so close, we could make no waves.

The prospectus, the final document written when all the checks were completed, had to describe the company and all its commitments in the minutest detail. It had to cover the entire range of views on its performance, and all the risks involved in its operations. These included such possible events as war in the Middle East, trade union strikes, and the chance that IBM might suddenly produce a computer model incompatible with our software. In other words we had to note each likely and unlikely, visible and invisible, potential obstacle or hidden snag so that no one could later say that we had concealed anything.

Dozens of people pored over the source material on which the prospectus was ultimately based; they checked, corrected, and rewrote. It was time-consuming work on a massive scale. The underwriters had their lawyers and accountants plus the huge accounting firm Arthur Andersen. On our side we had Yoni Glazer and a backup team drawn from the accounting firm Somekh-Chaikin. Our American lawyer, David Fox, and Amnon Shoham teamed up with our Israeli lawyer, Mickey Spigelman, and his crew. All in all there were more than thirty people involved, too many to fit into our Kiryat Attidim offices. Facilities were provided by Somekh-Chaikin, and it was in their offices that the prospectus was written up. We gave them access to all our correspondence and books, disclosed all relevant documentation. They took notes and produced drafts, making their respective contributions, adding comments, corrections.

In the course of reading the first draft of the prospectus something odd came to light. My academic degree and Galia's had been omitted from the listing of board members, even though we had both been careful always to include them after our names. Spigelman asked for an explanation and Amnon Shoham slyly provided the answer. "Benny doesn't have an academic degree, and after all, the company is Benny." We all had to be "brought into line," as he put it. Galia and I noticed that David Fox wasn't saying anything and decided to follow his lead for the time being.

The brilliant Benny was evidently suffering from "status anxiety." Not only was he responsible for the deleting of our degrees but also saw fit to crown himself "chairman of the board" in addition to his recognized title of CEO. Since our specific roles within the company were never formalized, Benny took advantage of a loophole. On this issue we didn't cave in to him. After a short, tense discussion, Benny accepted the lesser title of co-chairman and CEO. In line with my role I was named president of the company in Israel and chairman, and Galia the company's president in the U.S. That is how the three of us were listed in the prospectus. The problem was solved with a compromise.

Outside of business, life carried on and made its own demands. Summer was approaching and I had promised our third son, Ramon, that we would go for the family's traditional excursion to the U.S. before his Bar Mitzvah. In July 1992, I instructed my partners to continue with the public offering while Matia and I took Ramon for a ten-day trip to Toronto, then to Orlando and New York. Quite a few eyebrows were raised when I announced my decision to go on a vacation at that particular moment.

Email didn't yet exist, so there were faxes and phone messages waiting for me at every hotel we checked into. I got back from the Bar Mitzvah trip at the beginning of August, happy and well disposed, eager to wrap up the final draft of the prospectus, only to find a somewhat alarming note from David Fox on my desk: "In a public offering there cannot be two classes of shares. I am halting everything. Please give this your urgent attention." When had this arrived? Last week. Why was I not made aware of it? How come that on the one and only urgent matter that came up during my absence not a single fax was sent to me? I was bristling with rage. How could it be that no one had realized how important this was? I phoned David right away and promised him an answer as soon as I had one. Before even going into the detail I knew that this obstacle would not be easily removed.

At a certain stage in 1988 or 1989, we had decided to enable the employees to participate in our success and at the same time bind them more firmly by giving them a special class of shares. We didn't know how to raise funds, and we didn't know what options were or how to use them. We wanted our employees to benefit from the success of the company without giving them the right to vote. The holdings were equally divided between Benny and Einav Computer Systems (Galia and me) and it was a delicate balance. We therefore issued non-voting shares that enabled us to pay the employees a dividend of approximately 20 percent of the company's profits. Now, just as we were about to be listed on the stock exchange, David Fox was telling us that whereas a private company could have ten different classes of shares each with its own slightly different entitlements, a public company should have only one class.

To solve the problem would require a big effort on our part. We would have to approach the income tax authorities and work with them to find a formula that would quickly turn the special shares held by our employees into common stock. We enlisted the help of Professor Arieh Ovadia, an expert in the field, whose view was that the value of non-voting shares was 87 percent of the regular shares. His opinion was accepted by the authorities and on that basis we turned the "inferior" stock into regular shares. Relieved, I notified David Fox that the obstacle had been removed and that we could go ahead with the offering.

Our ignorance about options, plus our failure over the years to raise funds, meant that we were not saddled with additional partners and the majority of shares remained in the hands of the founders. At the time of the IPO the employees held only about 1.5 percent of the company's stock, an absurdly small number by today's standards when it's common for the employees to own 10-20 percent or even more. Our workers were OK with this because they too were of the "wilderness generation." Only two senior members of the staff, Avi Cohen and Ariel Gordon, felt that they had lost out as a result of the swap. I told them "OK, you're right. First of all agree to the change so that we can proceed with the flotation. After that I promise that we'll compensate you." Following the offering I formulated an agreement that satisfied them.

Both had been instrumental in the success of the company. Because of people like them we felt that we were more able than our competitors to conquer new markets, including America. After Benny Weinberger founded the company, Ariel Gordon was the first hire. Ariel is the archetypal scatterbrained genius: bright, naïve, dyslexic, with an exceptionally high IQ and all that comes from it. Once he absentmindedly brought his daughter to the office instead of taking her to kindergarten. Until the little girl asked him, "Daddy, when are we going to my nursery?" he hadn't even noticed. Despite the quirks, Ariel's leadership in the development of product was organized to a tee. In the first years, together with Avi Cohen, he was in charge of technological development. Subsequently Ariel was named director of research and development with responsibility for the bulk of the recently developed products, while Avi, who had originated Control M and was head of the support team, became director of technical support.

Avi Cohen, the young soldier who had participated in writing the GS Daily program—the basis for the development of Control M—was 4D's fifth employee. Avi was larger than life and brilliant. He had a devastating sense of humor, eccentric principles (he never took a loan), and was a confirmed bachelor. Quite often colleagues tried to fix him up with dates, but to no avail. His Yekke meticulousness, his commitment to precision, his discipline, his insistence on maintaining well-ordered processes in every aspect of a program all contributed greatly to our success as a company, especially abroad. Then we realized that the quality of his design, his careful planning, the excellent manuals that we produced under his supervision combined to give us a decisive marketing edge.

Just before the draft prospectus was finalized, another obstacle was discovered. The team checking our documents found the letter Benny wrote in 1983 to the university where we had done some of our initial development work. In it he offered them 3 percent of Control M's future profits in lieu of rent for their development stations. At some stage he also sent them a check in the sum of eight thousand shekels. I had identified this arrangement as a potential obstacle as far back as 1988 or 1989—long before we thought about a public offering. By then, the upgraded Control M was our most important product and I knew, now that the letter had come to light, that we had a real problem on our hands. Not only was there an agreement of sorts, a payment had been made, meaning that we had began to implement it. In relation to the IPO it meant that 4D, in effect, had a silent partner, one that was likely to become very noisy indeed.

Yosef Gottstein, head of the computer center at the university, was the person who had signed the agreement with us. Well after we had left he continued to demand payment. Every few months he phoned asking for Benny but my instructions were that he be put through only to me. "What's going on? You signed, why aren't you paying?" was the invariable question to which my standard response was "I'm not sure we need to." From his hesitancy, I had realized that he too was unsure. "Let's talk," was his standard suggestion. "Why should I talk to you?" I would say. "Even if I reach an understanding with you we would have to go to somebody more senior and he perhaps wouldn't agree. You don't have the authority to make decisions. Your signature is on the agreement but above you there is a financial director and above him the head of the university. I will be happy to talk to you, Yosef, I am not angry with you in the way that you are angry with me. But we can only talk business in the presence of someone authorized to come to an arrangement with us." This telephone ritual repeated itself every three months. To his "Why are you speaking to me in that way?" I would reply, "I'm not, I'm being polite. It's just that you have no authority." And now that waltz of the offended was about to begin all over again.

When the agreement with the university surfaced in the course of the audit for the prospectus, I phoned David Fox to fill him in. His reply was brief with a noticeable tone of anxiety. I knew exactly the questions on the tip of his tongue: How did a silent partner suddenly pop up? Why didn't you mention him earlier? This was serious. At best we'd appear irresponsible, at worst, liars and fools. I told David, there is no silent partner and promised to dispose of the issue before the prospectus was finalized. And to myself I added, show- off, making false promises, you haven't arranged anything yet.

Just a few days after we'd discovered this particular obstacle, there was a call from the university to arrange a meeting on the subject. I fervently hoped that the timing was purely coincidental, that they didn't know about our going public. Naturally I couldn't ask. As I requested, Gottstein came to the meeting with the institute's financial director. I had been preparing for this day for two years and knew that I needed a witness. I invited Itai Ben Dor, a senior member of our marketing division, to join me and briefed him as to his role. "Itai, you sit at the meeting as if you were part of the furniture. Say nothing. If it becomes necessary to testify about what transpired there, you will be able to do so."

We met in their offices. According to Gottstein we owed them 3 percent of all our revenue from the sales of Control M, plus interest. How much is that, he asked. I kept my poker face. "Benny made a mistake and signed, that I admit. But the agreement referred only to the first version of the product. We stopped selling that four years ago. You're talking about Control M, right? Well it's obsolete." I went on to say that in my view a university shouldn't profit from software products. If it rented us two development stations for seven or eight months we should be looking at the value of the rental. I went on and on and Gottstein disagreed then agreed, and all the while I knew full well that unless I could get back to David Fox with a solution I was in deep, deep, trouble.

I also knew that the university needed cash and decided that I should offer an inducement that might help to oil the wheels. After about two hours I declared, "Let's take a break. But before we do"—I throw in the bait—"clearly I'm not leaving here without making a payment. So how much are two development stations worth over such and such a number of months? Thirty thousand dollars? Fifty? I'll pay for that and we'll call it a day." And indeed, their ears pricked up. After consulting among themselves, they said. "OK, we're ready to accept a rental fee. But not $50,000 dollars. We want $200,000." The moment a figure was mentioned I knew that I was home. We could talk.

We continued negotiating for another forty-five minutes, at the end of which I offered them $100,000. They went into another huddle and came back asking for $120,000. "Just a minute, we need a break," I said quickly leaving the room with Itai in tow so that they wouldn't see the grin on his face. When we went back in I OK'd the $120,000 but in three installments—$40,000 a year. And they agreed. They agreed! All the way back to the office Itai couldn't stop giggling. My smile was saved for my five o'clock telephone call to David Fox in New York, in which I was going to tell him how I had dismantled the ticking bomb.

It should be noted that if my suggestion of a rental fee had not been accepted, the consequences for us would have been very painful indeed. Control M and its derivatives, in different and more advanced versions, continued for many years to be the source of 70 percent of our revenues. In 1999, for example, the 3 percent stipulated in the agreement would have amounted to no less than two million dollars. Instead I made them happy with $120,000 and extracted us from a very complicated mess. After the flotation, Yosef Gottstein phoned me. He had read about it in the papers. "You made a reasonable deal," he said to me. "Right, and so did you," I retorted. And that is the truth. Every year a new version of Control M was launched and the previous models taken out of circulation. That was my interpretation of the situation and they accepted it. It wasn't a bluff.

By September 1992 we had surmounted all the obstacles and were set for the public offering. The prospectus in perfect English had been fully edited and was ready to be printed and published. In ten days time the company would be floated on the New York Stock Exchange and we could celebrate our achievement.

On September 23 a courier came to our offices and handed me a letter. It was written by a lawyer representing Motti Glazer, from whom I had parted umpteen times and, more than a year earlier, had made sure that the separation was absolute and final. Now Motti's lawyer was claiming that 50 percent of my direct stake in 4D as well as 50 percent of the shares indirectly held by me as part of my holding in Einav Computer Systems belonged to his client. How could we possibly have forgotten such a fact? How come we failed to remember that he was a partner. Trembling, I phoned David Fox in New York for the third time, and prepared for the worst. This time he would really hit the roof, what with all these last-minute hitches, and call off the flotation. He did sound subdued and asked me to have the letter quickly translated into English and faxed to him so he could consult with his partners.

As we were biting our fingernails they read the letter and looked into the matter in depth. David phoned back with their conclusions. This wasn't a serious obstacle, and certainly not one that could delay the offering. "Don't get agitated," he said amiably. "On the eve of a flotation there is always someone who comes out of the woodwork and tries to get something by extortion." I hoped that he was right, that we could also overcome this crisis without adversely affecting the issue. But in my heart of hearts I was less sure than he. I knew Motti Glazer only too well and had that sinking feeling that this was just the opening chapter of a new saga.

Chapter 21

Due Diligence

The news published in September 1992 that EDS had acquired a 2 percent stake in 4D is what got Motti going, since it meant that the value of the company's issued shares would be $100 million dollars. He claimed that at the time of our separation this was something I hadn't told him.

The claim was false. During 1991 we had meetings and discussions during which the idea of a public offering was raised. Benny and Galia were told that such a move was premature because 4D's future remained unclear. About a year after the partnership with Motti was dissolved, the company's fortunes improved markedly and it was valued accordingly. Motti wouldn't admit that he had been foolish to reject my proposal that Einav Systems be "frozen" and insisted instead on us parting for good. Unwilling to admit that he had lost out because of his own poor judgment, he chose to smear me. My former partner managed to spoil my mood but I didn't take his complaint too seriously. After all there had been a final and binding arbitration award. Until the arrival of his lawyer's letter on the eve of the public offering, my thinking was that he would make a bit of a fuss and then clam down.

By means of "deception, fraud, and falsehoods," his lawyer wrote, I caused the naïve Motti to hand over to me his share of Einav Computer Systems-4D. Therefore, the separation was null and void. Receiving such a slanderous letter is unpleasant and insulting. Until David Fox allayed my fears, I was also worried that it would endanger the flotation. Mickey Spigelman responded to this offensive letter: "Motti Glazer was fully aware of 4D's intention to float the company on the stock exchange and spoke about it openly," especially, I might add, during the many arbitration hearings we sat through.

The company was floated on New York's NASDAQ exchange in October 1992. Like a bunch of kids, we were very excited. Here we were joining that elite group of pioneering Israeli high-tech companies listed on the American exchange. At first 4D's shares were traded at $12.Then slowly the price climbed until a few months later their value had risen to $20 a share. The flotation had raised $35 million and our joy knew no bounds. In our Kiryat Attidim offices I hung up a wooden ruler borrowed from my youngest son, Yoav, sticking a thumbtack in the number that the shares closed. Every morning the ruler was marked with the previous evening's fix in New York. The future began to look rosy. Then our son Ramon's Bar Mitzvah coincided with the share amount reaching $13. Lucky thirteen.

Motti and his family were not invited to the Bar Mitzvah. The friendship between our two families had faded along with the deterioration of business relations between him and me. There was no letup, however, in the correspondence between the lawyers. In Motti's name, his lawyer chose to ignore the facts and informed us that his client demanded a general meeting of Einav Computer Systems-4D to discuss the company's future. He wanted to give the impression that it was business as usual, that the parties had never parted, that Motti hadn't received hundreds of thousands of shekels and my shares in the subsidiary companies, and that he was still a partner. Spigelman's response was that since the separation agreement, "Your client has no standing in the company or its business." And so it carried on. The exchange went back and forth over a period of several months while Motti's hostility and my resentment were barely disguised by the legalese of our representatives. Every response we sent kindled the hope that Motti would back off. But he didn't.

In April 1993, when the shares on the NASDAQ hovered around the $20 mark, Motti sued me, Meir Arnon, Galia Streiker, and the registrar of companies. He asked the court to return the position of the company to what it had been prior to the separation, that is, to annul the separation and regard him as a full partner in Einav Computer Systems-4D. He claimed that defendant number 1, Roni Einav, had fraudulently removed from their jointly owned property an asset (4D) which had been under his management, and had, by deceit, concealed its true worth, which amounted to tens of millions of dollars. Further, he accused me of acting in bad faith, of deception, making false pretenses, and exploitation. The second defendant was the subsidiary, Einav Computer Systems. He accused Meir Arnon, defendant number 3, of deception, Galia Streiker, defendant 4, of fraud, and the registrar of companies, defendant 5, of the unlawful registration of a company. According to Motti the "exit"—Meir's departure from Einav Computer Systems-4D five years earlier, and the purchase of shares by Galia and me— was a conspiracy by the three of us to deprive him of his rightful share in 4D. He claimed that at that time, when, as everyone could see, not least the banks, we were on the ropes, we knew that the company was destined for success, and that is why we had driven him out. According to Motti his scheming partner Roni Einav had led him down the garden path. How else could a partner and company director explain his ignorance about his own company?

I was cut to the quick. He had sullied my good name, portrayed me as a liar, and himself as the innocent victim. There was one small detail that he conveniently omitted in his lawsuit—his accusation was groundless! A year and a half earlier he had put his signature on a final arbitration award. In his award the arbitrator had stated that both sides were forgoing "all claims and demands of any kind" that one party may have now or in the future against the other party "in any matter related to the company, the partnership, and/or in all the other companies mentioned above." Heaven forbid that he had deliberately concealed this from the court. It had simply slipped his mind. Had he been truthful, his petition would most probably have been rejected out of hand. Though I knew all the facts back to front, it in no way lessened my humiliation or the adverse publicity. I had no option but to respond. The question was, how? I consulted with Mickey Spigelman and came to a simple conclusion. You can't lie a little bit. You either lie or you tell the truth. And I hadn't lied. To prove this I had to go to war against Motti.

In September 1993, that year of high promise when the State of Israel signed the Oslo Accords and took a big step toward peace with our neighbors, judicial war between Motti and me was declared.

The court very quickly rejected Motti's suit against Meir and the registrar of companies. That forced him to present an amended petition solely against Galia and me. "More lengthy than necessary or desirable," as the judge put it. Clearly puzzled, she pointed out that Motti had gone to great lengths to create the impression that his role only covered his areas of expertise and that he didn't know what a company share was. Yet in cross-examination he stated "… there was a great deal of overlap between roles and during a certain period we had shared an office." Given all of that, how could anything possibly have been kept secret?

This story certainly wasn't good for my health. So far as business was concerned 4D continued to grow, our innovations were successful, and sales surged. In the wake of the Oslo Accords, Israel gained enormous worldwide support and all doors were opened to her. Yet instead of participating in the joy around me, I shuttled between the lawyer and the court, where I was interrogated as if I were a criminal.

The hearings lasted for three years. During that time I learned to get on with my life. When the Oslo Accords were signed we drank a toast to the future in the office. At home, my wife said, "Perhaps now we will build roads in Palestine and be able to drive to Jordan and Iraq." The diplomatic outlook appeared brighter than it had ever been. More and more countries in Europe and elsewhere in the world did business with 4D including one Muslim country, Malaysia.

But once the joy of the Nobel prize for peace and all the talk of a "New Middle East" had subsided, problems began to surface. After a lull, terror returned to the streets of Tel Aviv, and evil-minded demonstrators called Prime Minister Rabin a murderer. On the 4th of November Yitzhak Rabin was assassinated. The young lit candles and grieved, the whole country mourned its catastrophic loss. I, to my sorrow, had no option but to continue my litigation with Motti.

Business was booming, but we also learned by our own experience what it meant to be a company listed on the exchange, and what a terrifying roller coaster ride we were on. Yoav's wooden ruler was eroded by the sharp ups and downs of the NASDAQ. At the end of 1993, after the Oslo Accords, 4D's value soared to $250 million. Within six months it had plummeted to less than $40 million; within one quarter it rose to $82 million. We had no regrets about the flotation. We had raised money and were now in the big league. Our reserves allowed us to fix things, but we soon discovered that to be a public company was like living in a glass house. Every move we made, every error, was visible to the naked eye.

That same year Benny made a mistake in reporting the company's earnings in the United States—an error that was to be very costly to us. Suddenly we also became pawns in an international geo-political game over which we had no control. I was not the only one who occasionally secretly yearned for the freedom we had had as a private company.

The Motti story dragged on. He never stopped hoping that the court would rule in his favor and that we would in the end be forced to give him—to "return to him" as he would put it—a part of the shares in 4D. After every stage in the proceedings that ended in our favor I prayed that he would stop, that he would realize this was a pointless escapade. I prayed that attrition would achieve what reason had failed to. Had he not sued me and instead come to me after the flotation, admitted that he'd been a fool and asked for my help, I would have given him something for the sake of the friendship we once enjoyed. But he insisted on claiming that I was a swindler and had lied to him. I couldn't live with that under any circumstances. So our legal war continued. This was merely the end of chapter one.

Chapter 22
Laurels

When do you know that you've reached the peak? The scientist knows he's there the moment he makes his discovery. An artist can sense which of his works will become a masterpiece. And in software? In software there are no summits. You go on improving versions and strive to develop new products. You sell more, your profits go up, and market analysts sing your praises. Empowered, you gallop ahead at breakneck speed. And yet, there is no single achievement that you identify as "the one," the pinnacle of your life's work. The first sale of Control M in Israel was a moment of triumph; the superb marketing operation in Europe was a major success; the setting up of an independent company in the U.S. had all the hallmarks of a peak but was, in fact, only the start of a new ascent. In 1991 when we landed a contract with a large client we felt we had conquered a mountain, yet we continued to strive upward and onward. We made bids for more proposals and entered more competitions—many of which we won. Our product was superior to that of our competitors. And we had something that others didn't—a winning original concept known as IOA.

IOA was a simple and clever idea. Once in place each one of us asked himself why he hadn't been the first to think of such an obvious concept. It materialized in the middle of a routine day at work, as we sat in our comfortable office in Kiryat Attidim with not a care in the world, each under his own desk lamp and at his own computer.

We had already successfully developed a second product, Control D, and another software item, also to be called Control something-or-other, was in its final stages of development. Among ourselves we joked about our takeover of the word "control" together with the entire English alphabet. We had already gathered a couple of laurels but were not relaxed enough to rest on them. Each of us searched for new ideas, something unique that would give us a competitive edge. One day in 1988, Benny called me into his office. As I entered the room he was sitting at the computer grinning from ear to ear. Pointing excitedly at the screen he said, "We built the products with parts that are common to them all for reasons of economy, right? It turns out that they interface and are compatible. Control M and Control D combine to form a complete architecture that will automatically activate computer centers." What's he so excited about, I thought, and then recalled what happened at the customers' get-together in Venice earlier that year. A presentation was canceled and Ariel Gordon suggested that we instead present our range of interlocking products, which is what we ended up doing.

"What we've got here is OA, Operations Architecture!" Though Benny didn't shout "Eureka!" my pulse began racing. I said to him, "This is either a brilliant idea or total nonsense. In any event, two products are not enough for an architecture. Not just in the IDF, but also in the world of automation, everything good comes in threes. It's worth our while to complete the next Control quickly and put at least four or five products under the same umbrella. In the meantime, mum's the word. I'll check out the idea as soon as I can, and you prepare a lecture on—What did you call it? OA? That's too short. It has to have three letters." We ran through a series of acronyms and settled on IOA, Integrated Operations Architecture.

Who was the most appropriate person to try the concept out on? Jan Ofschoor, who we expected to meet in October at the planned B&BE kickoff in Berlin. Until then we decided on maintaining absolute silence, in case our brilliant idea turned out to be utter nonsense. On the first day in Berlin I invited Jan for a swim in the hotel pool. After letting him have the better of me in two races, I told him about IOA and asked for his opinion. His response was thrilling. He said it was an outstandingly clever idea. I rushed through the hotel's corridors in my bathrobe to grab Benny and give him the encouraging news before he went down to deliver his lecture. "You ran to tell me that? I know it's brilliant." How on earth could I have thought that he needed encouragement?

His lecture was outstanding. There are certainly advantages to the sort of unlimited self-confidence that Benny possessed. He exuded inspiration and captivated his audience. He compared the operation of a computer to an automobile production line. If you wanted the line to be fully automated, there had to be a connection between all the machines. How did that apply to our field? If the job runs satisfactorily in the operator's computer but gets stuck in line for the printer, the document won't be produced on time and won't be sent to its destination on the due date. In other words, we will have done only half a job. If the job is ready to be run, but has to wait for data files or the instructions of a tired operator in the middle of the night, that in itself precludes automation. We would overcome all that with a range of related products. With them we'd create a computer center in which all workstations operate in a fully coordinated and automated way: the bank's computer software, or that of any other customer, would receive all the data on time, the documents would be produced in sync, sent to their destination and arrive punctually. Most hitches would be forestalled and those that did occur would be dealt with by the computer itself. Thus the computer center as a whole would justify its existence. To set up such a center you need IOA, a file of compatible software packages programmed to manage a comprehensive automated production line. We had those, others didn't. Every one of our competitors' programs was developed separately, and in most instances by different teams. We already had a software package. Stage one of our IOA, and stages B and C were underway.

Benny's Berlin lecture was enthusiastically received, and the interest moved quickly from the theoretical to the practical. As well as being technologically innovative, our IOA also had a tremendous marketing advantage because whoever bought the concept wasn't buying a single software product. They were buying everything that had been developed around it. In effect, with the help of this concept the customer was locked into our range. If he had bought Control M there would have to be exceptional reasons for him not to buy Control D a year later. And if, after a while, we introduced Control R it would be worth his while to buy that as well.

Since our client base kept on expanding we thought it would be a good idea to speed up the development of new products at the rate of one per year. The sales personnel were enthusiastic about IOA. The analysts liked the idea and praised it highly. Gartner, the world's leading authority in the field of software, praised IOA as far back as 1989, calling it a revolutionary breakthrough. About a year later we were given an added boost by IBM's launch of its new strategy known as "system view," based on principles similar to those of IOA.

By 1991 we had already developed five controls compatible with the integrated system. Some difficulties arose with the new versions we were launching every year. All the different components of the IOA had to play in harmony. But not all the clients bought all the updates to all the controls at the same time. Sometimes they updated one, but continued to use a previous version of another. We were afraid that as a result there would be incompatibilities. This didn't happen because our strong development teams made the existing versions compatible with the new ones, a very complex undertaking. And it didn't take the customers long to appreciate the advantages of the method. Instead of having to learn about an entirely new product every time they made a purchase, and invest precious resources in it, they applied the tools and knowledge they already possessed to integrate the new product. This greatly lowered the overall cost to the customer and simplified the handling of programs whose usage was inherently complex.

The method found favor with the development team too. It made the launch of new software more economical. Installation and operating instructions to customers were also simplified and any improvement made to one product often contributed to several others. Above all, IOA facilitated data sharing between the various programs and decision-making based on the collected parameters produced by the system integration. This gave us a decisive qualitative edge over our competitors and, over the years, our customers eventually bought from us an average of three or four out of the eight we offered, which was good. One of those customers, the jewel in our crown, was EDS.

For us the deal with them was a turning point. EDS is a giant multinational company with computer centers throughout the world from England to Singapore, from Texas to Japan. They had been using CA's software until CA began to demand huge sums for the franchise. In a fit of anger EDS decided to change horses and approached us with a tempting but complex proposal. If we would develop a conversion program for all CA's programs, they were prepared to switch to our software in all their forty computer centers throughout the world. Once again CA was unknowingly involved in determining our fate. As always we first said yes and left the questions for later. We signed the deal with EDS and worked at a frenetic pace to develop the required modifications.

The company's operations were highly centralized, producing one master operating tape in Texas and distributing it to all their centers worldwide. We were given the task of training their Texas instructors in the use of our software. Aside from the size and quality of the deal, the very fact that we were selling to EDS brought us to the attention of the upper echelon of American business. If they were buying from us then clearly we were the best of the best.

Between 1987 and 1991 the sales of 4D shot up twenty-two fold and the number of workers in the company grew by a factor of fourteen. In the U.S. and Canada the company was still small but widely represented because the branches that Tone had opened in Chicago, Dallas, New Jersey, Washington, Atlanta, and Toronto were easily absorbed by us.

By 1988, we decided to initiate a launch (kickoff) of our very own. The first event was at the Laromme Hotel in Jerusalem. We all went out for dinner at a restaurant named Bangkok, where, in my cups, I promised that when we had a thousand customers to our name all of those present would be invited to dinner in Bangkok, the city. We then had fewer than 100 clients so the risk I was taking wasn't very big.

The next launch was scheduled for January 1991 at the Dan Caesarea Hotel but was postponed because of the outbreak of the first Gulf War. It finally took place in October 1991, when we were able to present the restructured Israeli company under my full management and the company in the U.S. managed by Benny and Galia. For the first time we were in a position to give the product developers in Israel and some of the international sales personnel the same business card.

Our management team had the right mix of professionalism and intuition. The pace at which we were expanding was right. The year 1991, which began with a deep internal financial crisis and the thunder of war outside, ended with a profit of $2.6 million on a turnover of $7.8 million. At the end of 1992, after we had completed the share issue and become a public company registered on the NASDAQ, our sales rocketed to $ 17.3 million—nearly three times what they had been the previous year—and our profits soared to $7.1 million. In addition to EDS, our list of clients included AT&T, Boeing, Toyota, Mitsubishi, Samsung as well as the U.S. Air Force and U.S. Army.

This impressive roll call of the high and mighty confirmed the magic touch of some of our excellent sales personnel in the U.S. The most successful among them was Bob Sacko, nicknamed "the great." He was a tall man, always smiling, assertive, and an avowed basketball fan. Bob was considered an oddball because he never quoted a price, usually the first thing that a customer asks for, but his results spoke for themselves. He had extraordinary charisma and a sales pitch all of his own, which, it transpired, wasn't at all bad. He'd say to the customer, "You like the look of the product? Then let's show you what it will do for your business." In most cases he closed the sale after a few months' demonstration or a trial period. A clever salesperson has to know how important a product can be to the customer and the sort of benefit he is likely to gain from it. At this, Bob excelled. In his most astonishing sale, when we thought that he was negotiating a deal of around a million dollars, he signed off on a transaction worth no less than seven million.

The most original of our sales staff was a short ultra-Orthodox Jew named Kurt Nirenberg, whose bailiwick was the Pentagon. The match may sound strange, but Kurt was undoubtedly one of the most talented people in his field. Before he came into the picture the Pentagon's purchases from us had been sporadic. They used our products and those of our competitors. At one point they wanted to decide whose products would be their standard. We hoped and prayed that this prestigious and powerful customer would choose us. The difficulty was that the sales cycle to a huge body such as the U.S. Department of Defense could stretch over a two-year period, and the salesperson involved would need to have great staying power to see it through. We sent Kurt, who immediately reached the right people, established contact, and became a welcome visitor.

I was curious to find out how it worked, what kind of interaction evolved between this religious Jew and the top brass in the U.S. armed forces. It was hard to imagine him sitting in his traditional clothing, opposite them in their uniforms, downing their beer. Once when he came in to report to me I decided to ask. First we chatted, discussed Operational Research, minefields, simulations. At an appropriate moment I popped the question. "Tell me, Kurt, when you're with these American generals, what do you talk to them about?" "Anything, so long as it's not about the software," he replied. "They don't understand software. We talk about simulation, minefields, just like I do with you. Then we eat together."

"Just a minute. What do you mean you eat together? There's no kosher food at the Pentagon."

A mischievous smile sprung from behind Kurt's beard. "They eat and I talk," he replied with a wink.

"Well, and ...? How does that help you to sell?" I wasn't following.

"Ah," said Kurt, "they very much appreciate the fact that I don't eat."

After a year and a half of Kurt fasting at the Pentagon the generals continued to vacillate, and our man despaired and left. Somebody else finalized the sale a few months later and scooped the bonus. It was a sizable transaction, worth more than four million dollars. Kurt was angry but there was nothing to be done since his replacement was unwilling to share. Salespeople are protective of their clients and their commission. In due course Kurt overcame his disappointment and returned to work with us in the U.S. and then in Israel, where he did well for himself and enjoyed the influence he had on the company. Even Benny learned a thing or two from Kurt. I once overheard him reprimanding a man from technical support: "Talk to the client about baseball. Don't bore him with technical stuff he doesn't understand, then we'll get around to solving his problems."

After Gartner had first singled us out for praise, clients began to approach us directly. We had become famous for Control M, and we had a major innovation, the IOA. Subsequently this model became the standard. Competitors realized that this was indispensable for success in the implementation of technological infrastructure.

Though we were not good at telemarketing, in America we couldn't have managed without it. Sound marketing strategy is to know in advance where there is a chance of making a deal, which companies have the right budgetary allocation, who the right people are. You have to filter out the irrelevant, and decide on the timing of a proposal. Or, like Bob Sacko, you make no proposal at all until you are sure that the time is ripe—an art form all of its own.

At the beginning of 1993 we convened again, this time in Zichron Yaacov. This was the first time since the IPO that the entire company was able to meet up in Israel. Everyone was invited to share with us the changes and achievements that stemmed from our having become a public company. We began with socializing and pampering ourselves a bit, after which came a series of lectures. Itai Ben Dor from marketing asked: "Are we satisfied with ourselves, with the products, with the sales? What are our hopes?"

We wanted next year's success to be bigger, and wished to increase the American share of the pie. The company in the U.S. at that time had only 315 customers. Despite its successes it remained a less significant part of the business compared to the European side, where sales were far bigger and where we had 459 customers out of a worldwide total of 1,015. We knew that the global market for our products was fifteen times greater than we had thus far achieved, and that our potential for growth was far from exhausted.

Benny philosophized a bit about the ins and outs of software developing. Galia didn't much like lecturing and pushed her husband to the podium in her stead. Ariel Gordon gave a rousing speech about the importance of technical support so that all our staff would realize the heavy responsibility that rested on their shoulders. "If the Control products crash for twenty-four hours," he declared in the tones of an evangelical preacher, " a bank such as Credit Suisse can simply evaporate." In other words we had to function perfectly at all times to avoid causing heavy financial damage, or even, heaven forbid, life-threatening ones. This is more or less what transpired during our conference. We ended it tired and content and returned to the serious business of work.

Although we had only just begun to grow we felt confident enough to invest a bit in ourselves. In Kiryat Attidim we replaced our labyrinthine eight hundred square meters in building number 5 with two floors in building number 7. We organized an air-conditioned computer center, with backup air conditioning, a proper laboratory, a library, a cafeteria to seat forty-eight, and an instruction center with room enough for twenty-four participants. Everything was updated and improved.

In the U.S. the marketing and sales setup was expanded so as to achieve the targets set at the launch, to increase sales by 40 percent. If the sales manager there had been working on a half-time basis, his hours of work were now upped to time and a half.

Toward the end of 1993 the figures indicated that our growth had been phenomenal and that this was going to be a truly exceptional year. It looked as if the investments had justified themselves. The annual sales turnover had reached $23 million, a significant increase when compared to the $17.3 million in 1992. On December 29 of that year the results for September were published: half a million of our shares changed hands. In *Globes* it was reported that the brokerage firm Oppenheim estimated that "in the light of the significant growth shown by the company the share value is likely to reach $35-40 in the coming twelve months, up from $22.75."

Could the upward movement of our profit curve continue? We were in seventh heaven. Just two years earlier we had been on the ropes with all three managers having to put up personal guarantees. Profits did indeed go on rising. Toward the end of the year they reached $6.6 million. In less than three years we had grown sixfold. Our self-confidence improved beyond all measure.

In March 1994 we convened 4D's third annual conference in Israel. This was a few days before the publication of the final results for 1993, and before the gathering storm cast its shadow over my relationship with Benny. Again we talked about our performance, the challenges that lay ahead, and our expectations. We had no idea of what was lurking just around the corner. At the event itself, I gave a summary of what had been done in the course of 1993, Galia spoke about the U.S. end of things, and Benny reviewed the planning for the year ahead and declared that by the end of the decade there would only be three independent software companies in the world: CA, Microsoft, and 4D. This led some to believe that his overconfidence had finally gotten the better of him.

We knew that in the course of 1993 the company had become somewhat routinized, that the start-up spirit was running out of steam and needed to be revived. How do we do that, what would we have to change, how many employees did we think we would have at the end of 1994? These were all the issues we considered, defined, and presented to those assembled.

It was during this period that the PC became widely popular and we decided to take a leap into the unknown. We wanted to adapt our software programs, which until then worked on mainframe computers (a central computer, MF, with an MVS operating system), to also work on personal and middle-sized computers as well as with other operating systems such as

VMS OS/2, Windows, and Unix. Our idea was to permit the customer to schedule procedures on the operating system of his choice, and all would be made accessible via one entry gate, a kind of organizational command post, which we labeled Enterprise Control Station. This move required considerable developmental investment, but we felt that it could determine our future. And we were right. Later on this expansion propelled us into a leading position, whereas companies that did not make the leap lagged behind. Customers such as Fidelity, US Airways, and AT&T wanted to try us out, and very quickly we had close to sixty installations. In the contracts we undertook to add operating systems on demand.

We were so thrilled that we failed to notice that the product was not yet stable enough. Instead of making new sales, the sales personnel and technical support teams in the U.S. kept chasing their own tails, servicing these prestigious customers just so as not to lose them. Consequently we lost money.

Ariel Gordon tells the story:

When I was sent by Roni to salvage the situation the first thing I did was to rehabilitate technical support. Next I put a stop to the installations of the new product. The third thing I did was to focus on closing a deal with the major potential customers who were not yet in the bag.

As it turned out, the accounts for the last quarter of 1993 showed that yearly profits had slumped to $1.9 million. Most of what we had sold—and we sold a lot—went to cover our quickly escalating expenses. We had allowed this growth in outgoings on the assumption that sales would continue to rise at the previous pace. Conclusion? The company was being mismanaged. We did poorly. Undoubtedly the ship had set sail on a perilous course. Even if we got lucky and didn't capsize we were already paying dearly for our errors of commission. How come we plummeted so quickly?

Between 1989 and 1990, Benny was in Tel Aviv overseeing every aspect of development, while Tone in the U.S and B&BE in Europe distributed and sold our product. Marketing was not our responsibility. But from the moment Benny moved to the U.S. his influence over development decreased. Others took his place, and he concentrated on U.S. marketing.

The process itself was right except that in the U.S. Benny was overreaching—that was clear to everyone except Benny. He once said to me "Roni, when we compete—we win." And so we did. However, because we succumbed to the illusion that we were already selling more than enough, in some cases we didn't even put in a bid for the proposal. Sometimes we didn't even know about it because we lacked proper business intelligence. When I saw that Benny was not reaching all the targets he was supposed to, I suggested he hire someone to help. I wanted him to have other professionals at his disposal, so that he could share the workload.

Then disaster struck. Benny hired some people who had worked for big companies and had no understanding of the limitations a small company faced as it was growing. The wrong man in the wrong place—heading the list—made two mistakes. Firstly, with Benny's encouragement, he set up a marketing system for a product that was not yet ready (ECS). Then he enlarged the workforce on the assumption that the earnings per worker would continue to be what they had been in the past. And wonder of wonders, the opposite happened. In 1994 our turnover was $28.3 million with an operating loss of $23.2 million. Any sensible person seeing those figures would know that something was seriously wrong.

The July 1994 issue of *Enterprise Software Magazine* published a list of the hundred best independent software vendors (ISV) in the U.S. The list was of companies that only sold software products, ranked by their sales volume. We were proud to have been included in it for a number of years. First and second places on the list were occupied by Microsoft and Computer Associates, its closest rival. Oracle was in third place, Novell in fourth. These were companies with a turnover of billions. Next came software giants such as the Texan BMC. B&B, under Paul Newton's management, was in 32nd place with sales that year of close to $120 million. In this august list we were ranked far below them, of course, revealing that we were facing great difficulties.

The bad results for the end of 1993 and the beginning of 1994 upset the delicate balance among the three directors. Galia and I asked ourselves where we went wrong and what should we do about it. Not so Benny. This was a dreadful year. In the good times that preceded it, sales per worker topped the $200,000 mark, whereas in 1994 they were almost half that sum. These results were a wake-up call.

Looking back, I think that our expansion was too rapid and too steep. My brother Amnon thought that I had erred in relying too much on Benny and by giving him a free hand in the U.S. Whether that was true or not I don't know. And as if all of that weren't enough, Benny made some procedural mistakes which on the face of it didn't look serious but, as we were about to discover, in a public company every small deviation from regulations is nothing short of a catastrophe.

A public company must file a report of earnings every quarter. In the report for the last quarter of 1993, published at the beginning of 1994, Benny included sales that were not finalized. A sale in progress with an American sub-agent, for example, was entered by Benny as revenue. The distributor reported it as a done deal, though he hadn't yet completed the transaction. That was one mistake. Another distributor sent in an invoice before the due date and this transaction was also included in the quarterly report. These were deals Benny was sure of and therefore didn't hesitate to give an instruction for them to be incorporated in the report.

There is always a potential discrepancy between the profit forecast of a company and its current revenues. A public company is expected to forecast its sales and profits conservatively, and to notify the public indirectly and through market analysts. If the company sees that its forecast is not, in practice, being realized, it has to publish what is called "a profit warning" so that investors know that profits will be lower than forecast. Obviously a profit warning causes the share price to fall, and company directors try to avoid it. In our case, Benny's profit forecast was reasonable and based on real future sales, though we were procedurally not allowed to enter them yet. When the mistake was discovered and published we were asked to amend the report and did so. But the snowball had begun to roll, and we along with it.

On March 21, 1994, a class action was filed against 4D and its directors, Benny, Roni, and Galia, as well as against Michael Karish, the company's finance manager. The plaintiffs claimed that we had published false and misleading statements about the company's forecasts, its revenues, and its profits, and that in doing so had breached U.S. Securities law. From one moment to the next we were transformed from winners to criminals. When we had recovered from the initial shock and had begun to deal with the new reality, we realized that such petitions are routine in the U.S. and are filed far more frequently than in Israel. Certain attorneys specialize in them and even earn a good living from such cases. The lawyer who starts the process buys a symbolic quantity of shares in a company he has marked out as a target and lies in wait for every possible slip-up. The moment he becomes aware of an error he approaches other shareholders and proposes that they file a joint petition and that he represent them. The court has to approve him officially as the representative of the other claimants.

That is exactly what happened to us. The lawyer was from San Diego. He bought our shares, and waited for his chance. When Benny's error came to light he pounced. Our laurels sprouted thorns.

Chapter 23
Childhood Heroes

Karl May, Jack London, and Mark Twain opened my young eyes to distant worlds filled with hair-raising adventures. *White Fang* and *The Adventures of Tom Sawyer* were stories I read over and over again till I could recite them in my sleep. Also included in my private pantheon were Yigal Mossinson's unforgettable Hasamba series, whose copies were snatched from the library shelves the instant they got there. The Hasamba group's top-secret cave was located in my childhood turf by the sea, where the Hilton hotel stands today. The cave played a vital role in the stories of Yaron Zahavi and his band of budding soldiers.

The war that Yaron waged against the British Mandate in Palestine appealed to me because it existed on the border between the real and the imaginary. Hadn't I seen the "red berets" wandering around our front yard on the eve of the War of Independence, eavesdropped on the grown-ups whispering about a concealed weapons cache? Once I woke up to the sound of a Czech rifle being fired from the first floor, taking aim at Egyptian warplanes en route to bombing Tel Aviv. Perhaps there really was a cache of weapons in our building. I so wanted to believe that there was, that the boring tenants were in reality clandestine heroes led by my very own father.

At the end of 1956, I was twelve, and in my own eyes, a grown-up. My adventures were played out within walking distance from home, two square kilometers that incorporated a whole universe and overlapped what was then the center of Tel Aviv. Within this area resided our entire tribe—family members from both sides, and most of my friends. We lived on Shimon Hatarsi. Ilan Kotz, my friend from kindergarten and football who lived in the next apartment, used to chat with me by leaning out of his window. Aunty Sima, Uncle Artek, and their four children, Dangi the pilot, Gadi, Ruthie, and Naomi lived less than a kilometer away. When Dangi got married he moved to an apartment nearby.

All our activities took place within the confines of the two square kilometers that comprised our universe. My grade school, Ussishkin, was across the street from our house, so that my mother, by just looking out of her window, could see whether or not I was playing truant. Uri's high school was inside the area and the United Youth movement's northern branch was on its very edge. The school and navy cadet group attended by our little brother, Amnon, were there too, and the Maccabiah stadium, which we sneaked into to watch football, was within walking distance.

In our quarter everybody knew everybody. For children it was a safe zone, as well as an unexplored continent jam-packed with temptations. Just walking down the street was adventure enough. The streets were either dirt roads or gravel tracks with potholes and hardly any traffic, so we could play there to our heart's content. In winter, Ben Yehuda, Nordau, Ibn Gevirol, and even a bit of Dizengoff Street became muddy with huge puddles in which frogs and tadpoles swam freely. Behind our house the puddles were so deep that daffodils grew in them. We put on our black rubber boots, the most essential footwear in the Tel Aviv of that time, and every day set off to explore and discover our sodden continent. The fast-flowing Yarkon often breached its banks, transforming already substantial puddles into real swamps. Rolling around in them, spattering mud in every direction, and bouncing stones on the sea's shimmering surface, are all remembered as unequaled pleasures. When we'd had our fill we would rush home to dry ourselves by the paraffin heater and get clean, quickly, before Mom got back.

In the winter of 1956, after the Sinai Operation, the Yarkon burst its banks, this time also flooding Shimon Hatarsi Street, water reaching all the way to the fence around our house. There wasn't a dry meter left for us to play on or even stand on and we, who were so used to playing in the street, had nowhere to go. Ilan Kotz suggested we go to Tel (mound) Kodadi, on the northern bank of the Yarkon, close to the river's estuary, where the ground might be dry.

On the way to the mound we waded through puddles, belting out a song of praise to our army. The Sinai campaign had ended not long before, and its outcome was the subject of endless discussion among our leaders. We were not interested in politics, but Ben Gurion's words about our soldiers on the radio filled us with pride. "Blessed are the mothers who have such sons," he said. We sang for joy, happy that we had been freed of the blackout and could once again play outside until late in the evening. At the ruined fortress we got organized in the dry corner and took out the marbles. Then we decided that whoever won a round in the game would tell a story. When I'd won ten grushim it was my turn.

Two family tales of heroism came to mind, one with a sad ending, and one that was happy. The sad story was about my uncle David Weintraub, Dad's only brother. He was an idealistic Zionist who worked in Tel Aviv's port area. On April 1, 1948, he was among those unloading Czech weaponry smuggled into the country on board the vessel Nora. An Egyptian aerial attack on the city killed him. I don't remember my uncle, I was too young, but it was one of our family's most important tales and I was proud of it.

The happy anecdote was about my cousin Dan Gonen. He had taken part in the Sinai campaign, an outstanding pilot who flew Mystère jets and had taught me to build model airplanes. Nicknamed Dangi because of his ginger hair, he was the shining star of the extended family and much admired by me. He was three years older than Uri, thirteen years older than I. He trained to fly in France, and in the Sinai campaign shot down a number of enemy planes and also forced an Egyptian Mig 15 to fly in the wrong direction until it was out of fuel and its pilot was forced to abandon it. This was the story I decided to tell. No one else in the group had a cousin who was a daring pilot and as they listened, my friends' eyes opened wide in admiration.

Twilight. We began to feel the pangs of hunger as the rain came down with ever-increasing force. On the homeward journey we deliberately delved into the deepest puddles, startling the frogs and having a great time. I wanted to surprise my mother and get back in time for supper before she had to whistle for me to come. Within the family we had a beckoning whistle. Mom never shouted "Roni come home," like other mothers did. As I got close to our street, thinking how to spend my windfall of ten grushim from the game of marbles, I looked up at the glass door on our balcony and saw that the table was already set. We ate at seven, and whoever didn't come on time had to suffer the consequences. There was no telling off anyone, and no shouting. Once, when Uri was still living at home and I came an hour late, all Mom said was: "Pity you didn't come on time. Uri wanted to take you along." I was terribly disappointed that I'd missed him. Eating a cold omelet mattered not.

So the table was set when I looked up, but my mother was standing beside it gesturing at Ilan Kotz's older brother, Giora. What was Giora doing at our house? I sprinted up the stairs and entered the apartment through the already open door. Mom looked ashen. "What's happened? Has something happened to Uri?" I blurted out. The only telephone in the building was in the Kotz apartment and they took messages for all the neighbors. "Uri? No, no," muttered Giora. "There was a call from Uncle Artek. It's Dan. He's been—wounded."

Dangi? Dangi wounded? "How? Where?" I was screaming my head off. Amnon emerged from the nearby room. Seeing him, my mother burst into tears. "Tell the truth, come on!" I shouted at Giora, who stood there looking lost and badly shaken. And he did. "Dangi was killed in an air accident. His plane crashed in the south. Uncle Artek phoned to tell you."

I remember that my mom put on her black rubber boots. I remember her dressing Amnon in his coat and buttoning it crookedly. I remember that I led her down the stairs because she was unstable and I was afraid that she would fall. She didn't even notice that I was covered in mud. I don't remember her telling Giora to phone my father. We walked to Dangi and Aviva's apartment. I held on to Amnon because Mom's hands were trembling. I remember that I tried to bypass the puddles so that my little brother wouldn't get dirty. My dad opened the door for us at Dangi's and gave Mom a hug. I remember Dangi's wife, Aviva, very pregnant, saying over and over, " I want to see him," and Gadi, his younger brother, trying to comfort her. I remember feeling a void in my stomach, and in my heart and in my soul.

After Dangi was killed, Mom lost her joie de vivre. This happened in December 1956. In April 1957 I turned thirteen but my Bar Mitzvah party was postponed. Today Mom's condition would be tagged as "slight depression," caused by us having joined the ever-expanding "family of grief."

Chapter 24

Troubles in America

Success has many fathers and no lack of mothers, godparents, and adoptive parents. Its brother, failure, is an orphan. In April 1994, the board of directors and the company's management began to try to allocate the blame for the crisis and start to fix the damage. Benny, in Benny's view, was blameless. And yet he was the CEO, the general manager, custodian of our interests in the United States. Who else was around? Galia? Benny blocked her involvement. The newly appointed sales manager? He was answerable to Benny. The accountant? Followed Benny's instructions. That left me, president of the company in Israel and chairman of the board. After my fiftieth birthday in April 1994, Benny tried to deflect attention from himself by forcing my exit from the company.

How do you bring about such an underhanded move against your own partner and patron, the very person with whom you had come this far? Benny approached the company's lawyer, a friend of mine, and tried to convince him to have a heart-to-heart with me and persuade me that I was already fifty and it was time for me to stop getting in his way. Benny's way. He pushed members of the board to go along with this. The board had a membership of eight. When we started out as a company Benny and I agreed that he would nominate four people to the board while Galia and I would name an additional four. This balance was put to the ultimate test in that time of crisis.

It was spring. Passover came and went. During May there were many long meetings that began at 5 p.m. and ended in the wee hours of the morning. As obligated by both the current situation and the law, members of the board were concerned with the good of the company. Yet as appointees of the management's two warring factions, they found it difficult to come to a decision. The issues raised at the meetings were painful and unpleasant. What was to be done about our losses in the U.S.? How were we to deal with the class action there? The board vacillated. They didn't want to bring to a vote extreme proposals that would end in a stalemate and paralyze the company. They wanted me, Benny, and Galia to present a proper recovery plan, one agreed on by the three of us.

After the first meeting we tried, and came to the second with a plan of sorts that didn't satisfy the board. The trio convened once more, this time at my initiative. "Maybe we are not good enough managers for a company of this size," I said. "Perhaps the three of us ought to resign and bring in professionals to replace us." I thought that exchanging all of us for a professional management team could be a good compromise. The blame and humiliation of the failure in the United States would be equally shared and, most important, the company, our property and our responsibility, would once again be afloat. Galia was close to agreeing, Benny was adamantly opposed. Under no circumstances was he prepared to consider such an option.

But we couldn't return to the board empty-handed. Somebody had to accept responsibility. I decided to take the rap even though responsibility for the U.S. slip-ups in reporting and registration did not lay with me. I was to blame for having not questioned Benny more closely about his report of sales in the U.S.; I was to blame for trusting him and for only waking up when the house was already ablaze. I was to blame even though it was his job as CEO and not mine to check those sales reports. This was his direct responsibility and that of the accountants in the U.S.

In May or June the board reconvened and made a number of decisions. One was that I, who until then had fulfilled two roles—president of the company in Israel and chairman of the board—would remain as chairman but resign my operational role as president, with the exception of two areas of responsibility which I had insisted I retain: managing relations with Europe, which accounted for some 20 percent of our sales, and overseeing relations with Japan. Against his will, Benny's role was also pared down, and a member of the board, Rafi Oz, was appointed to supervise him in matters related to finance. The board's third decision was to appoint Avi Cohen as chief operating officer. On the surface everyone swallowed their pride for the sake of the company, and so that we could move on.

The class action against us went into high gear and was conducted at a cost that by Israeli standards was astronomical. The legal fees were at least four hundred dollars an hour and we were billed for some three hundred hours a month. On average we paid out over $100,000 a month, a very expensive show. Representing us in court was Skadden, Arps, which had been with us from the time we first set foot in the U.S. Until the class action came up, we had worked with David Fox and Amnon Shoham, two of the firm's specialists in financial-legal issues. When we approached them about the class action they turned us over to Jonathan Lerner, an expert in this field. In Israel, 4D's board asked Benny to represent the company against the plaintiffs. Even though the evidence indicated that he was the number one culprit, he was nonetheless the man who had been there and who knew what had transpired in the U.S.

Our shareholders, through the lawyer from San Diego who had launched the suit, accused us of causing them losses of between $30 and $40 million. They claimed that because of Benny's erroneous (fraudulent, as they put it) reports, they had bought our shares on the basis of incorrect information. The blunder in the report published in the U.S. was at the root of the entire problem.

The claim was exaggerated but the moment it was published the share price really dropped, causing havoc in the market—a tailspin that was completely out of control. In the American press the class action was summed up as dangerous. "A judgment against the company or an out-of-court compromise is likely to have a negative impact on its financial results." At the time of the IPO, the share value was $12. At its peak the price reached $25. Now it had plummeted to a low of $3.75 a share. The plaintiffs calculated the compensation due to them by the difference between the price they paid at the time of purchase—before the erroneous information was published—and the realistic value following the publication of that information. According to their arithmetic we had caused them overall damages of $30 million. Their lawyer demanded immediate compensation. We had then about $15 million in the bank.

We were in the eye of the storm and Benny had still not mended his ways. He continued to air his own versions, orally as well as in written reports. Even though we were continuing to lose money he came out with an announcement that, inter alia, declared that the company had "achieved its plan." The business plan had indeed included a provision for financial loss—sometimes you take such a possibility into account. But what about common sense? To make that kind of announcement in our situation could easily be construed as misleading. What on earth were we to do with him? I began to despair.

At that same time an interesting situation opened up in Europe, my direct area of responsibility. Our distribution contract with B&BE was due to expire in October 1994. In the original contract of 1987 and its extension drawn up in 1991, a clause was included that was worth millions to the distributors. In principle, the clause stated that if we chose not to renew the contract, then B&BE would continue to receive their part of the payment for maintenance of our programs even though in fact they were not doing the work.

In the negotiations preceding the expiration of the first extension in 1994, they appreciated this clause that was so beneficial to them. For us it was problematic because we planned to set up an independent distribution network in Europe. The clause meant that for an entire year we would be working for them, to a certain extent. They would continue to earn millions from customers we serviced.

When we signed the agreement in 1991 we were desperate for their letters of credit. We needed them to get out of the financial hole we were in after the crisis with Tone, and so agreed to the draconian clause. But given that it was liable to cost us $50 million and more, we now wanted to wipe the slate clean and initiate a separation from B&BE, so that we could set up an independent distribution network whenever the time was right. Benny thought we should do it immediately. Because Europe was my turf I called the shots. Over a period of two or three months, I conducted tense negotiations, the sole purpose of which was to sever relations with the Europeans as peacefully as possible.

At the same time we took steps toward the setting up of an independent distribution network. Even if we didn't establish it right away and chose, instead, to sign a new distribution agreement with B&BE, it was better that the negotiations be conducted when we already had the infrastructure of an independent network. We appointed Michel Koder, a Frenchman experienced in the sale of software programs similar to our own, as manager of 4D Europe. We also began hiring workers for the new branch and took on about ten people in other countries on the continent.

We were unable to give the go-ahead because we had not yet retrieved the distribution rights from B&BE, but 4D's

European infrastructure was laid. With a great deal of effort I closed the contract separating us from the Europeans peaceably. It was agreed that we would pay them an additional year's maintenance and with that our liability to them would end. For the signing of the contract, Han Bruggeling, Ian White, Galia, and I met in Düsseldorf. Our delight at the smooth ending was mixed with sadness because, after all, we had enjoyed a very fruitful working relationship with B&BE.

The separation was a complex maneuver, which had gone well, and I thought that the atmosphere would now be clearer. But that was not to be. Benny declared that we must become an independent company in Europe now. The crisis in the U.S. and the class action were at their height. We were still bleeding. We had not yet reached a settlement with the American shareholders, as we tried to reduce their claim from $30 million to a sum we could manage. Why was independence in Europe such a burning issue? The infrastructure had been created, Europe wasn't going to sink in the ocean. I tried to appeal to my partner's common sense. But Benny stood his ground, continuing to press his demand. At that stage I realized that he was unstoppable and that things couldn't go on that way. A company couldn't be properly run with two heads. Still, until a solution was found I had to prevent another rash move that would mire us in more complications in Europe.

On the day our separation from B&BE came into effect, the last week of July 1994, I phoned Han. I got him at home in the middle of a party. I said to him, "Yesterday we parted, right? Now I am asking you for a proposal to reestablish the relationship. Just send me a simple, clear suggestion. Let's first agree on the royalties and then negotiate the rest." When he had recovered from the surprise, that same evening, he sent me a very good one-page proposal.

True, it was not done in accordance with procedures—I didn't consult Benny, the CEO—but I believed that the move could be our salvation. I acted in accordance with the principle once described by General Yoram Yair, who sat in the row behind me in high school. There were moments when an officer had to take responsibility and carry out an operation without waiting for clearance, even if that meant deviating from the accepted protocol. He had to first verify the success of his mission and explain his decision only after the fact. That is what I did. I presented Han's proposal to the board and got its OK to continue the negotiations. The board gave its blessing because it couldn't in good faith do otherwise.

It was also decided that our next meeting would be in the U.S. I was going to make every effort to present the board with the best possible agreement. I set up a team to join me in the European negotiations. It included Galia, Michael, the company's CFO, and Rafi Oz. Benny, who was kept in the loop by Rafi, continued to oppose the move, and worked tirelessly to torpedo it. He distributed a thick document to board members entitled "Why 4D must not continue its association with B&BE." When the document didn't succeed in frightening the board into submission, Benny escalated his campaign against me. Throughout the negotiations he kept adding superfluous clauses. I allowed for most of them just so that we could continue, even though the negotiations could have collapsed over any one of the substantive issues on which we had not as yet secured agreement. After all, the only thing we had agreed on in advance were the royalties.

When we reached the stage of drafts going back and forth between Tel Aviv and Amsterdam by fax, and it appeared that the new agreement with B&BE was taking shape, Benny and I were no longer on speaking terms. I reported any progress directly to the board.

Somehow we managed to agree on a draft just one week prior to the scheduled meeting in the U.S. Despite the pressure of time I decided that the whole team should go to Amsterdam to close the deal with B&BE, and return to Israel on the Thursday afternoon in time to travel to the U.S. the following week. We arrived in Amsterdam on Wednesday, October 5, and began to discuss the clauses in the agreement with the distributors' representatives. We quickly deadlocked because Benny prevented me from closing, while from the U.S. Paul Newton effectively blocked his representative, Han Bruggeling.

The first day ended in great disappointment and the two teams—already old friends—decided to go out for dinner and drown our sorrows in wine. We met again the next day at 9 a.m. in B&BE's offices. Negotiations continued until 3 p.m. and we succeeded in closing most of the issues, except for that of the quarterly advance payments. We agreed that I would go to the U.S. to try and conclude the matter with Paul Newton and from there travel on to the planned meeting of the board.

The next morning I was sitting in Mickey Spigelman's office. I gave him the agreements drawn up in Amsterdam, plus various related notes, and he began polishing it into a draft agreement. Though utterly worn out, I then traveled to Haifa with Matia for a long-standing weekend date with friends, and continued to work with Spigelman by phone and fax. The next day I flew to California, a journey that, door-to-door, took twenty-two hours. Paul Newton and I agreed on a method of periodic checks. While our direct sales in the U.S. continued to rise it would mean that there had been no disaster in the market and B&BE would stand by its commitment to pay us a quarterly advance of $3 million dollars.

I sent this addendum to Spigelman so that he could incorporate it in the final draft. To my mind this was a good agreement that would provide us with much needed security and, given our shaky situation, was ten times better than our setting up an independent distribution in Europe. Now it was my job to present it to the board so that it could vote on a proposal.

At the board I didn't have a guaranteed majority. Benny and I each had half the votes. I knew that he was seething with anger because I had bypassed him and he was lying in wait, readying himself for an ambush.

Chapter 25

A Place at the Top

The plan to boost our spirits by holding the next board meeting in the U.S. did not materialize. It was not as simple as I had thought. Galia discovered some possible complications of the tax laws and the compromise was to hold the meeting in Tijuana, Mexico.

We all met up in California and convened for a first evening meal in the hotel. All, that is, except for Benny. He was conspicuous by his absence. It was a bad sign. Galia reported on the traveling arrangements to Tijuana and the booking she had made for a hotel with an appropriate conference room. We all then retired to our own rooms.

The next morning I went to have a word with Benny at the company's offices in nearby Irvine to which we had moved after the IPO. Until then we had worked out of two modest suites in Costa Messa rented by Galia with her personal credit card. The elegant brass plate at the entrance to our new office building bearing the name New Dimension Software filled me with pride. It was a far cry from the small tin sign that I had myself put up at the entrance to our humble office on No. 7 Derech Hashalom.

In 1995, I should mention, we were forced to change our company name from 4D to New Dimension Software, Inc. A French company with the same name sued us, claiming that it had been the first to register it in Europe. We filed a counterclaim in the U.S., where we had preceded the French in registering the name. Since it was abundantly clear that one or the other of the companies would have to capitulate and that our claims were a waste of time and money, I asked Michael Karish, our CFO who was an accountant and a lawyer, to propose a compromise. In return for a million dollars, we would relinquish our claim and change our company's name. A negotiation ensued at the end of which we settled on a payment of three hundred thousand dollars, plus enough time in which to make the change comfortably, and permission to use advertising and informational material bearing our former name for a further eighteen months.

Our new offices were on the tenth floor of an impressive American building in Irvine, California, surrounded by lawns and flower beds. Each member of the staff had a spacious office with panoramic views of the local landscape. The floors were of marble and the reception desk mahogany. The icing on the cake was a well-dressed receptionist who smiled at you as you entered and addressed you as "sir" in polite, genteel tones. We had come a long way from the Tel Aviv cubicles with the loud receptionist and creaky floors. As I walked in, everyone rose to greet me. The doors to all the offices were open. Only Benny's was closed, another ominous sign. For all the well-mannered smiles of our American employees and their "how do you do" and "have a nice day," the tension in the air was as thick as the smog that drifted from Los Angeles.

Taking a deep breath, I knocked on Benny's door and invited him out for lunch. We have to talk before the board meeting, I said, resigning myself to an uneasy meeting. Though I left it to him to choose the restaurant, he went into the first one he saw, didn't even wait for us to order and declared that he was completely opposed to the new agreement with B&BE. There was no point in arguing with him. Other lunches in different times came to mind, and in a different mood, but I kept the nostalgia to myself.

I asked him what he expected would happen at the meeting and whether there was something we could agree on in advance. "A new board," was his response. "We appointed them. Let's dismiss them and select others." All in one fell swoop—Benny's way. Nodding vaguely in consent, the truth was that the idea didn't appeal to me at all. It seemed more like a ploy than a solution. We ate and parted without reaching an understanding, not even a symbolic one. He was sounding me out, and I him, but we remained in the dark about each other's true intentions. Benny then didn't show up for dinner, at which we were all supposed to get together. Also noticeably absent were two other members of the board: Benny's cousin, David Green, and his friend the lawyer, Amnon Shoham. Rafi Oz, another one of Benny's appointees, did come to the dinner.

In the months prior to the meeting Rafi was on the team negotiating the new agreement with B&BE and was obviously coming to the realization that it was in the company's best interests. Rafi understood that given the crisis situation, it would be a mistake to open up an additional front in Europe. My hope was that he would obey his conscience, put the company's good first, and give me his vote at the meeting. The fact that he joined us for dinner was encouraging.

The next morning we set off for Tijuana in three vehicles. In the first were seated "my" board members, Galia and Professor Yehuda Kahane (an expert on finance and insurance from Tel Aviv University); in the second car were Benny's supporters, Amnon Shoham, David Green, and Benny himself. Rafi Oz, who was the last to leave the hotel, made for the third car, the one in which I was sitting. We were on our way. At first we chatted a bit about Mexico—a country Rafi had never been to. I knew he was struggling, wavering between his duty to the company and his allegiance to Benny. It was an open secret that before our departure for the U.S. Benny had worn him to a frazzle.

"Listen Roni," he said with a sigh, "last night after dinner I phoned home and consulted my lawyer. I am an appointee of Benny's and he is saying that if I don't vote in line with his instructions, I must resign from the board. I am sorry, but I don't want to be caught up in this imbroglio." From the pocket of his jacket he extracted an envelope and handed it to me. "I hereby notify you of my resignation effective immediately."

At that very moment we crossed the border. Concentrate, I urged myself, don't shoot from the hip. A desert landscape helps the mind to focus. Look at the view and try to think clearly. "Listen," I said to Rafi, "I don't exactly understand the implication of such a resignation and I don't want us to make a procedural mistake. Keep the letter in your pocket for a while. You've come this far, wait." I was bursting to tell Galia and my supporters the news of the bomb that was ticking in Rafi's pocket. They must be in the know before the meeting. But not on a cell phone. I didn't want anyone to overhear.

We arrived in Tijuana late in the afternoon. The moment I got to my room, even before taking a shower, I contacted my supporters and updated them re the Rafi Oz situation. They also had no idea of what to do about this unexpected development, and thanked me for buying us all a bit of time. I invited Galia over. The air-conditioning in her room wasn't working, and in mine it worked intermittently, which was some consolation. We decided to phone home and ask Mickey Spigelman for advice. How should we act if Rafi Oz goes through with his resignation? Should we or should we not bring up my proposal for a vote? Mickey said that we should. Over the phone he dictated the precise wording to ensure that whether my proposal was accepted or rejected it would not be legally flawed.

The next day all members of the board were in attendance except for Nahum Rozman, who joined by phone. Michael Karish was also present, though he couldn't vote. I arrived with the good final draft for a new European agreement but had no idea whether there was a chance of getting it passed.

The meeting opens. I, as chairman, put current issues on the agenda to the vote. Then comes the day's hot item: a new agreement with B&BE or launching 4D Europe. I take the plunge, comparing the risks of going it alone in Europe to the security that the nearly completed agreement offers. I encourage the board to debate the issue, study the draft I had brought with me. I answer questions. Benny raises objections and extols the virtues of his counterproposal, which he has named "The Omega Plan."

After a three-hour discussion it is time to vote. Who is for the new distribution agreement with B&BE? Galia Streiker, Professor Kahane, Nahum Rozman, and, of course, Roni Einav. Just a minute, a surprise—Amnon Shoham is also voting for the proposal. Excellent. Now it's Rafi Oz's turn. His hand hovers over the jacket pocket with his letter of resignation. I fix my gaze on the water jug. The general mood is bleak. And then I hear Rafi's voice. "I too am for it." Yes, yes, yes! Who is against? Only two: Benny and David. The ayes have it. The minutes record that the draft of the new agreement is good for the company and I am asked to improve a couple of clauses. The board also authorizes me to complete the negotiations with the Europeans and to begin dismantling the independent infrastructure that we had already set up on the continent. I'd done it!

I hold back my sense of satisfaction, and proceed to the next item on the agenda. Rafi Oz raises his hand, pulls out the resignation letter and places it on the table. The board accepts his resignation. I close the meeting and invite everyone to the bar. Amnon says something to Benny apologetically. Benny turns his back on him and goes into a huddle with David. I want to invite Amnon for a drink with us but fear that the invitation would be misconstrued. He goes up to his room. Rafi Oz also slinks off. They are stopped by Galia for a moment to be informed of our scheduled time of departure. Those of us who linger on in the bar down margaritas to cool body and soul. The emotional tempest of the past several days that we had all been hiding from each other is over. Now there is no further need for words. We share the same feelings of relief. Things have been delayed and postponed but now we have closure, and all is well again.

On the way back Benny, David, and I are together in the car. I am next to the driver, they sit in the back. In the mirror I see Benny close to the window, silent. A sign, perhaps, that in the end his good sense has prevailed? Suddenly he speaks. "In my view this was a very bad meeting. We should have set out to conquer Europe in the same way that we conquered America." I turn to respond, but don't make it in time. "You should know," he says looking at me with hostility, "with the decisions passed you have destroyed the company."

It was mid-October 1994. At that time I didn't yet understand where he was headed. How sad. People often fail because they don't realize how close they are to success when they take the wrong turn.

During that journey from Tijuana, as I surveyed the monotonous landscape on my side and Benny ignored it on his, I tried to fathom the deepening rift between us. My conclusion was that his brilliant intellect notwithstanding, he was unable to acknowledge his failings. Even when he did, he was only paying lip service. He was quick to spot the mistakes of others and as long as they were his underlings he would easily forgive them. But I was his equal, the witness to his mistakes. That could not be forgiven.

After we had crossed the Mexican border on our way back to California, I was reminded of a parallel Israeli experience, a scene I glimpsed from the air after the Six-Day War. The point at which yellow turned green was the border between Egypt and Israel. That border did not need marking. The demarcation was obvious as barren wilderness suddenly gave way to lush irrigated fields. Here too with Benny there was first a change in the coloring of the landscape, then a change of smells. He noticed neither.

On the way back to Israel I stopped over in Paris. There was no time to waste. I froze any further extension of the European company and told Michel Koder to begin laying people off, including himself. In Israel the winter of 1994 was already upon us. My son Liran, then a captain in an elite unit, met me at the airport. He listened intently to my account of the dramatic events of the previous two weeks. "You are playing control games just as we do in the army," said the next generation. "Except that you do it wearing three-piece suits."

Outwardly I continued to coordinate things with Benny, but in practice I achieved what I had set out to achieve. He refused to accept the board's verdict and continued to put spokes in the wheels. I made sure that he was briefed on every detail of the negotiations with B&BE, except for the exact timing of the expected signing so he wouldn't try and torpedo it. Ten days after the meeting in Tijuana we signed the new agreement with the Europeans and, as is customary, immediately issued a press release. Benny, the CEO, was quoted in the release praising the agreement. He did this under duress and that enraged him further still.

It was abundantly clear that we could not continue like this. In a business partnership, as in marriage, it's best to do things by agreement. It is easy to agree when you are successful, but when things go wrong and you're losing money, tension and conflict arise. In our case, Benny didn't think that we had failed. He also didn't think he was part of the problem, and therefore categorically rejected every suggestion to put things right in a rational way. He had turned down my proposal that the three of us resign and later on refused to accept my European solution, despite the fact that a majority of directors concluded that it was good for the company. At that stage I already faced the truth of our partnership: in spite of his many talents that had produced numerous achievements over the years he was now an obstacle in the way of New Dimension's recovery and future prosperity.

On the 25th of October, 1994, about a week after our return to Israel, a further meeting of the board was set, at which I planned to propose Benny's dismissal. Since it was an item on the meeting's agenda, it was hardly a secret. The board had the authority to fire the CEO. In effect, with four directors on my side, I would have the required vote. Benny knew that I was going to the meeting with four sure supporters. He had only three secure votes, himself and two others, Rafi Oz having resigned. Clearly apprehensive he initiated a series of moves to postpone the meeting. He even suggested that we go to the U.S. for arbitration. I said no. A day before the meeting, Amnon Shoham, a nominee of Benny's and his friend, sent in a letter of resignation. I didn't understand the logic and to this day I don't know what went on behind the scenes. In any case, the meeting wasn't postponed despite the further resignation.

The board members convened, and were joined by Mickey Spigelman, who, for the previous six months, had been attending our meetings because of the tension between us all.

Because I wanted maximum privacy, the meeting took place in our instruction center on the roof floor of the building, opposite the cafeteria. For the same reason, the gathering was fixed for 5 p.m., a time when many workers would already have left. Benny had spent most of the day in the office frenetically copying documents. After the arrival of the board members I went down to call him to the meeting but he was nowhere to be found. We waited half an hour, but there was no sign of Benny. David, his relation, also didn't turn up. And then a phone call came from Benny announcing that he was resigning from the board. Another call from David informed us that he too was resigning, effective immediately. At 5:30 the meeting began with only four members of the board.

The four began to read the company's articles of incorporation in order to understand what they should do in such circumstances. Mickey Spigelman, who was well acquainted with the rules, explained that for a quorum to be legal, at least five members of the board had to be present. It was apparently Benny's hope that as a result of the resignations we would not have a legal quorum and therefore be unable to hold the meeting. Or, that if we held it without a legally constituted quorum, our decisions wouldn't be worth the paper they were written on. A company that doesn't have a functioning board must convene a general assembly to nominate a new board. Benny thought that at a general assembly he had a chance of defeating Galia and me, or at least of ending up with a tie. I asked Mickey Spigelman for his advice and he suggested we find a fifth member. It appeared that the articles permitted not only instant resignations but also instant nominations.

I considered phoning Matia but first went downstairs to see if by chance someone was still there. The stations were all unmanned. In a room by the entrance I could hear a rustling sound. Michael Karish was still working. "You are still here," he said with a smile. "Can you give me a lift? My car is in the garage." "Of course," I replied, "but first there is a little problem and I need your help." I explained the situation. "I am inviting you to be a member of the board. You are not committed to anything. We will bring up issues for a vote. You can vote as you wish and also abstain. I need you there so that we have a legal quorum and the company can function. At the earliest possible opportunity I will replace you in an orderly way." After a bit of hesitation Michael agreed. We immediately nominated him to be the fifth member of the board, a legal quorum was formed, and the meeting was formally opened.

There were a number of items on the agenda: the budget for 1995, Europe, an analysis of the performance of the management and of the CEO. Then the proposal to fire Benny from his job as CEO was put to the vote. The main argument for it was the damage he had caused in his reporting in the U.S. and his responsibility for the class action that stemmed from those reports, and which had cost us a fortune. Four of the five voted in favor. Michael abstained. The vote was recorded in the meeting's minutes. The next item on the agenda was the proposal to set up a committee to search for a new CEO. It was agreed that in the meantime I would act as temporary CEO. The meeting was brought to a close. There wasn't a single member of the board who voted for the dismissal easily, but business is business. We were experienced enough to know that the operation we had performed was vital to the health of the business.

Everybody dispersed to head home. Galia gave Michael a lift and Mickey Spigelman stayed on to go over the meeting's decisions. I took the minutes and locked up the instruction center, thinking: Benny has to be notified.

From the rooftop the new Tel Aviv could be seen in all its splendor. Tall skyscrapers in clusters of twos and threes towered over its once modestly low silhouette. The friendly skyline of my childhood city was no more.

Phone Benny.

On the way back to my office I looked at the pleasant set of rooms in building No. 7 Kiryat Attidim, where we had moved after we had begun to prosper. There was Michael Karish's office. Usually he was the world's most fastidious person, with everything neatly closed and locked up in cabinets and drawers. Today he had left one file drawer open. I peeked into the multitalented Ariel Gordon's office, a confusion of paperwork, booklets, reports, a child's toy. Only Ariel knew how to find something in the chaos. Here was where Avi Cohen, a real genius, sat hermit-like, blinds closed so that nobody can peep in on him. And my office, at the far end of the floor. The desk facing the open door, a picture of Matia and the children, smiling. On the right-hand wall a copy of the check we received after the NASDAQ listing. On the opposite wall, New Dimension's logo in Japanese.

Mickey Spigelman finished the paperwork and joined me. "What, you still haven't informed Benny? It's already nine o'clock." Had so much time elapsed? Steeped in thought, I simply hadn't noticed. I dialed the number. In his Raanana house, Benny lifted the receiver. Without beating about the bush I said, "We decided to fire you." Then I read him the wording of the board's decision. He was in shock. That option hadn't been included in his plan.

Six weeks later the board appointed Professor Eli Talmor to replace Michael Karish as a director, and these five members remained in place until 1999. And so from November 1994 until March 1999 that was our board, except for one temporary member who was added later because of Benny, but let us not put the cart before the horse.

Benny refused to accept the board's verdict. The negative publicity in the media and the damage it caused the company did not deter him. In the general assembly he convened in Spigelman's offices on November 5, just a few days after his dismissal, he tried to get the tables turned. His argument was that since the general assembly was the body that appointed the board, it was not within the board's authority to dismiss the CEO. Only the general assembly could do that. Attending the assembly were the three of us, Benny, Galia, me, and a few other small shareholders who had bothered to come. They, in any case, didn't have the power to decide the issue.

It was Benny who had established the rule that appointing a new board required a 66 percent majority of those attending the assembly. In other words all three of us would have to agree on the move. Benny had 34 percent; Galia and I together held 34 percent, leaving a total of 32 percent in the hands of the small shareholders. Benny's reasoning for putting this rule in place at the time was to prevent the imposition of a board on him that wasn't to his liking. At this fateful juncture, when he failed to convince the small shareholders to take his side, his own decree boomeranged.

After Benny's dismissal we began to search for a new CEO. I set up a search committee of five, among them a bigwig, Harvey Krueger, from Lehman Brothers, New York, a similarly important figure from Israel, the highly reputed economist Amnon Neubach. I wasn't planning to step into Benny's shoes. Nothing could have been further from my thoughts. I honestly believed that the company now needed management of a different kind.

The search went on for six months before we found the right person, Dan Barnea. Dan, an electronic engineer by training, with managerial experience, was my age. When we began to work together we discovered that we had both gone to the United Youth movement and even had been members of the same North Tel Aviv branch. How Israeli! All the members of the search committee agreed that he was an excellent man with leadership qualities and good interpersonal relations. He was appointed CEO of New Dimension in June 1995. We thought that we could now relax. But then Benny issued proceedings against us.

Chapter 26
Hubris

Benny sued the company in Tel Aviv. In the U.S., the class action against us for which he was principally responsible continued. That did not make him reconsider his litigation against us. He sued me, Galia, and the three other board members who had dismissed him. The claim was identical to the one rejected by the general assembly, that the quorum of five that had dismissed him was not legal. He made a further claim, that I had conspired with Rafi Oz in Tijuana, to persuade him to resign, thereby upsetting the balance within the board.

With hindsight I am able to look at this episode with relative equanimity, though at the time it was not easy. I worried that if Benny succeeded in court the results could be serious for the company and for me personally. The emotional toll was already heavy.

Officially Benny was still part of the company. We had been advised that while the case was in court, we should continue to pay his salary. For three whole years he went on receiving twenty-one thousand dollars per month. Even after his dismissal he was still the principal shareholder.

The court soon rejected Benny's claim that I conspired with Rafi Oz to ensure Oz's resignation. As for the claim about the illegality of the quorum of five that dismissed him, the judge wrote: "The one who in the final analysis created the opportunity for the group Einav/Streiker to gain control of the board was the plaintiff himself, in that he resigned (and caused his friends to also resign) … If the plaintiff's entire objective was to paralyze the board so that it wouldn't be able to dismiss him from the role of CEO, he has no one to blame but himself." Secondly, the judge ruled, so long as the general assembly had not appointed a new board, the board of five served as an interim legal board and its decisions, including the decision to fire Benny, were legally valid.

During the court proceedings two things happened, one important the other funny. The important one was we reached a compromise in the Class Action in the U.S. It happened on the 26th of April 1995, about a year after the suit was first launched. We brought it down from thirty million dollars to seven million. Three million five hundred thousand dollars was paid immediately and the balance was to be paid in shares or cash in a year's time. The main beneficiary was the lawyer who had instigated the suit. Its conclusion was a first step on our road to recovery.

The funny thing that happened is linked to the makeup of the board, the issue of Benny's suit. Since his dismissal he had not set foot in the offices and had no direct information as to what was being done in the company. In the course of the litigation his lawyer complained that the board was doing as it liked. The judge asked him what was it that bothered him: "That they are screwing your client?" To which Benny's lawyer replied, "No. But they might." To put his mind at ease the judge appointed a sixth member of the board, a lawyer, whose entire role was to safeguard Benny's interests while the case was still ongoing.

Parallel to Benny's lawsuit against us in 1994, Motti's litigation dragged on. When those proceedings first began early in 1993, my lawyers asked Benny for information that would strengthen my defense. As my then partner in the management of a successful company he willingly confirmed in an affidavit what I had said: If there was something that Motti didn't know, it was entirely due to his lack of interest.

At that time the lawyers were planning to call Benny to the stand as our main witness. But after the class action in the U.S. and his dismissal at my instigation he went wild and moved heaven and earth to get his revenge. He informed Galia and me that if we didn't agree to rescind his dismissal he would support Motti's suit. Galia warned him that if he didn't stop threatening her she would go to the police. I didn't take him too seriously. I was wrong. The moment he realized that his demands wouldn't be met, he changed sides and volunteered to testify on Motti's behalf. He calculated that if Motti won thanks to his testimony, and again became a small shareholder, it could give him a majority in the general assembly. The chance to win by a knockout so blinded him that he "forgot" to tell Motti's lawyers that in the not too distant past he had met my lawyers to testify on my behalf. They discovered this only in court.

It sounds incredible but that is what happened. The situation became unpleasant and dangerous. If Motti's claim had ended in the way Benny hoped, the latter would have obtained the necessary majority to oust me and Galia and do as he pleased. Except that in the course of questioning, his lies were exposed.

Motti Glazer's suit went on for four years, until 1997. Sitting in judgment at the Tel Aviv district court was Hilla Gerstel, then a young district court judge, who dug deep and checked everything thoroughly. From a certain point in time the hearings in Motti's case overlapped Benny's litigation, which kicked off at the end of 1994. The court case with Benny went on until 1998. Together the two cases lasted for five years—no easy burden to bear. Two court hearings, a lot of time, money and emotional energy.

Motti Glazer had once been my friend and then ceased to be. Benny Weinberger was my partner and then wanted to continue without me. Motti brought Benny to me and then tried to oust him. Benny had then asked for my help and patronage, and got both. How did I become their common enemy? What happened to us along the way? Wise men will hold forth about the evil influence of money. Perhaps Motti would not have felt cheated if the sums involved had been small. We had, after all, parted by mutual agreement and he received everything he demanded and more. Others will say that power corrupts and that is also true. One thing is for sure—this stretch of five long years was no bed of roses.

The verdict in Motti's case singled out Benny Weinberger. In the judge's view "Benny Weinberger's evidence lacked credibility and displayed a great desire to hit out at Einav and Streiker and to profit from joining forces with Glazer." The verdict was handed down in August 1997, exactly six years after the separation agreement between Motti and me. That same year Israel was swept by a wave of terror. The national mood was at an all-time low. Ramon, our third son, was serving in a Patriot missile unit and there was a real fear that he would soon have to fire those weapons in action. The only good thing I could look forward to in that bitter period was a verdict that would clear my name.

In her findings the judge noted that Motti's claim not to have known about things that were published for marketing and advertising purposes was not believable. In cross-examination it turned out that he knew "much more than he was willing to own up to." It was he who had initiated the separation from me, whereas I had suggested merely freezing Einav Systems so that I could devote my time to the affairs of 4D. He gave up on the company and handed it over to me "because he didn't like it or its activities and was even hostile to it," regardless of its worth. Just as was the case in his exit from Liraz, what interested him was Einav Systems and not the value of the company that was being sold. It was Motti who had acted in a "non-straightforward manner when he realized his option to separate," because he believed that 4D wasn't worth a dime; he agreed not to check the value because he thought he was giving me nothing in return for a great deal; it follows that if, after 4D became a great success, he realized he made a mind-boggling mistake, "and had no one to blame but himself." These are the main findings published in a judgment that ran to seventy-six pages.

In her findings the judge was also critical of the way in which I had dealt with the share dilution agreements and the shares of Meir Arnon, indicating however, that this was a matter of secondary importance. On the other hand, the summary of issues from 1988 and 1989, including the mutually agreed waiver of all claims, which was intended to rebuild trust between us and which Motti had signed of his own free will, was found to be substantive and binding. His demand to return to the status quo of 1984, prior to Meir Arnon's withdrawal, was, wrote the judge, absurd. Motti should have demanded financial compensation and then his claim might have had merit.

This nightmare haunted me for three long years. It was the first time in my life I had seen the inside of a court, the first time I had been questioned under oath. Unlike Dickens's *Bleak House*, the case didn't drag on for generations but certainly went on for far too long. In the end victory was mine. The price tag was three hundred thousand dollars in legal fees and a great deal of heartache and nervous strain. It is not pleasant to be called a crook and a liar. It was very unpleasant to be questioned in a courtroom. But we got through it. The court ruled that Motti had to pay Galia, me, and Einav Computer Systems twenty-five thousand dollars each. I couldn't have cared less about that. I just wanted to forget him and all the odious situations he had forced me into. And then I heard a rumor through the grapevine that he intended to appeal to the Supreme Court.

A day after he had lost the case in the district court I bumped into his wife in the elevator. Both families were still living in that same building in Ramat Ilan. She was clutching a huge black garbage bag. She hadn't been able to seal it because it was filled with shards of glass from broken bottles and smashed utensils. I could well imagine what had gone on in their house when Motti was told of the judgment. They must have spent huge amounts of money on the case over the years, and now Motti was going to waste even more on a hopeless appeal. His usually well-groomed wife looked as if nothing mattered to her any more. Even the tears had dried up. "I don't need your money," I told her. "I will waive what the court ordered you to pay just as long you end it all now. Enough is enough. Tell him to stop." I wasn't gloating. This gave me no pleasure. Apparently she convinced him because Motti changed his mind and didn't appeal.

Now only the case with Benny was still on, but life also went on and business even flourished. We began to recover from the mess in the U.S. In the class action they compromised and we paid 20 percent of what they had originally claimed. Most of the deals that were disputed because of Benny's erroneous reporting—which led to the suit—came to fruition. Thanks to the new management team that included Dan Barnea, Galia, the U.S. manager Darrel Bittenheuss, and me, our sales volume reached almost $100 million in some fifty countries. We had 2,500 top customers, our net profit reached approximately 21 percent, and yearly growth was close to 50 percent. All of this is to say that the harmonious management, the industriousness, intelligence, dedication, and vigor of us all produced the hoped-for results. The share price that had fallen during the crisis began to rise from a low of $3.75 to $4.50 then to $6 and $7 per share and upward to $25. At the end of 1998 beginning of 1999 it shot up to $52.50 and at times even neared the $60 mark.

However, success didn't persuade Benny to back off. Even when he saw Motti losing, he continued with his suit until he himself was the loser. I thought that that was it, at long last this unnecessary episode was over. Unlike Motti, Benny took the ultimate step and appealed to the Supreme Court.

It is hard to explain Benny Weinberger. He is a talented and ambitious man and was a central figure in the setting up of 4D-New Dimension and the development of its products. That I do not forget. But his appointment to the post of CEO of a public company in the U.S. was a mistake. Having said that, one cannot ignore the fact that megalomania is part of the game. You cannot do what we did without at least a bit of megalomania. Successful entrepreneurs are revolutionaries whose burning self-belief and ability to break with convention enable them to move mountains. It is not easy for me to speak in Benny Weinberger's defense but his infinite faith in his ability even when subjected to ridicule helped the company to take off. "The start-up spirit" goes forward against all the odds. When it deviates from the area of development and manifests itself in such areas as accountancy, management or, god forbid, the law, when there too the conduct is in line with the dictum that "what isn't forbidden is permissible," that spirit becomes an ill wind that blows no good.

Megalomania is perhaps not the right word. "Hubris" is the more appropriate term, the quality that makes you great is also sometimes the very one that is responsible for your downfall.

Chapter 27

The End of the Beginning

When we were children in the middle of the twentieth century, the past was known, the future predictable, and the present changed slowly. Now, in the Third Millennium, the past is no longer what we thought it had been, the future is unpredictable, and the present is changing rapidly. The making of business decisions, a process once entirely rational, has also had to adapt itself to swift change. Fortunately I'd already encountered Games Theory back in the sixties, based projects on it, and taught the subject to grad students at Technion. The paradoxical facet of decision-making was familiar to me. When the selling of New Dimension came up, the point at which I chose to begin this story, theory turned into practice and my awareness of this aspect of decision-making played a major role in how things turned out.

The philosophy that developed around the subject— sometimes known as "positive uncertainty"—posits that a person making future-related decisions at a time of uncertainty would be well-advised to use not only his rational judgment, but also his intuition. He should formulate an opinion, and be prepared to change it in the course of making his decision. The manager of a business bases his routine managerial decisions on the rational and the practical. Yet I quickly discovered that for decisions involving big changes affecting the company's future,

I'd better adopt a positive approach to the problem of uncertainty. Instead of trying to bend reality I learned to flow with it. I made it a habit to combine the traditional rational method with an intuitive, creative approach, keeping in mind the paradoxical principles involved in the decision-making processes: As *Ethics of the Fathers* states, "All is foreseen, and freedom of choice is granted. The world is judged with goodness, but in accordance with the amount of man's positive approach." That's what also guided me when Rick Gardner of BMC surprised me with his acquisition offer in November 1998.

I don't presume to possess the scientific tools to analyze all the business decisions I've ever made, or even the one I began to formulate after my encounter with Rick Gardner. As for those etched in my memory, I can say that they were a combination of rational thinking and intuition. Founding Einav Systems, for example, was a wholly intuitive move, the fulfillment of a dream with no proper business plan or profit forecast. Taking on Motti Glazer as a partner was a rational decision stemming from necessity. Founding 4D-New Dimension was, to a great extent, an adventure. The decision to invest in developing the GS Daily before obtaining proper approval was definitely intuitive and irrational, perhaps even a gamble. Business decisions that are mixed up with personal disputes are, of necessity, emotional and irrational. How much emotion was involved in my decision to part from Motti Glazer? Did my resentment affect the quality of the decision? It was irrational and financially unwise to agree to his inflated demands, but I was willing to pay any price just to be rid of him. The future, of which you can never be sure, justified me both on the personal as well as on the business level.

The selection of 4D's overseas distributors was a complex undertaking fraught with uncertainty because we had to make quick decisions that would impact on our future in alien territory. The decision to select Tone as our U.S. distributor was fortuitous and intuitive from start to finish; in the decision to sever ties with them rationality was already at play—we'd learned from experience.

Perhaps character is fate and whatever it is that shapes you plays a part in your business decisions. Could it be that the Israeli tendency to swift improvisation in rapidly changing situations just happens to match the philosophy of "positive uncertainty"? It's hard to know. What I do know is that as we came away from the meeting with Rick Gardner, during which he had clearly shown interest in acquiring New Dimension, all three of us, Dan, Galia, and I, saw that the situation had just changed before our eyes. Suddenly we were no longer discussing compensation but facing a far more fateful decision. And we instinctively curbed our inclination to shoot from the hip. We must take our time and discuss the issues in an orderly and rational way. This time it was doubtful that intuition alone would do the trick.

I'm dwelling on the subject of decision-making in times of uncertainty because, to a great extent, it has charted my course. According to traditional decision-making strategy, one has to focus on clear goals, gather facts, be aware of them, forecast results objectively, and act in a practical, rational manner. Applying that strategy involves a lot of time and money, resources that were in short supply when I first started out in the software business. The alternative approach was far more suited to my Israeli temperament and to my particular business environment. Be focused, yet remain flexible. Be aware but also skeptical. Be objective and at the same time optimistic. Be practical but don't let go of your dreams. In other words, once you've defined your goals, relate to them only as options and be open to the possibility that more attractive targets may emerge, as indeed they did in Europe, when we switched directions and teamed up with B&BE even though we already had an agreement with other distributors.

According to this approach, while knowledge is power, the imagination is sometimes fired by the absence of knowledge.

The combination of imagination and ignorance is what drove us to float the company on the NASDAQ without knowing exactly how it would transform our lives. It's very important to be objective, says the alternative approach, but being optimistic and believing in your dream is far more important. Be practical, but don't forget that intuition is also real and has the power to be not only reactive but also proactive. We discovered that fact when we set up the company in the U.S., even though we weren't sufficiently financed to do so. For New Dimension it was the dawn of a new era. In the second half of the 1990s, when we grew and became established, we increasingly relied on rational considerations.

The Einavs celebrated some important family milestones in the last decade of the twentieth century. Our eldest son, Liran, got married in August 1996. Our youngest, Yoav, had his Bar Mitzvah in December of that year, after which we took him on the customary trip abroad. Zach, our second son, graduated with honors in economics and accountancy. Ramon, our third son, enlisted in the air force and served in the antiaircraft Patriot missile unit. In 1997, Liran went to Harvard for his doctorate in economics and did outstandingly well. Matia and I visited him and his wife in the U.S. often. Occasionally we arranged European vacations to Prague, Athens, and Paris for New Dimension's employees, and not for a moment did we stop investing in the company, developing and expanding it. Until I got that phone call from Koichi San in November 1998, our business continued to run as usual.

New Dimension's growth stemmed mainly from the increase in sales, but also from the acquisition of other technologies that complemented our own and opened up new markets. In 1997, we established a presence in Mexico and sold well there. We also tried to expand distribution to India, but that did not work out. The very big deals we made in the U.S. that year became a matter of routine, and included prestigious companies such as Visa, Blue Cross, and Hartford. By investing just a few million dollars, we got U.S.-based Enlighten Software to sell us Tandem technology, which complemented our own capabilities and provided us with an additional array of customers. We acquired security technology for our subsidiary, Eagle Eye, from EDS Germany and successfully attached it to Control SA. That same year, we signed a special agreement with Memco, the Israeli firm specializing in security software. Memco was founded by our former consultants, Eli Mashiah and my friend Israel Mezin, and after the agreement continued to develop in parallel to New Dimension. (In 1999 Memco was acquired by Platinum for $570 million. A few months later Platinum was acquired by CA.)

What motivated mergers in the field of organizational software in medium-sized companies such as ours was the need for continuous growth. Big industries, giant corporations, prefer to reduce competition by swallowing up the smaller concerns. The small organizations are guided by the maxim, "If you can't beat them join them." Buyers in our field, banks, industries or governments, are always happy to minimize the number of suppliers with whom they have to negotiate. They don't want to buy a hundred software products from a hundred different manufacturers. They'd rather buy a hundred products from two or three sources. The large software firms are aware of this and are constantly on the prowl for smaller manufacturers with products complementary to their own. Size has clear advantages. The distribution and financial systems are already in place, and an additional product is barely noticed. Thus, when you approach the customer you can take advantage of your size and the highly varied inventory of products at your disposal.

At the bottom of the list of the one hundred largest software companies published annually by the journal *ESP* is the company with the lowest sales figures for that year: sales of ten or twenty million dollars. At the top of the list are usually Microsoft, CA, SAP, and Platinum, with sales in the billions. In the middle are dozens of companies whose annual sales figures range from forty to seventy million dollars, and a few that sell in the hundreds of millions. In 1999 we reached a sales volume of one hundred million dollars. We were operating in Israel, the U.S., Australia, and Mexico, and were about to penetrate the Brazilian market. Ours was a successful, brilliant, growing company. It was natural that potential buyers would show interest. In the early 1990s, however, we weren't thinking of selling.

Not only was I uninterested in selling the company, I'd never even sold any shares. After we'd recovered from the crisis in the U.S. and our share price had resumed its climb on the NASDAQ, valuations of the company also kept rising. In the early '90s, for example, it was valued at $300 million and the share price was $25. Let's say that on that day I held two million shares. Two million times 25 comes to 50 million. Why not sell 200 thousand shares for $5 million? I could live well off that, buy myself security, and keep on working.

I didn't sell. Not one of the trio, Benny, Galia, or I, sold any of our shares. At that juncture it felt like a betrayal, like leaving a kibbutz. Not only was the notion of selling the company out of the question, so was the idea of selling shares. We had reached maturity in the organization's development, we were doing well, and the future seemed bright.

From my perspective, all also seemed to be well on the personal level. After Benny's dismissal, I continued to serve as chairman of the board in a company whose workforce had grown to 500. Had I followed the conventional path, who knows whether I would have landed such a job. I loved the work, I was liked, and I had achieved a level of success. On average we sold a product a day. Every quarter we earned millions of dollars. Our success rate in winning bids and proposals was extraordinary. Customers paid handsomely for an automating virtual robot—a "smart pack" contributing orderliness, profits, service reliability, and other related benefits to their organization. They willingly paid us a hundred thousand, a million, even millions of dollars, for a computer tape and some literature.

With every additional success, the interest in buying us grew, and the pressures mounted. The company was no longer a small private business at 7 Derech Hashalom in Tel Aviv. It had become part of a global economy. The moment you attain that prestigious status, you have to accept the idea that in the international galaxy of software houses, New Dimension is but one planet, albeit a bright one, and subject to its inner forces. Thus, whether to sell or not to sell your successful company isn't necessarily a question that arises at your convenience. Nor is the response as obvious as it may seem. You're being offered a lot of money, so why not take it? The answer involves business and personal considerations that are difficult to untangle even in a harmonious management team. In our case the endless dispute between Benny and me made those answers particularly hard to come by. I also had patriotic and humanistic considerations: loyalty to the employees, the technology, the country. "People are duty-bound not only to their family, but also to their nation," my father had long ago told me.

As long as the three of us were unable to reach a joint decision, we continued to maneuver between the forces around us. And we hoped that when the moment arrived it would suit us. The first such moment came in October 1997.

In Israel, there was a law to encourage industry by exempting companies from capital gains tax if they went public and their shares remained unsold for five years after the offering. We were concerned that the law and the exemption would be scrapped before our IPO. Fortunately, they were only voided on January 1, 1995, twenty-eight months after we were listed on the exchange. From 1993, when the share price began to soar, as well as after our fall and subsequent recovery, the option of selling merely floated in the air, a far-off but tangible dream about striking it rich. On the other hand, since we'd just begun to reap the fruits of our investment in the U.S. and enjoy success, we were in no hurry to sell.

In 1996, for example, we received a serious offer from Boole & Babbage USA. The CEO, Paul Newton, Han Bruggeling's boss, made a special trip to Tel Aviv to make the offer, but the price wasn't right. Or perhaps that was the only rational excuse we could come up with since the gap between the parties was but one dollar. At the time Han said to Newton, "If it's a bad deal, it's a bad deal, and if it's good, it's good at $11 or $12 per share." Today I believe that even if his offer had been $12 we would have rejected it, either because the time wasn't ripe or because our internal dispute was at its peak.

The IPO was followed by wave after wave of offers to purchase. For a variety of reasons we rejected them all. In retrospect the main reason was hidden, even from us: we were simply not ready to part with our baby. In 1993 things went in the opposite direction. When our share price was reaching for the sky, and B&B's shares were falling, they proposed that we buy them. In 1998, we tried to negotiate a merger with our long-standing German competitor, Beta Systems, but their greed stood in the way. With Platinum, who showed interest in us, the talks never got down to specifics.

In our spheres there are occasionally such ripples, movements in various directions around the galaxy. After experiencing a few powerful surges, we realized that we couldn't escape them forever. Galia also realized this, as did the members of the board. Only Benny remained entrenched in his disregard. Therefore, the crisis we experienced divides our company's history into two periods: up to the end of 1994 (Benny's dismissal) and after. From the moment he went to war with us to demand his reinstatement (early 1995), it was a new ball game. Whereas before the dispute he'd rejected purchase offers for sound reasons, during the trial he turned offers down out of spite for Galia and me even if the price was OK.

A whole year went by before Benny's appeal to the Supreme Court was heard, a year during which New Dimension grew and blossomed, bought Enlighten, did business with Memco, had a disappointing love affair with Beta, and sailed on to bigger deals, clinched more repeat sales and registered other fine achievements. I described the situation in an affidavit presented to the Supreme Court in response to Benny's appeal:

"When the petitioner resigned from the board, the company was recording heavy losses of some $20 million in the U.S. and the share price on the U.S. Exchange was about $5; since the appellant [petitioner] left his managerial role and the paralysis that had plagued the company and caused it such serious damage had ended, the company has flourished. Its profits have risen steadily and in 1998 will reach more than $15 million while the share value (as of 10.12.98) has climbed above the $34 mark. This is how the respondents [me] have turned the plaintiff—posing as victim—into an extremely rich man. The value of his shares having risen sevenfold (from approximately $20 million to about $140 million!). And all of this the fruit of the labor of the respondents ... The appellant ... is asking to hold on to the reigns of power, to have the situation turned back to that which existed on the eve of his resignation from the board, where he had veto rights over every board decision and every company activity. He used it to paralyze the company, which was plunged into a difficult crisis and vast losses."

We had reached 1998. Benny was drowning in paperwork and lost his appeal to the Supreme Court. This time his pride was wounded. How could such a thing happen to him? He, who was always right, had pinned his hopes on the judicial option, milked it dry, invested in it years and a fortune, how come he had been defeated? The blow was harsh and final. There was nowhere else to go. He was forced to accept that his dismissal had been confirmed not only by his bitter enemy, our board, but also by Israel's Supreme Court. He would never again be New Dimension's CEO, a bitter pill to swallow. And so 1998 turned out to be not a bad time for us to consider fresh proposals for the sale of the company. This time the right one came when Benny as well was in the right mood to recognize a good thing when he saw it, aware of his changed status, and less arrogant, though no less sure of himself. This time a miracle happened, a record high confluence in the high-tech galaxy, when our share price soared to about $50—almost twice the price it had been when the company was jointly managed—and coincided with Benny's agreement to consider the sale of New Dimension.

The potential buyer was a surprise: BMC, the eighth largest software company in the world. We had no shared activity with them and we weren't in any way their competitors. As a result we hadn't taken them into account in our most recent list of potential buyers.

After the meeting in Germany with Rick Gardner, the meeting with which I began my story, we began a kind of tango—a dance that we kept going from November 1998 until March 1999. At first it was a cautious tango of mutual attraction, not yet love or marriage. A tango danced on our side by Galia, Dan Barnea, and I, while Benny, who had given the green light, continued to sit it out. Our hope was that he would come and join us.

Meanwhile business went on as usual. So long as the deal wasn't in the bag it could easily be undone. At the beginning of 1999 we concentrated our efforts on ensuring that our customers were ready for the dreaded millennium bug. Financial organizations throughout the world were being operated by our software—banks, industries, service companies, armies. We couldn't allow all their operations to grind to a halt. In December 1998 and January 1999 we were pleased to read articles by the renowned analysts at Goldman Sachs, praising us and forecasting an annual growth in dozens of percentage points. New Dimension was, they wrote, a shining star in the software galaxy, and constantly upped the expected target price of our shares.

BMC kept forwarding to us reports of its revenues and various successes. Nor did we hold back on our achievements. Unexpected outsiders intervened to upset the dance; Platinum suddenly sued BMC, claiming priority in the purchase of B&B. In light of this new development BMC reordered its priorities by postponing the completion of their purchase of B&B and focusing instead on us. So rather than slowing down, the tango's tempo quickened. Two steps back—they realize that B&BE is mainly based on our products and perhaps they made a mistake in choosing to buy them instead of checking us out first. A very clandestine tango, it has to be said, conducted in the fashion of a military operation, with highly secret code names in the correspondence between us and them to avoid any small detail leaking before everything is signed, sealed, and delivered. BMC's Texans choose the code name "Ranger" and labeled the entire operation "Project Warp," perhaps because they had deviated from their original intention of buying B&B.

And so Ranger continued to tango with us. Two steps forward. We pay them a visit in the U.S. We send out big delegations— twelve people. They pay us a return visit with a delegation of nine. We say, look, we can improve your company because the number of products of yours and ours that overlap is close to zero. New Dimension will be a good fit for you. Their response: that's right and the embrace gets tighter. And so the tango continues, closer and closer, with increasing synchronization, as the right balance is found, the advantages are recognized, mutual points of attraction established.

BMC checked us out with a fine-tooth comb, which was why the tango lasted for so long. Once they were satisfied, it was time for the financial negotiations to begin, in February 1999.

In Israel it was cool and pleasant, and in New York Dan Barnea, who had gone there with Mickey Spigelman, was frozen to the core by Manhattan's icy winds. The negotiations took place in David Fox's office. Two American lawyers, Watson and Brinkley, together with an Israeli lawyer, Professor Ya'acov Ne'eman, arrived to represent us, the intended.

It was morning in New York, evening in Tel Aviv. I was sitting by the phone in Kiryat Attidim. The big windows reflected the twinkle of lights being switched on in the city. Only about half of our employees were still at their computers. The rest had already gone home. Over an already cold cup of coffee I waited for updates. The phone rang. So quickly! The deal must have collapsed. Dan Barnea is on the line. "Listen," he begins, "Professor Ne'eman thinks the deal will have to be taxed at source. Which means that we will have to transfer 17 percent of the purchase price directly to the income tax authorities, and then work out with them if we are entitled to any refund." "Very bad news. Stay on the line," I say, and link him into a conference call with Benny, who is at home in Raanana. "No way. If that clause is included, there's no merger," Benny says without hesitation. "You are prepared to kill the deal over this clause?" Dan wants to make sure there is no misunderstanding. "Yes," Benny and I say in unison (a small miracle in itself).

Dan hangs up and returns to the negotiations. Two hours later he calls back to say that the parties have agreed to clean up this thorny problem before the deal is signed. Bravo. The negotiations may proceed. "On the issue of price," Dan says hesitantly, "I have bad news and good news." The price of our share was then drifting between $48.50 and $58.00, on the ascent. "BMC's proposal is $52 a share," Dan says. "Is that the good news or the bad?" I ask and he replies, "That's the good news. The bad news is that they want to buy for cash."

This is the place to note that ever since the issue of the merger had first arisen, I had argued on many a board meeting that money wasn't everything. We also had to consider national and human issues. We needed to find a good home for the people and for the technology we had developed. For me the core issue was keeping the developmental work in Israel. In order to ensure this, we had to insist that half the purchase value be paid to us in shares of the purchasing company, so that our voice would count in meetings of shareholders. I told Dan, "Tell them that we want half the total value in cash and half in their shares." When he got back to me he reported, "They're not prepared to give us shares. Their shares are dropping in price just now and it's not worth their while to give us shares. As for keeping the developmental work in Israel, they are inclined to agree to that."

After several more transatlantic consultations I said to Dan, "In that case, I can live with a cash payment, but don't agree to $52.00 a share. Agree to $54.00." The two-dollar difference amounted to the not-negligible sum of two million dollars less for me. "Keep fighting on that second front," I instructed him and signed off. About half an hour later Dan was back on the phone: "Roni, they're offering $52.50. Do you agree?" I agree. Yes. I overrode the personal consideration. That was the extent of the financial negotiations.

The discussions in New York stretched into the night. David Fox stayed with them all the way through and did a truly magnificent job, while Mickey Spigelman kept a close eye on every detail. In the end the deal included not only the price but also the issue that was no less important to me: a formal undertaking to leave the development team in place in Israel and to expand it in years to come. In addition BMC undertook the allocation of options and the covering of all expenses incurred in making the deal—a clean sweep. BMC also agreed to keep the name of the company and its original blue color emblem. The new logo agreed on was New Dimension Software, A BMC Company. I gave my consent, as did Galia and Benny. Together we held 68 percent of the shares in the company. The buyers needed another month to obtain the agreement of other shareholders and additional option holders, because for the purposes of a buyout you need to be over the 90 percent threshold.

We still had pending the problem of the options promised to our board members. Already in 1996 three of them began to complain—the two professors, Talmor and Kahane, and Nahum Rozman, the engineer. This was during the period of change in management, the various crises we had to deal with, and their resolution. The three claimed that they were investing a great deal of work without being properly compensated. Indeed, despite the threats and pressures they had been exposed to, they had spared no effort. They were entitled to a reward over and above the standard payment. However, because we had agreed in June 1995 to give the newly appointed CEO, Dan Barnea, share options to the tune of 250,000 and the promise of an additional 250,000 subject to the performance of the company under his management, our options bank had been emptied. I proposed that they get 10,000 options per year if and when such options became available, but the three board members demanded double that amount. We decided to go to arbitration, from which I expected a compromise to emerge.

The arbitrator awarded each of the directors 50,000 options per year. I was not pleased with this decision, yet felt so overwhelmed by the other problems that I simply had the arbitration award signed and filed in 1997. When the deal with BMC came to fruition, a lawyer representing the three board members approached BMC on the subject. The company agreed to a compromise whereby in exchange for their approval of the sale of New Dimension and a relinquishment by each of them of their 150,000 options, they would receive $7.5 million. I mention this in order to say that good people also expect to profit and profit handsomely. Money, as they say, makes the world go round.

All the required agreements were obtained, and the procedure was complete. As fate would have it BMC bought us at the same time as they acquired B&B. And the whole move had stemmed from the controversial compensation clause in our distribution agreement with B&BE. What irony! Contracts, after all, involve thousands of matters that never come to pass and suddenly one little hypothetical clause became crucial. I fought over it for reasons that at the time were important and against the fierce opposition of most of my colleagues. Three years later it became the springboard to another sphere. But if asked what was more important to me, the sale of the company or the listing on the NASDAQ, I will admit that without a doubt the important event was the NASDAQ listing. A sale, even when one is talking of very large sums of money, is at the end of the day a purely commercial event. The listing on the exchange was a dramatic breakthrough, a steep ascent in the wake of which we turned from being just one more celestial body in the software galaxy to a glittering star.

On March 11, 1999, as winter turned to spring, the contract with BMC was signed and an official announcement of the merger published. This was a very important event indeed, the biggest cash purchase in the history of Israel's high-tech industry. BMC was invited to send its representatives to Israel for a meeting with Prime Minister Benjamin Netanyahu. We were lionized by the media, interviewed, photographed. It was the kind of hullabaloo that until then we'd experienced only vicariously, following news about the economy.

As I have already said, success has many adoptive parents. Rick Gardner, the main best man, sent an amusing message of congratulations: "It is not long since our meeting in that village near Frankfurt. I am sure that you are proud, and rightly so. I am hopeful that with Dan's help we will also succeed in the future to keep the home fire burning and even to fan it. To success." Dan Barnea was delighted: "For Roni this deal is as if God had put all the stars on parade and marched them to his tune." The implication was that in all those years I hadn't sold any shares and suddenly I had sold them all at the right price, and had mended my relations with Galia and with Benny and the three directors. Somehow everything worked out in the best possible way. At long last I had peace of mind. The future of my extended family was assured for another four generations and there were also options for new beginnings.

That is the story. We set off on our way with an Israeli dream. After a few years we reached the "NASDAQ stock exchange" with a company worth $120 million, which we sold seven years later for close to seven hundred million dollars.

"After all the years and all the memories I move on with mixed feelings," I wrote in my letter of parting to New Dimension's staff at the beginning of 2000. "I go on my way with many achievements to my name and hardly any failures, many friends and some enemies, 2,500 customers, most of them satisfied—particularly since the first of January 2000. To be quite honest, I went further than I'd expected. New Dimension has been my biggest achievement thus far, thanks to you, a very special group of highly dedicated and ambitious people. I am proud to have been a member of this family. Today I am more experienced, more mature, and richer than I was on the day we began our journey. Yet I remain close to you in spirit and intend to remain close also by my physical presence. In the future I shall no doubt need your help and with joy I will stretch my hand out to you, if and when required. My new office will soon open in the building opposite and I will be pleased to invite you all to a festive launch in about a month's time. Be seeing you, Roni."

Roni A. Einav is one of the pioneers of the Israeli high-tech industry. In 1983 he founded "The Fourth Dimension Software," where he served as CEO and Chairman of the Board until it was sold, in 1999, to the American company BMC. Today, Mr. Einav heads Einav Hi-Tec Assets, which focuses on investing in high-tech start-ups. Mr. Einav, MSc in Industrial Engineering (The Technion, Israel), served in the Israel Defense Forces as a weapons analyst. Born in Tel Aviv, he is married to Matia, and is the proud father to four sons, and a grandfather. In his spare time he travels in Israel and abroad, reads, visits museums and rides his bicycle.

Dr. Miriam Yahil-Wax is a dramaturge, writer, translator. She is a published poet and critic, and an award-winning translator of some 50 plays and novels (Dickens, Lessing, Doctorow, Oates, Guare, Molière, Stoppard, Gorky). As dramaturge of Gesher Theatre, she co-adapted and translated Doestoevsky's *The Idiot* and Babel's *Odessa Stories*. She collaborated with J. Sobol and H. Levin, served as dramaturge of Haifa Theatre, and was Artistic Director of The National Youth Theatre. A lecturer at Stanford, UCSC, Haifa University and Tel Aviv University, she holds a Ph.D. in Drama (Stanford) and an M.A. in English and American Literature (TAU).